Introducing
Psychoanalytic
Theory

Introducing Psychoanalytic Theory

Edited by

Sander L. Gilman

BRUNNER/MAZEL, *Publishers* • New York

Library of Congress Cataloging in Publication Data

Main entry under title:

Introducing psychoanalytic theory.

   Papers presented at a lecture series
sponsored by the College of Arts and Sciences
at Cornell University.
   Includes bibliographical references and
index.
   1. Psychoanalysis—Addresses, essays,
lectures. I. Gilman, Sander L. II. Cornell
University. College of Arts and Sciences.
[DNLM: 1. Psychoanalytic theory. WM 460
I64]
BF173.I48   1982   150.19'5   82-9477
ISBN 0-87630-312-2   AACR2

Published by
BRUNNER/MAZEL, INC.
19 Union Square
New York, New York 10003

Preface

Understanding psychoanalytic theory is difficult enough for the trained psychoanalyst. It would seem an impossible task for the university undergraduate. Because so many students had difficulty in comprehending the basic structures of the human psyche, the College of Arts and Sciences at Cornell sponsored a lecture series on psychoanalytic theory for its undergraduates. While the course was initially conceived for those students in premedical specialities, it quickly became evident that the course was of substantial interest to a wide range of students (and faculty) in the humanities and the social sciences.

Many areas of intellectual investigation from literary criticism to clinical psychology presuppose a working knowledge of Freud's theories and their further development during the past 40 years. In the normal course of a university education, however, the interested nonspecialist usually has little chance to study Freud. To enable this interested nonprofessional to have access to Freud's views in the light of our contemporary understanding of them, a series of classes was held by members of the Department of Psychiatry at Cornell Medical College; psychoanalysts from the New York Medical College, Upstate Medical College, and the University of Chicago Medical School, as well as humanists from the University of California at Berkeley, the University of Chicago, Massachusetts Institute of Technology, and Cornell, also participated. The fruits of these lectures are collected in this volume. I wish to express my thanks to Alain Seznec, dean of the College of Arts and Sciences, as well as to the various contributors, for making this project a success.

This volume is so structured so that it can be used either as a textbook or for self-study. It begins with the most basic and accepted views of Freud's theories and their legacy and builds upon these earlier chapters. The contextual chapters assume the information provided in the earlier chapters. They reflect the interest in psychoanalytic theory as expressed in other contemporary disciplines (philosophy of science, intellectual history, literary criticism, and sociology). All these chapters deal ex-

v

pressly with Freud's theories and reveal how these theories have been distilled into the broadest spectrum of humanistic investigation. They can serve also as points of departure for discussions concerning Freud's importance in his time and ours.

Note: Unless otherwise indicated, references to Freud's works are to *The Standard Edition of the Complete Psychological Works of Sigmund Freud* (London: The Hogarth Press, 1953-1974), cited as *SE*.

Contents

Contributors

MARIANNE HORNEY ECKARDT, M.D.
*Clinical Associate Professor of
Psychiatry, New York Medical
College*

LAWRENCE FRIEDMAN, M.D.
*Clinical Associate Professor of
Psychiatry, Cornell Medical College*

SANDER L. GILMAN, Ph.D.
*Professor of German Literature,
Cornell University; Professor of
Psychiatry (History), Cornell
Medical College*

OTTO F. KERNBERG, M.D.
*Professor of Psychiatry, Cornell
Medical College*

FRANÇOISE MELTZER, Ph.D.
*Associate Professor of Comparative
Literature, University of Chicago*

ROBERT MICHELS, M.D.
*Barklie McKee Henry Professor of
Psychiatry, Cornell Medical College*

U. H. PETERS, M.D.
*Professor of Psychiatry, University
of Cologne, Germany*

BERNARD RUBIN, M.D.
*Professorial Lecturer, University of
Chicago Pritzker School of Medicine*

MICHAEL H. SACKS, M.D.
*Associate Professor of Psychiatry,
Cornell Medical College*

MICHAEL H. STONE, M.D.
*Professor of Psychiatry, University
of Connecticut*

JOHN A. TALBOTT, M.D.
*Professor of Psychiatry, Cornell
Medical College*

SHERRY TURKLE, Ph.D.
*Associate Professor of Sociology,
Massachusetts Institute of
Technology*

BARBARA VON ECKARDT, Ph.D.
*Assistant Professor of Philosophy,
Yale University*

PART I

Basic Concepts of Psychoanalysis

Chapter 1

The Basic Propositions
of Psychoanalytic Theory

Robert Michels

I

Psychoanalysis is about ninety years old, and thus close enough to its origins that its meaning is often discussed in terms of those origins. It was the discovery, or invention, of a single man, Sigmund Freud. The story of his interest in psychoanalysis and the development of it as a system of thinking about human behavior contain the key concepts of psychoanalysis as we think of it today.[1]

Freud said that psychoanalysis was three things: first, a treatment (in today's terms, a therapeutic method of psychiatry); second, a method of inquiry—a way of exploring a subject matter, collecting data, interacting with a piece of the world in order to develop ideas and concepts about it; and third, a theory, a scientific structure, a body of knowledge, a set of hypotheses and models, a way of thinking about an interesting area of the world. These three things are different but interrelated. Here I shall emphasize the second and third—the method and the theory. However, for Freud and most psychoanalysts, psychoanalysis above all else is a method of treatment. The theory and the method of inquiry are secondary. Its greatest strength and its greatest weakness stem from the central role that psychoanalysis as a method of treatment plays in the conceptualization of psychoanalysis as a theory and method of inquiry.

Nineteenth-century psychiatry was important in the history and development of twentieth-century psychiatry. In fact, the dominant ideas in contemporary psychiatry can be traced to the nineteenth century. Our current concepts stem from Eugen Bleuler and Emil Kraepelin, both born within a year of Freud's birth in 1856.[2] Psychoanalysis, however, did not grow out of nineteenth-century psychiatry and Freud himself was not really a psychiatrist. Psychoanalysis has features that are so antithetical to nineteenth-century psychiatry that it was inevitable that Freud, the developer of psychoanalysis, would be a nonpsychiatric physician. The nineteenth-century psychiatrist was interested in patients whom he believed to have diseases of the brain or nervous system. These diseases might be bacteriologic, or degenerative, or their precise biologic nature might not yet have been identified. Of course this general approach was not unique to psychiatric diseases; it was true of much of nineteenth-century medicine. After all, Freud worked only a few decades after the relationship between microorganisms and infectious disease was first discovered.

The nineteenth-century psychiatrist believed that a group of people suffered from these diseases of the nervous system, that their symptoms were delusions, hallucinations, abnormal patterns of behavior, and deterioration of emotional or intellectual or cognitive functioning, and that these symptoms had roughly the same relationship to the underlying disease process that the rash, fever, and cough of measles, chicken pox, or pneumonia had to their underlying disease process. If one wanted to understand measles, he would not contemplate, introspectively or empathically, the meaning of the patient's rash. He would not do so because no one believes that the spots have meaning, except that they indicate the tissues are affected by the virus that causes the disease. Similarly, the nineteenth-century psychiatrist, wanting to understand the psychiatric diseases of the time—dementia praecox, or dementia paralytica, or senile dementia, or hysteria—would not study the meanings of the funny things that patients said and did, because he believed that they did not have any more relationship to the basic disease than did the shapes of the measles spots.

He would see the psychiatric patient's symptoms as clues that the organ system involved must be the brain, the organ of the mind, and that the study of the disease must involve the dissection, culture, and analysis of the brain. Furthermore, since nineteenth-century psychiatrists were as humane as their fellow citizens, or, for that matter as twentieth-century psychiatrists, they were concerned with providing humanistic support for their patients suffering from these illnesses, just as they did for patients suffering from tuberculosis, leprosy, or rheumatoid arthritis. However, there was no reason to spend a great deal of time listening to the insane things that psychiatric patients were saying. Out of this nineteenth-century psychiatric stance grew much of scientific interest, but not psychoanalysis.

Freud was a neurologist, a specialist in diseases that at the time of his practice were most often seen in ambulatory rather than hospital medicine. He had an office where he saw outpatients. Freud was ambitious, well regarded, and desirous of making a success at the private practice of medicine in the competitive world of Vienna.[3] Therefore, he did something that doctors have always done. He was kind to his patients, polite and friendly; he talked and listened to them, recognizing that the treatments he offered were of relatively little efficacy but exploiting the placebo effect of tender loving care, concern, interest, and friendship. Freud's patients were largely young, as neurologic outpatients tend to be; they were largely female, as were most patients with the neurologic problems of the late nineteenth century; they generally came from relatively high socioeconomic classes (medicine was at least as elitist then as today—perhaps more so); and they were verbal. He collected fees from them (institutional psychiatry is still conducted with patients whose fees are largely paid by third parties, while outpatient medicine more often involves the patient paying the doctor directly). Most important, Freud's patients were not mentally ill. They were not "crazy" or insane. Since the diseases involved were believed to affect parts of the nervous system which had to do with motor and sensory function rather than those which controlled thinking, Freud's patients were presumed to have normal mental function, and it was appropriate to talk with and listen to them. This exchange provided the context for the development of psychoanalysis in which it was natural and desirable for the doctor to listen to his patients and talk back to them, to develop a relatively symmetrical relationship with them, rather than a hierarchical superior-inferior one, to pay attention to what they said, and perhaps even to think about it. This was not nineteenth-century psychiatry. Indeed, some would argue that it still is not psychiatry. But it is nineteenth- or twentieth-century ambulatory medicine and it is the setting that gave birth to psychoanalysis.

In summary, psychoanalysis derives from medicine, not from psychiatry. Nineteenth-century psychiatry, perhaps uniquely of the medical specialties, could not give rise to psychoanalysis, while other areas of medicine were more likely to do so.

Freud, working first with the case material of his older colleague, Josef Breuer, and then with some cases of his own, made a surprising discovery. It contradicted what he had been taught by the leading neurologist of the era, the great Charcot, and what was said in the textbooks, and it opened up the new field of psychoanalysis. The discovery was, in the metaphor that I used earlier, that the spots did have meaning, that his patients' symptoms were not simply clues to an underlying biologic process, but had human communicative meaning. He discovered that the motor or sensory patterns that were disturbed in the neurologic patients he had been treating had significance as communications, memories, thoughts, fantasies, wishes, or fears—concepts that derive from the world of persons rather than the world of organisms. He discovered that his patients were disclosing the basic pathophysiology of their disease process to him and that by doing so they were changing the disease itself. He discovered that talking to the patient was more than the setting in which the treatment occurred, that it *was* the treatment, and that the patient's disease could be transformed into words, rather than simply described by them.

The history of psychoanalysis, from that point on, is an elaboration and a discussion of the rules for discovering meanings, for formulating them, for verifying them, for using them in the therapeutic endeavor, for tracing their developmental origins, and for looking at their multiple ramifications and manifestations in every possible area of behavior. The basic foundation remains unchanged. What were first thought to be signs of an organic process are now seen to be symbols of a process of meaning that can be understood by appropriate principles of interpretation.

What did Freud actually do? He started by seeing patients with primarily physical symptoms, neurologic patients called "hysterics." He used the various biomedical treatments of the time: sedation and electrical stimulation. He found, as have many before and since, that the treatments did not work very well. However, most important, he listened to his patients and talked to them. He discovered that they characteristically told stories or reported memories or experiences that were significantly connected with their symptoms and isolated from the rest of their mental lives. In the process of talking with his patients he made a second observation: Symptoms were modified by the telling of stories. The patients might not be permanently cured, they might relapse, but nonetheless a connection existed between the symptom and the story that was associated with it. Freud began to believe that if the memories or mental contents that had been split off from the rest of mental life were rejoined with it, the related symptom would disappear. He thus developed a model of treatment in psychoanalysis. It consisted of finding the meaning of experiences that were separated from the patient's conscious continuum of mental life and then integrating these experiences with the rest of the patient's psychological functioning. Pathology or neurosis was seen as the consequence of the sequestering or walling-off of one part of an individual's experience from the rest.

II

After this brief history we can discuss some basic concepts of psychoanalytic theory. First, psychoanalysis is about the psyche, the mind. Psychoanalysts are interested in what goes on in the mind. This is different from such other ways of looking at human beings as behaviorist psychology, which in its purer form sees "mind" as a term that has nothing to do with scientific psychology but has religious or spiritual origins. For Freud and other psychoanalysts, behavior is a product of the mind, while for the behaviorists, the mind is a hypothesis used by some students of behavior when they are not able to understand phenomena. Psychoanalysis deals with mental concepts—experiences, wishes, fears, fantasies, thoughts, and impulses.

Related to the central role of the psyche in psychoanalysis is Freud's concept of "psychic determinism." For the nineteenth-century physician or scientist, the world followed the rules of strict physical determinism. The state of the universe at any given time determined the state at any subsequent time, and if one knew the details of the state at $time_1$ and the relevant natural laws, one could predict the state at $time_2$. This view of the world left little room for the concept "mind," for if the state of the physical universe was completely determined by its prior state, this would include the brain, which at one and the same time was part of the physical universe and had some special relationship to what we call "mind," an entity *not* part of the physical universe although it is related to "brain." This is the age-old "mind-brain" problem of philosophy (*not* "body-brain," a relatively easy dilemma), and several strategies exist for approaching it: mysticism, interactionalism, parallelism, and linguistic analysis, to name a few.

One might argue that "mind" is an epiphenomenon of "brain" and that strict determinism governs brain events while brain events lead to mind phenomena. This, however, contradicts commonsense psychology, which observes that mind events appear to cause other mind events. I feel angry; I attack you; I feel guilty; I apologize; I feel better. Each of these mind phenomena might only appear to be a part of a causal chain and in fact may not be any more related to the preceding or succeeding mind state than the progression of behaviors in an epileptic seizure. Common sense, however, suggests otherwise and argues for what might be called "psychic" determinism.

Commonsense psychic determinism is "loose" rather than "strict," however—that is, there are a number of seeming mind events which it does not claim to explain. In addition to the seizure phenomenon mentioned before, these include such everyday experiences as dreams, slips of the tongue, and simple forgetting—all explained by common sense as meaningless, merely noise in a complicated system. Certain other experiences cannot be explained but are far too important to be dismissed as trivial. They interfere with the individual's pleasure and adaptation and at times seem to "take over" his mind without being a product of it—the symptoms of mental illness. Here our commonsense approach reverts to a strict physical determinism: Something is wrong with the patient's "nerves" or "brain" and the pathologic mind phenomena occur as a result.

Psychoanalysis accepts the psychic determinism of commonsense psychology but applies it with the strictness of a scientific world view. Not only is everyday behavior psychically determined, but so are both the trivial and apparently meaningless experiences of dreams, slips, and forgetting, and even the most bizarre and manifestly inexplicable phenomena of mental illness. Psychoanalysis expands commonsense psychology by expanding its view of the mind to include more than conscious experience, to include the powerful unconscious forces that shape the trivial phenomenon, the pathologic experiences, and so much else that is important in human life. Psychic determinism, therefore, becomes the counterpart of the dynamic unconscious; together they define the psychoanalytic paradigm that says that human action can be determined in terms of inner experience and that the causal relationships long assumed to link everyday experiences can be extended to embrace the extraordinary phenomena of mental illness, if one recognizes the hidden recesses of unconscious mental activity and their powerful impact upon behavior.

This brings us to an important distinction, often neglected in discussions of the elements of psychoanalysis: the difference between the concepts of "descriptive" and "dynamic" unconscious. It has long been known and little challenged that trivial experiences exist outside of conscious awareness. People forget things and later remember them. They must have been stored somewhere in the interval. The existence of a descriptive unconscious is beyond question and of relatively little psychiatric interest. The concept of the dynamic unconscious, however, signifies something more important and more interesting—that there are powerful forces shaping mental life outside of awareness. Further, they are powerful in shaping certain specific areas of mental life: dreams, parapraxes, and mental illness. In summary, psychic determinism is a universal rule of mental life that requires for its universality the recognition of an arena of mental life not previously recognized, that of powerful but unconscious dynamic forces.

The next question concerns the nature of these powerful unconscious forces. Psychic determinism and, to a considerable extent, the notion of dynamic unconscious forces are really not discoveries, but inventions. They are conceptual tools that Freud created to map a hitherto unknown terrain. However, the next step did involve a discovery. Freud's patients talked to him, and as they did they told him stories about emotionally loaded, painful, disturbing experiences in which they felt shame, guilt, or discomfort. Their symptoms were influenced by this talking, and he came up with the notion that the experiences they told him about were linked to their symptoms, that the *meaning* of the experience—the tension and mental conflict associated with it—made it pathogenic.

As Freud explored these experiences, he learned that they tended to cluster about certain themes and that the dominant theme was sexuality. Freud discovered what does not seem surprising to those who were educated in the era of his impact: The topics that disturbed people most, that they were guilty and ashamed about, that they were in conflict about, and that they tried not to think about, had to do with sex. That was an important discovery in the nineteenth century. He further discovered that his patients' sexual experiences stemmed from events that happened surprisingly early in their childhood, from an age we have not usually associated with sexual concerns. He suggested that neurosis is the unfortunate adult sequel of traumatic infantile or childhood sexual events. At that point, however, his young science had a disturbing surprise. The stories that his patients had been telling him were not true. The traumatic experiences they had related had not occurred.* We

---

*Recently some have questioned whether Freud might have gone too far in rejecting the historical validity of his patients' accounts of childhood sexual trauma. Adults do molest children, and such experiences probably do predispose to psychopathology as the children mature. Nevertheless, psychoanalysts came to recognize that childhood sexual wishes and fears are universal, as are neurotic phenomena in adult life that can be traced back to them. It is the universality of the derivatives of childhood sexuality that is the strongest argument for the endogenous source of these sexual fantasies.

now believe that he discovered this first in his self-analysis, in his exploration of his own memories from childhood.

Freud then faced an interesting dilemma. He had reported the relationship between traumatic sexual experiences in childhood and later neurosis, and it turned out that he was wrong. There were three obvious courses of action. First, he could retract his earlier assertion. He did not do that. Second, he could try to conceal his error. He did not do that. Third, he could hold to his theory by reinterpreting the data, the usual initial scientific response to data that disagree with a theory. Freud did just that. His patients reported memories of traumatic sexual experiences in childhood, memories that appeared to be false. However, it was true that they reported them. His error was in believing the reports, but his genius was in recognizing that false reports were even more interesting than true reports. True reports would only tell us about the extent of perverse adult sexuality. If an adult molests a child we know something about the adult, but we know very little about the child. However, if the child imagines being molested by an adult, we have an insight into the child's mind. Freud's discovery was that sexual fantasies are so intense and so pervasive in the first decade of life that they lead to memories of events that never in fact occurred. Freud took the false reports as a clue to the sexual imagination of the child and by doing so transformed the discipline.

From that time on, psychoanalysis was interested in the inner world, in patients' experiences, rather than in the external events of their lives. The transformation of events into experiences is influenced by the individual's developmental stage, transient mental states, symbolic elaborations, and many other factors. No two children experience the same thing, regardless of how it looks to the outside observer. The "truth" becomes what is experienced rather than what "happens." After this discovery, the major determinant of behavior was no longer seen as the events of the outside world, but rather as the inner dispositions of the individual, and in psychoanalytic thinking this came to mean his drives and their various transformations. Freud's concept of drive encompassed the various demands that the body places on the mind.

Clearly, there is no logical inconsistency between an interest in the external stimuli or triggers to behavior and the inner dispositions or motives that shape it, but the schools of psychology that have organized around these two issues have taken quite divergent courses.

A logical extension of the principle of psychic determinism is that each state of the individual's mental life is determined by earlier states. This means that the very earliest states, infancy and childhood, are extremely important in shaping the way in which the individual organizes all subsequent experience throughout life and, consequently, that early childhood mental life is a central area of inquiry for psychoanalysis. Again, this challenges a view of commonsense psychology that regards infants as empty-headed, with real mental life not beginning until the development of language. For Freud, by the time the infant is able to talk full sentences, the structure of the mind has largely been determined.

A link exists among the three concepts of dynamic unconscious, drives, and the importance of infancy. The central notion is that normal adult mental life, commonsensically understood as the result of conscious processes having to do with everyday adaptive tasks, has major determinants that stem not from the current tasks of adulthood but rather from desires of childhood which have never been gratified. These largely consist of frustrated childhood wishes for pleasure and gratification, the derivatives of sexual drives, which persist unconsciously in the adult mind. The validation of this model is based on the role of these unconscious infantile and largely sexual determinants in explaining dreams, parapraxes, and psychopathology in the framework of psychic determinism.

III

This is a simple statement of the core psychoanalytic model. One can view the first few decades of Freud's work as an exploration of this model with its formulation outlining almost all of his works. The basic structure is: " 'Blank,' an area of human behavior, can be understood as determined by unconscious forces stemming from infantile sexuality, as transformed by a variety of mental mechanisms." Each of Freud's works substitutes a different area of human behavior for "Blank." We have *The Interpretation of Dreams (1900)*, looking at dreams, *The Psychopathology of Everyday Life (1901)*, looking at parapraxes, *Jokes and Their Relation to the Unconscious (1905)*, looking at humor, *Three Essays on the Theory of Sexuality (1905)*, looking at sex, *Studies in Hysteria (1895)*, looking at neurosis, the Michelangelo and Leonardo papers looking at artistic creativity,[4] *Totem and Taboo (1912-1913)*, looking at religion and culture, the clinical papers looking at character structure, and others. In some of these areas, such as neurotic symptoms, dreams, or parapraxes, Freud explored a field that had been previously outside the sphere of psychological understanding and gave it new meaning. In other areas, such as art, religion, or culture, Freud discussed an area of human behavior which had many meanings and added a rich new dimension to our understanding.

The prototypic formulation introduces another important psychoanalytic concept, that of mental mechanisms. The unconscious infantile sexual determinants of experience are not directly manifested in behavior but are disguised or transformed, so that one must learn how to discern or interpret their influence. These rules of transformation occupied much of the interest of psychoanalysis after its first few decades. In effect, psychoanalytic interest moved from the sources or dynamic origins of behavior to the study of the transformation of these forces into behavior, such as psychopathology. This shift marked the birth of what was to become ego psychology, the study of the mental structures that control, channel, inhibit, delay, and transform the basic dynamic forces of the mind, rather than the study of the origins of those forces.

The history of psychoanalysis is marked by this shift from its initial focus on the drive origins of behavior, which later come to be called the "id," to the mechanisms for transforming those drives, mechanisms encompassed in the term "ego."[5] In that shift we discovered that most things in which we are interested were not the result of the direct expression of a drive, but rather the result of the drive or its derivative wish as one component of a complex structure that also included fears aroused by the wish and a mental mechanism or structure that organized the wish and the fear into a unified product. When we examined this product, a unit of behavior such as a symptom, we did not see the drive or wish or fear in pure culture; instead we saw a complex mental structure that represented a compromise between a forbidden wish and the fear that was the source of the forbidding, along with the mental mechanism that created the compromise.

Freud's final revision of the basic model was in 1926.[6] In it he regarded human behavior as the result of a wish—usually based on unconscious forbidden infantile themes—that came into conflict with a fear, again usually an infantile fear. That conflict was associated with anxiety, the built-in response to the anticipation of a dangerous situation. The anxiety triggered a defensive operation (for Freud, repression was the prototypic defense mechanism). Infantile wishes were never erased—they continued to be present and active throughout life—but they were often controlled by repression and remained unconscious. If repression was not sufficient and the wish continued to disturb the individual, other defenses were called into play. These might result in symptoms or in other forms of psychopathology, such as inhibitions, the avoidance of situations that might stimulate the neurotic conflict, and various character traits. These considerations, however, take us far from the basic propositions of psychoanalytic theory and introduce later issues in the development of psychoanalysis.

NOTES

[1]See the biography of Freud by Ernest Jones (1953-1957). *The Life and Work of Sigmund Freud*, New York: Basic Books.

[2]For the roles played by other nineteenth-century psychiatrists, see Henri Ellenberger (1970). *The Discovery of the Unconscious: The History and Evolution of Dynamic Psychiatry.* New York: Basic Books.

[3]See Frank Sulloway (1979). *Freud, Biologist of the Mind: Beyond the Psychoanalytic Legend.* New York: Basic Books.

[4]Sigmund Freud, (1914) "The Moses of Michelangelo." *SE* vol. 13, 209-236, and (1910). "Leonardo da Vinci and a Memory of His Childhood." *SE* vol. 11, 59-138.

[5]Sigmund Freud, (1923). "Ego and Id." *SE* vol. 19.

[6]Sigmund Freud, (1926). "Inhibitions, Symptoms and Anxiety," *SE* vol. 20, 87-175.

Chapter 2

Development

John A. Talbott

Discussion of developmental stages might most usefully be opened by asking why we should care about development in the first place. Most psychiatrists' time is spent primarily treating adults, not children, so why be bothered about what goes on in childhood? A hypothetical example of the type of patient I see in my clinical practice might provide the answer.

A 20-year-old college student came to see me because of his inability to begin writing his senior honors thesis. He had done all the research and had all his notes neatly organized; yet every time he sat down at the typewriter, his mind went off to things in the dormitory room he needed to fix, to someone he needed to telephone, to things he hadn't done outside, to the bank book he hadn't balanced, and so forth.

I asked him if this had ever happened to him before and he said it had not. I asked him what he was feeling while he sat idly at the typewriter. "Distraction," he said. "Well, is that all?" I asked. He said he also experienced a feeling of struggle. He felt a certain resistance to writing the thesis, he said, and a little anger at having to do it for someone else. In fact, he told me voluntarily that he had gotten furious at his professor during a conference for "assigning him too difficult a subject." Of course, the student himself had decided on the topic, yet

16

he blamed the adviser for the turmoil and torment he was now going through.

I asked him if he had ever felt these feelings of struggle and resistance about doing an assignment and the accompanying anger at someone for holding him to it. He said he had and began to discuss past assignments that he had resisted doing, papers that he put off writing until the last hour and then had to finish overnight. He acknowledged his difficulty in deciding on research subjects or topics and a great deal of disappointment in himself.

He recalled that when he received his high school diploma at graduation and no fireworks went off, he discovered that he was left with only a diploma and began to question for whom he had worked so hard. He experienced a feeling of anticlimax. I merely asked, "Has anything happened like this before?" He then recalled a very poignant episode when he had experienced the same feelings of frustration, annoyance, control, struggle, and resistance.

One day he had been assembling a small windup child's toy with a screwdriver and was having trouble. His father, who he knew could fix the toy rapidly, came along and was going to take the toy from him and fix it. My patient had an intense memory of the struggle between trying to do the task himself to please his father and knowing that his father would be angry if he failed and would then take over and fix the toy himself. These feelings of immense shame, disappointment, and anger resulting from the incident were felt keenly now, even though he was only three-and-a-half years old at the time.

This fictitious, yet typical, case study tells us something about why child development is important to us, even when we are dealing with adults: Adult problems clearly have their origins in childhood. We see development as a number of phases and barriers which have to be negotiated during a lifetime. We see that each task along the timeline is a different task, each with its own hazards, rewards, possible bad outcomes, and resultant problems.

The first person to really address development in depth was Sigmund Freud. Freud formulated his ideas on child development from such clinical examples as the one I just related. He based them on the experiences of patients he was treating or consulting on, and, as I did, he frequently noted the origin of problems in early childhood.

If he were dealing with the fictitious student I described, Freud might have construed the problem a little differently than we would today. He might have seen this student's primary problem as a struggle between producing and not producing something of value for a parental authority figure and linked it to the struggle over the parent's dominance of the child during toilet training. Today, I think we would talk more in terms of mastery, control, and struggle over autonomy, and use such words as dependence and independence. But while we have broadened the sense that Freud used, we still think in much the same terms, and we still consider events that occur early in life extremely important.

Freud would have called this event a "fixation point," because the patient was not totally successful in carrying out one task of that phase of development and this mini-scar remained to haunt the person and to be revived later.[1] One has the opportunity in each developmental phase to master tasks, to fail at them, or to partially accomplish them. Obviously, it is impossible to look at this situation in totally black-and-white terms. None of us has completely mastered all the tasks of childhood, adolescence, or adulthood. There are always partial solutions. That is one reason our personalities are mixtures of different elements, since simple one-to-one correlations found reading Freud or others really do not exist.

For example, some works on dream theory implied that an airplane in a dream meant something specific and that if someone dreamed about an airplane, you could go to a index of dream-symbols and find out exactly what it meant. Clearly, that is not so. You have to find out from the dreamer what things mean, a lesson that was brought home to me vividly early in my training. A hospitalized patient who was thought to be suicidal told a dream to her psychiatrist during a session. The dream was that the patient was with a group of people who were singing. After relating this dream, she asked for a weekend pass for a visit outside. The psychiatrist thought that the dream meant that she was happy and could safely go out on a pass. He gave her the pass, and she committed suicide during her leave. In retrospect, those singing people clearly were heavenly angels.

The moral behind this anecdote is that in psychiatry you cannot assume any set of equivalencies. Moreover, you really have to find out what specific things meant to the patient in the past, when the crucial event occurred, and what the individual task difficulty was. You cannot overgeneralize.

In essence, then, we still believe, like Freud, that events happening during life sometimes are partial successes but often are partial failures that leave some scar that can be opened again at a later time by any number of influences. The influence may be a nonspecific stress, such as joining the army, going away to college, or leaving home—events that always will take a certain toll. Or it may be a stressful occurrence that is specific to the earlier difficulty and that will open the very same sore.

Also, all the little bits and snatches of difficulty that we have throughout our lifetimes add up to form the personality structure we all walk around with. Freud would explain that our fictitious student's difficulty during the anal period resulted in rigidity, obsessional thinking, difficulty making decisions, conscientiousness, inflexibility, and so forth. At times, not only these personality traits, which live on through our lifetimes, but discrete symptoms that pop up, such as procrastination—as in an inability to complete a paper—make obvious the lingering effects of an unsuccessfully resolved phase. The reason to bother with development, then, is that the adult personality we have to deal with today is directly related to what happened in the past.

In pre-Christian times, there were two predominant theories of child development, one being predeterminism. That is, it was thought that each germ cell would go on to recreate its own type of germ cell; hair could grow into hair, nail into nail, but not hair into nail. The other was an Aristotelian concept of epigenetic development, which posited that development could progress sequentially; one moved from A to B to C to D, which is much more like classical developmental theory.

Today we see both theories interacting and there is still much disagreement over which type of development people undergo. For the most part, we now believe in an unfolding of events, going from a cellular level to an organ level to a systems level, with events shaping the final appearance of the systems. We know, for example, that there is a critical period in infant development during which he or she can develop language ability. If that critical period is passed without the proper stimulus being applied, the child cannot speak. Children reared by wolves or other wild animals are examples of this phenomenon.[2] Also, personality, as we now think of it, clearly is a combination of interactions, not simply a psychological unfolding. A person's final personality is the result of the interaction of personal experience and social focus on his basic psychobiological makeup. When we look at the adult personality, we tend to see it as an intermingling of both emotional and intellectual forces.

FREUD'S BASIC PREMISES

An examination of Freud's ideas on child development is dependent upon several broad concepts the reader may not yet have been exposed to. Let me mention several premises because my discussion depends on an understanding of them.

The first premise is that of psychic determinism. In the opinion of most psychiatrists, nothing in the mind happens by chance. Everything is determined by something else; everything has meaning. Slips of the tongue, feelings, thoughts that pop into one's mind—all have meaning. For example, last night at home I was telling my wife how marvelous it was that I now have two airline schedules. I was looking up a flight and I remarked how convenient it was to have one schedule at home and another one *here*. And she said, "Yeah, that's one of the problems." I had meant that I had one at the office and one at home. I tried to explain to her that this unconscious slip was still better than one I made two years ago when I tried to open my home door with my office key, which I felt was a much graver error. That act, which I was really unaware of at the time, had a lot of meaning to us.

The second premise is that mental processes exist outside our consciousness. Many things are out of our awareness. Certainly, all of us are aware of such events as whistling a tune and suddenly realizing that it is "Oh, What a Beautiful Morning," rather than "Oh, How I Hate to Get Up in the Morning." We recognize that the tune matches our mood without a conscious decision to whistle it.

Freud also postulated a drive or instinctual theory. Early on he believed that the sexual instinct was the single organizing element around which behavior and development clustered. He believed that this drive was really an innate capacity to react to things in a certain patterned way. Take the primitive bodily example of a reflex arc. A stimulus occurs, that stimulus is perceived in the central nervous system, and finally some sort of motor action results. Touching a radiator, then knowing that it is hot and pulling one's hand away is an example of that patterning.

Also, certain internal stimuli and drives increase the level of bodily tension, precipitate some sort of action (and it obviously can be either a thinking action or a motor one) that is reduced, allowing one to return to a state of homeostasis. Freud called the quality that impels this system to act *psychic energy*. It is difficult to talk about psychic energy without conjuring up images of electrical or hydraulic models, but we really should take the term as Freud intended it and not become too concrete about his analogy.

Freud said one could invest mental energy in an object or a person but not directly. In other words, I don't invest energy in something; I invest it in the mental image of that thing in my mind. This is called *cathexis*. A cathexis is no more than a sort of investment. For example, Freud believed that the mother was central to the development of the child and that the primary object of the young child's drives would be the mother. So the mental representation the child has of the mother is a highly cathected mental image.

Later on, Freud moved from believing solely in a sexual drive to believing that sexual and aggressive drives are fused; thus he developed a dual instinct theory. For example, in the oral phase, Freud identified the libidinous sexual instinct as the oral-incorporative sucking aspects and the aggressive instinct as the biting, chewing aspects. Similarly, in the anal period he contrasted the giving-up passive aspects with the sadistic or fouling ones.

Freud followed this drive throughout the life cycle, yet I think it is fair to say that Freud, and until recently everyone else, paid most attention to the first few years and that the amount of thinking and writing which concerned the later years of development decreased incrementally.

As I mentioned earlier, at each one of the barriers or phases one has tasks to do, and one either fails or succeeds at those tasks. The thinking in Freud's time, and that of many experts today, is that an excess or a shortage of some important thing can lead to trouble later on in life. For example, if one either is deprived of or gets a great deal of oral satisfaction, then one craves oral satisfaction later on. The need certain people have to have something always in their mouths—a cigarette, whiskey, or whatever—has been explained in two ways: either their mother never fed them properly and enough, or else she kept them so pleased and happy that for the rest of their life they do not want to relinquish that way of dealing with life. One major criticism of psychoanalytic theory is that you can explain everything by it, thus opening a certain doubt about how specific you can be in predicting future behavior, since you can cover yourself by explaining anything that went before as caused by either too much or too little.

An instinct has four parts: the source, the impetus, the aim, and the object. Working backward, the object is where the instinct is satisfied, for instance, in the mother. The aim is what activity satisfies the instinct. The impetus is the amount of instinct, and the source lies in the erogenous zones Freud described. The erogenous zones, where in Freud's thinking the action is centered, include oral, anal, phallic, and genital areas. The cathexis or energy is thought to be attached to different areas at different times. In the first or oral period, the erogenous zone is the mouth; in later periods, the zone is the anus, and then the penis. In Freud's thinking, these zones are the centers of activity, and development shifts accordingly.

I mentioned that Freud thought of fixation points as small scars at a certain point of failure, the point at which something happened that didn't turn out well. These failures are of two types: one concerning the object (for instance, the mother) and resulting in a fixation; the second having to do with the method of gratification (for instance, oral sensations). Regression, of course, is when one falls back to a certain phase after having once moved past it. The classic example is that of a child who is growing up and doing well until suddenly a younger sibling is born and the older child begins to suck his thumb, wet his bed, or revert to some other earlier form of gratification.

Developmental problems have three consequences. The first consequence is the resultant personality structure. Certain things that happen or don't happen while a person goes through life become part of the final makeup of that person. For instance, events taking place during the oral period are thought to result in personality traits associated with dependency and depression. It is normal, when you are a year old, to worry about where the next meal is coming from, because you cannot obtain food by yourself. You have to be predominantly concerned with survival. However, it is not normal to spend one hundred percent of your time worrying about meals when you are 20 years old.

The second consequence is a specific, discrete symptom, for example, a compulsive need to check the windows before leaving home or to touch every slat in a picket fence as you are walking down the street. Again, when you are three years old, you have to check everything to make sure that you have done it right; it is normal to be concerned that you have not left things undone. But when you are 50 and still checking all the time, a problem exists.

The third consequence is a perversion. In Freud's thinking, perversions are the direct expression of problems at one of these early phases. For instance, in the phallic period it is perfectly normal behavior for a boy to look at his penis, exhibit himself, make sure that it is there. At 35, this behavior is not considered appropriate.

Just as the whole concept of an individual's development is a series of stages, so too the development of psychoanalytic thinking builds upon itself. We began with Freud's sexual, instinctual theory. Erik Erikson[3] later broadened it to deal much more with ego functioning and that part of the mind which deals with the world. Jean Piaget[4] dealt in a much more cognitive, operational framework. The three theories are complementary, however, not contradictory.

INFANT SEXUALITY

Reading this volume can give you some ideas about the Vienna of Freud's time. It is amazing to look back and see the amount of anger Freud engendered in his colleagues—to the point that they treated him like a leper—when he raised the possibility of infants having some sexual expression. Infants have been masturbating from time immemorial. I don't mean simply manipulating their genitals, but rubbing, rocking, and otherwise stimulating themselves. Also, incestuous experiences in childhood have gone on for many years. Noteworthy to me is that, while at first Freud believed his patients who described incestuous or sexual experiences early in life, he later decided that those stories were all fantasies or wishes and then retreated from his belief in childhood incest. In the last few years we have seen the publication of numerous books[5] showing that childhood incest really is not an unusual experience at all. In clinical practice today, I think the experience of incest is seen not as mere fantasy or screen memory but as a very likely occurrence.

In any event, infant masturbation and sex in childhood clearly show that people do not suddenly develop sexual interests in adolescence. Also, Freud in talking about sex was talking about pleasurable bodily sensations and not just sexual intercourse, which is the way we tend to think of sexual activity.

THE ORAL PHASE

Let us discuss the phases of development, as Freud saw them, the genesis of those phases, and the problems of each phase. Freud saw the mother-child relationship during the oral period as the primary experience of the child. He saw the child's need as hunger and his satisfaction as sucking. The earliest organized human motor activity is the child's sucking. If you touch the side of a very young child's lip, he will immediately begin to suck. It is a reflex right from the beginning. When you think about it, a very young infant spends most of his time sleeping and sucking. So naturally Freud saw this as the infants' whole life during his or her waking hours.

Later on, the child begins biting and chewing, and the mouth continues to have tremendous significance. The mouth dominates a child's life, as it certainly dominated Freud's thinking. For him, the whole issue of feeding was a fused one: the mouth, nipple, breast, and mother were all one, not differentiated. He coined the term *infantile omnipotence* to describe the feeling a child has at this phase. Freud arrived at an understanding of that feeling retrospectively through analyses and his own theoretical framework. One cannot ask a three-month-old child if he feels omnipotent. When a child feels hunger, dinner appears; the child no longer feels hungry, and he gains a feeling of tremendous power and satisfaction. The mother becomes an appendage to the child, not the other way around. Lest you think that sort of thinking is bizarre, remember pre-Copernican astronomy.

So one has hunger (which is a need), distress, or pain, and then one has food, which provides satisfaction, relief, and pleasure. Freud believed that if the mother is absent, the infant can hallucinate the gratification, an early way to begin to put things into one's own head rather than to be dependent upon the outside world. This represents a very primitive mental mechanism called *incorporation*.

We know that at six to eight months, infants begin to discriminate people. Something called *stranger anxiety* begins at eight months: A child will burst into tears when a stranger walks into the room because he or she recognizes that person is not the mother or caretaker. At this point the child delegates to the mother all his/her omnipotence, so the child remains the king or queen and the mother becomes a prime minister of sorts. "It's okay," the child says, "I'm still in power; she's just doing my bidding."

Defenses or mental mechanisms develop throughout childhood. One early defense is incorporation, "eating" the mother. Cannibalism is not merely the activity of a starving society; it also is done to acquire the strength of an enemy warrior. A second defense is introjection, the ability to put a mental image in your head and carry it around. A third is identification, to be like someone. Later, emulation, the conscious attempt to be like someone, comes into play.

What are some of the problems of the oral period? Oral anxiety, a fear of not getting fed or fear that the supplies will run out, commonly is traced to this period. Likewise, during the later biting and chewing period, the child also fears that other people may do that to him or her too, so a fear of being eaten up begins. This period of oral aggression and oral sadism, as opposed to the oral incorporation phase, comes later, usually after a year. Almost every playground has its "biter," a child who is always biting others and who the mothers or caretakers hate to have on the playground. There are two checks to that impulse to bite. The first one is very direct: If you bite and eat the cookie, then you don't have it anymore. The second is that if you bite your mother, you usually get a swat in return and you are in danger of losing her, so you learn sometimes to check that impulse. You learn that you want to have the mother or the cookie more than you want to drive it away. In this way, biting becomes identified as an aggressive act rather than a loving one like oral incorporation, and the child learns to begin to exercise some impulse control.

We associate several character traits with the oral period. Again, these traits go back to too much or too little, and classical psychoanalysts would consider things like overeating or undereating to come from this stage. The need to smoke (especially to chain-smoke), impatience, a feeling of "When am I going to get it?", and envy that someone else is getting it stem from this stage. So do the issues of self-confidence and optimism. When one is well fed and happy in this oral phase, the world will probably be one's oyster; if one was never fed properly and never got enough, life does not hold much. Hunger for intellectual knowledge is also seen as deriving from the oral, acquisitive phase.

Clearly, the tasks of parents during this phase are to give children the power to gain mastery and to help them grow so that they can become independent of outside supplies and gain a sense of self-esteem. These tasks present big problems. When children begin to feed themselves, they tend to drop about 99 percent of the peas on the floor while trying to get them into their mouths. Parents have to learn to be patient and inventive in figuring out ways to hold back anger, so that their children can learn to feed themselves. Otherwise, children who have been hand-fed all their lives will continue to expect to be hand-fed. Erikson,[6] as I said, continued the interest in this phase, but in a broader sense. Rather than focusing simply on the mouth (orality), he saw the phase as centering around the whole issue of trust versus mistrust, the relationship of the mother and child still being central.

In addition to the character traits I mentioned earlier, other pathological troubles can develop. Such real difficulties as alcoholism and drug abuse can be seen as oral difficulties, as can some psychosomatic difficulties such as ulcers, eating disorders, and hypochondriasis. Some personality traits, also seen as deriving from this phase, include the passive-dependent personality (always wanting things to come without having to ask), the passive-aggressive personality (always working against something), and the chronic depressive personality (ensuring that things will never work out, that things are always lousy, that you will never get fed).

The anal period starts in the second half of the second year.[7] Today we tend to see this period as much more linked to the whole issue of muscular development in the child. During the anal period the longer nerves become operative and both neurological and physiological development proceeds. Freud himself pointed that out. More specifically, Freud believed that the powerful stimulation in this phase from the anal mucosa was the central force, counteracted by the parent's wish to impose bowel training on the child. The important issue that potentially causes conflict is the parent's telling the child, "You can do it my way or your way; you produce now or you produce when you want to, which is in your pants somewhere else." At best, the child can reach a diplomatic concession without giving up self-esteem. Freud emphasized the whole pleasureful nature of fecal retention—that it feels good and that the greater the mass, the greater the pleasure.

Children have also been known to play with their feces and there are some playful aspects to defecation. At some point the child gives up these practices to a greater or lesser degree; he either represses the urge (pushing it down below the surface) or puts it into his character structure, most often through sublimation (which is another defense mechanism). Freud would see a clean, orderly person as having integrated that characteristic into his personality structure during the anal phase. Anger, too, enters the picture at this stage—anger at giving up, resistance, feelings of frustration, struggle, the feelings I described in the hypothetical case example.

Two really broad categories of negative results come out of the anal phase. Rather than a diplomatic concession and retention of one's self-esteem, one can go through the rest of life being either fearful, submissive, and dominated, or angry, defiant, and struggling. The diplomatic maneuver that says, "I am doing not only what mother wants, but what I want myself," gets you out of that bind by steering the course between the rage and submission. If that diplomatic maneuver does not work, and fear predominates, you become a passive, submissive, scrupulous, conscientious, orderly, neat, pedantic, precise person. On the other hand, if rage does occur, then stubbornness, frustration, procrastination, and overcontrol result. In real life people do not usually wind up all one way or the other; they tend to be mixtures of a number of these qualities.

Freud described that with a clean and neat person—whose home has everything in its place—there is always a bottom drawer that is messy. The personality structure described as having many of these traits is an obsessive-compulsive one in which rage and fear often alternate. At first, Freud saw aggression as coming from this period; he later decided that sex and aggression were fused from the beginning.

In classical psychoanalytic thinking at its most ludicrous extreme, professional choices are seen as deriving from the anal period. Surgeons are seen as anal sadists, painters as fecal smearers, and so forth. It makes amusing literature, but I think you have difficulty trying to prove it scientifically. Erikson, again, took a broader view of the anal period, focusing not on just toilet training, but on issues of mastery, muscular development, the ability to do and to control things oneself—ultimately, autonomy. The pathology that results from the period, in the classical view, is chronic hostility and an aggressive personality. I have described the passive-aggressive personality before. The army is full of passive-aggressive people. You go in and say, "Sergeant, would you please get this done today? It needs to be done." And he says, "Yes, sir," and the thing doesn't get done. He smiles you to death and you get furious, but he is working on it all the time. The aggressive person is overtly defiant, and that attitude is born, in Freud's thinking, in the anal period. Similarly, obsessive-compulsive symptoms begin here.

THE PHALLIC PHASE

The third and last erogenous phase is the phallic phase. Given the reemergence of the women's movement over the last 20 years, this is one of the most questioned aspects of Freud's thought.[8] The importance Freud placed on the penis is tempered by our current focus on society and on the prerogatives that males have (which may be symbolized in the penis), rather than vice versa.

Freud believed that children at this age are first able to differentiate the sexes, an ability that we now know exists much earlier.[9] Freud noted the tremendous importance of the penis. When you look at boys who are going through the phallic phase, of their sexual development, you will see them checking to make sure that their penises are still there. They have a tremendous need to make sure they possess what seems to count. Freud called the anxiety over loss of the penis *castration anxiety* and believed it to be universal. Little boys fear losing it; little girls know they have lost it and are furious about it. The penis is what gives Daddy his power and what weakens Mommy.

To Freud, the Oedipus complex is also universal. Every child goes through an Oedipal period in which he wants some sexual control over the opposite-sex parent—not necessarily sexual intercourse, but some bodily, pleasureful control. The male and the female, Freud said, have completely different ways of setting up that situation. The male has the mother already, and does not really need to switch to get her as a sex object, but he has the problem of a big, powerful male figure to contend with. Little boys at this age really do see how big their fathers are and they feel it very acutely. And if you are intimate with mother, woe will surely befall you. So, the child is on a razor's edge of whether or not to do something about his desire. He wants to get his pleasure, but he is also afraid his penis may get cut off if he goes too far. And so usually a resolution results in a diminution of the castration anxiety. The boy internalizes the father and identifies with him. He no longer thinks, "I want to knock off Dad so I can have Mom." Freud saw that resolution as resulting in the superego, in conscience. And he explained women's inability to exercise strong moral control by their not having gone through the same process. While this is no longer commonly accepted, it was one of the cornerstones of Oedipal thinking years ago.

As I have already said, Freud posited that women went through a different process. Freud himself went through an interesting process regarding his views about women. He started out saying that women go through the same process as men, that little girls go through the same process as little boys. Then he said that was not so, that you cannot understand women. Finally, he said that women go through a different process—that the woman has to shift her focus from the mother to the father, whereas the boy is able to stay with the same object. Freud explained this new belief with the theory of penis envy. Little girls become angry at the mother for depriving them of a penis, leaving them deformed, defective, and injured. The solution is, "If I can't have a penis, I can have a baby." Little girls also have a fear similar to the little boy's fear of castration. Little girls, he postulated, have fears of losing the love and affection of their parents. The little girl also makes a resolution and renounces the father in order to have a nonincestuous opposite-sex relationship, in the same sense that the little boy has renounced his wish for his mother.

There are problems that all children go through in this stage. They frequently are anxious and worried and have nightmares or scary dreams that are not nightmares. Freud's Oedipal theory presents several questions, and I shall mention but a few. The idea of penis envy being based on the organ rather than on the cultural and social elements is one. The absence of womb envy or envy of the woman's unique function is another. In addition, Freud's conception that women are passive and receptive and that males are assertive and aggressive is no longer universally accepted. Freud also assumed that drives organized all behavior around them. We now believe that the ego is the organizing force as the person goes through the developmental stages.

Arising from this phase, in Freud's eyes, are such problems as narcissism, which derives from the myth of Narcissus looking in the lake and falling in love with himself. Sometimes you look at couples and see clearly that, if the choice of partner was not narcissistic in terms of actions, it was in terms of appearance. One of the clearest examples of this phenomenon was the marriage of Mick and Bianca Jagger, who look like they came from the same mold.

Another problematic outcome is homosexuality, which is seen as a continued investment in the penis and in the same sex. Exhibitionism is another. Exhibitionists get pleasure from the reaction of the other people; usually it is a male showing his penis and a woman reacting. The action confirms for the man that he still has his penis. Voyeurism, too, stems from this phase. Little children want to know what others' organs look like, what goes on in sex. Again, at 35 that behavior is not usually considered socially acceptable.

LATENCY

Latency, for Freud, is really not a phase in the same sense as the others because he saw it as a stopping or time-out in development. Freud believed that there is a cessation in the biological push at this point, a view that is not held today. Actually, during latency, which comes somewhere between age six and adolescence at age 12 or so, there is a resurgence, frequently even an increase, of sexual feelings. Freud's second thought was that repression of sexual impulses occurs during this period. In our culture this is the case, but it is a culture-dependent issue. One reason Freud called this period latency is because the child's interests are mainly social ones. Children become very concerned with how the other children are doing and how they fit in. Their tie primarily is to the leader. When my daughter was nine years old, she and her friends adored their teachers; the teachers could do no wrong. Children at this stage are a group not in their similarities to each other, but in their common allegiance to their teachers.

Erikson saw the task during this period as being one of resolving the conflict between industry (by which he meant a turning from play to work) and inferiority. He saw, too, that cooperation, rules, and games are really very serious, the stuff of adult life, and that the pathology resulting from this period concerns difficulties in socialization and interpersonal relationships.

ADOLESCENCE

Freud saw adolescence as the beginning of the culmination, the pulling-together of the personality, accompanied by a tremendous increase in sexual drive. He said that being psychotic is normal during this period, just as we would say today that adolescent turmoil and chaos are commonplace. The stresses are enormous: bodily change, mental change, and appearance of new and increased defenses. Erikson has conceptualized this period in terms of an ego identity. The main task of adolescence, Erikson said, is to pull everything together and to feel that you are someone. The danger in this period is role confusion, not knowing how that personality is going to pull together. Much pathology attributed to this phase has to do with both the pulling together of the basic personality and antisocial behavior—delinquency and the like.

ADULT DEVELOPMENT

When I was in medical school, we had about a semester of lectures on development. I think it took our professor until the last lecture to get up to about age four-and-a-half. At that point he said, "And then there is adolescence, adulthood, and old age." That was the end of the series. If you review the literature, you will find that until relatively recently no discussion exists of development after childhood.

We are beginning now to elucidate the developmental stages of life beyond childhood and to consider that life does go on after adolescence. Freud conceived the genital phase as pulling together the oral, anal, and phallic stages and making everything work. He saw that the oral, anal, and phallic impulses individually could be expressed appropriately in foreplay as a part of adult sexuality.

But at this point Freud really stopped in terms of thinking that people could move on. The work that has been done on midlife crisis is intriguing and shows us, I think, a great deal about the continuing difficulties people have. It is obvious to those of us in our forties, say, that our friends drop off like flies, with divorces, new jobs, moves to Martha's Vineyard, and so forth, every other day. Like the case of infant masturbation, it is hard to understand how everybody for so long missed discovering something so commonplace. Part of the phenomenon is social, of course, since changes are now accessible and acceptable. But even so, one often can pick up the *Wall Street Journal* and read about the midlife crisis one day and about the number of 50-year-old stockbrokers who have quit and opened a shipyard or a poultry farm the next. Clearly, during certain times after age 20, you look at your life. After age 40, when you get a sense that life is going to be downhill from now on and that you have got different tasks to do, you realize you had better know where your pleasures are coming from, because you are not in the same position you were at age 16. Often this self-searching is caused by deaths or serious illnesses of friends or parents. Sometimes it seemingly comes out of the clear blue. Erikson would call the midlife problem a conflict between creating and producing, which he called generativity, on the one hand, and self-absorption or moving into oneself, on the other.

In the past, very little attention was paid by psychiatry to the problems of the aged. We treated the elderly like we treated children: With children you give them half the dose; with older adults you give them somewhat more. It is the same medicine applied in the same way. We did not see these age groups in any way as having different problems, struggles, and tasks to accomplish.

Erikson talks about maintaining one's ego (which he called *ego integrity*) against despair. And now studies of older age groups are getting funding and attention from the National Institute on Aging in Washington. You may know that, given our ability to lengthen life, the growth in population of those over 65 is going to be dramatic over the next few years. Myths we have held for years—e.g., that old people do not have sex, that they inevitably become senile—have been exploded.

PROBLEMS WITH FREUDIAN THEORY

I should now like to discuss some modern views of development and some problems in Freudian theory which have been exposed as it has been confronted with scientific evidence.

First, we now realize that life does not begin at birth—it begins before. We know that prenatal influences—the emotional and physical health of the mother, drug use, alcoholism, genetic factors—are important and have a profound effect on intelligence, temperament, and character. We also realize that environment is terribly important. We understand that each child is born with a unique temperament, that children are not all shaped by the same cookie cutter. And this helps us understand some problems in parenting.[10]

Take the example of a "laid-back" child of a "laid-back" mother—things will probably work out all right. But if you give a "laid-back" child an "uptight" mother, then you get problems. In a random sampling, the mother who has several children is going to have an equal number of "uptight" and "laid-back" ones. Unless she has considerable emotional resilience and flexibility, one child is going to get in trouble, whereas he might not with a mother of another temperament.

Second, we know that infant behavior can be conditioned by adults. Not all things that children do are spontaneous. Smiling and crying can be conditioned at six weeks. Children can pursue objects, they can respond to the female voice differentially, and they can move with caretakers or mothers.

A piece of research done 15 years[11] ago showed an interview on film between a man and a woman. Whenever the man would cross his legs, the woman would do the same; when the woman scratched herself, the man would then scratch himself. Even when they were talking about something bland, all this absolutely reciprocal and synchronous movement was going on. One of my colleagues at Cornell, Daniel Stern, wondered how early that activity begins.[12] It begins, he found, almost at birth, and you can see marvelous synchronous behaviors between tiny infants and mothers. They read each other totally. The mother herself does not understand what is going on, but that almost instantaneous movement clearly must be more than simple muscular activity—it has to be emotional and precognitive. Finally, the whole Oedipal question—does the child seduce the parent or vice versa—raises the issue of adult conditioning.

Third, Freud's concepts about the oral period presents some problems. The child does explore many things with his mouth, but largely because of curiosity and because the mouth is the system most ready for use at that age. We now see from animal studies and from observing infant behavior that human attachment, not mouth behavior, is the key issue. H. F. Harlow separated infant monkeys from their mothers.[13] He raised them, put them in either with warm, cuddly surrogate mothers that had no milk or with wire mothers that did have milk. The monkeys preferred the warm, cuddly holding object without milk over the wire object with milk. Harlow also showed that infant monkeys who grow up in isolation without some sort of contact really end up socially dysfunctional and unable to relate to other monkeys. So the thinking today is not that the mouth brings on all the attachment behavior, but that the attachment behavior has the mouth as one of its components.

Fourth, we see more clearly today that toilet training is but one of many acts of mastery and attempts at autonomy, control, and struggle in the second year of life.

Fifth, we see that sex-typing in the phallic period may not result so much from identification, as identification results from the social sex-typing. We give dolls to little girls and trucks to little boys. Girls can cook, not boys, and boys can roughhouse, not girls. Some of that typing depends on muscles, to be sure, but some depends on what is socially "right."

Sixth, we see that adolescence is much more than the simple pulling together of all those instincts along with a rise in sexual bombardment. The adolescent has to perform a lot of tasks: establishing independence from the family, making vocational and educational choices, adjusting to sexual development and maturity. All these are very critical tasks, and many people we see as patients have been unable to carry them out.

It is also perfectly natural that adolescents make a very narcissistic object choice—someone the chooser resembles, but also someone the chooser would like to resemble. Preadolescent chums, if you look back to before you began to date, have a strong bonding relationship that is very important in most lives. Adolescent rebellion and the adolescent's being able to turn toward others and away from parents are also critical. To look into one's life, to review it and see it as worthwhile, and to come to peace with oneself are also important tasks. These typical stresses occur in all phases of adult life.

In summary, early developmental theory has undergone several major revisions. We now see that during the infant's oral period we are dealing not simply with mouth behavior, but also with attachment behavior. The anal period is not simply a struggle over toilet training, but a complex phase involving muscular development and mastery. And, finally, we see the Oedipal period is not so much a wish to kill one parent off and take control of the other, but a longing to find a comfortable niche in one's family so that one can continue growing.

NOTES

[1]See the discussion of development in SE "The Development of Libido and the Sexual Organizations," vol. 16, 320-338.

[2]Lucien Malson, Wolf Children, trans. Edmund Fawcett et al. (London: NLB, 1972).

[3]See Erik H. Erikson, Childhood and Society (New York: W.W. Norton, 1964).

[4]See Jean Piaget, The Origins of Intelligence in Children (New York: W.W. Norton, 1963).

[5]On the question of seduction see, for example, Robert Fliess, Symbol, Dream and Psychosis (New York: International Universities Press, 1981).

[6]See Erikson's discussion of these in *Childhood and Society* as well as in his *Identity: Youth and Crisis* (New York: W.W. Norton, 1968).

[7]Sigmund Freud, "On Transformations of Instinct as Exemplified in Anal Erotism" (1917), *SE* vol. 17, 125-134.

[8]See Juliet Mitchell, *Psychoanalysis and Feminism* (New York: Vintage, 1975).

[9]See Sigmund Freud, "Three Essays on the Theory of Sexuality" (1905), *SE* vol. 7, 123.

[10]See Alexander Thomas and Stella Chess, *Temperament and Development* (New York: Brunner/Mazel, 1977).

[11]W.S. Condon, W.D. Ogston, "A Segmentation of Behavior," *Journal of Psychiatric Research*, 5, 1967, 221-235.

[12]Daniel Stern, *The First Relationship: Infant and Mother* (Cambridge, Mass.: Harvard University Press, 1977).

[13]H.F. Harlow and M.K. Harlow, "Psychopathology in Monkeys." In H.D. Kimmel, ed., *Experimental Psychopathology: Recent Research and Theory* (New York: Academic Press, 1971), 204ff.

Chapter 3

Affect

Michael H. Stone

"I'm sorry, Papa, but I think you're being vague and poetic again. It seems obvious to me that the phenomena of life, both material and spiritual, can be understood only through logical knowledge."
"But what about the heart? Where's the language of the heart, son, where's love?"*

SOME TERMS IN THE LANGUAGE OF EMOTION

Physicians and philosophers, throughout the centuries, have compartmentalized mental functioning into a small number of overarching divisions, whose distinctive features were often seen as belonging in pairs of opposites. Thus, the animal soul (thymos) of Aristotle and Plato contained the baser drives, instincts, and urges and was contrasted with the spiritual soul (psychē), the seat of loftier (including religious), feelings. Man was understood to have a capacity for methodical, goal-directed thought (Reason), a faculty that could be sharply differentiated from the "irrational." Bacon[1] spoke of Reason versus imagination. The imaginative and the irrational components of our thought were closely akin to—and in fact were the mental counterparts of—the otherwise

---

*Yuri Krotkov, *The Nobel Prize* (New York: Simon and Schuster, 1980), pp. 156-157.

more "somatically" localizable feelings or *emotions*. However one may care to define *emotion* (or the near-equivalent concepts of affect, mood, passion, feeling), the term clearly signifies some inescapable aspect of the human condition. This aspect often acquires pejorative overtones. There is something crude, animal-like, ill-considered to our feelings, as though Reason could ascend to the most pure and the most heavenly, were it not for the unwelcome intrusions from Emotion, emanating from the flawed but necessary body—upon which the Mind must, willy-nilly, make its precarious perch.

Since we shall be concentrating here upon the role of affect, both in everyday life and in psychoanalytic theory and treatment, we should discuss briefly the customary usage of "affect" and other related terms.

In psychiatric parlance *affect* and *emotion* (Lat. *e + movere*: to move outward) are used interchangeably in some contexts to denote strong, generalized feelings, psychical excitement, or various reactions with both psychical and physical manifestations.

Emotion, the less technical word, is used in general speech as well as in the psychiatric community to refer to the many specific varieties of generalized feelings—such as De Rivera[2] has enumerated—that we commonly recognize—love, hatred, joy, sorrow, envy, gratitude, to mention but a few.

Affect as an abstract concept may refer to the set of all emotions, to the subject of human emotionality in general—as in the title of this chapter. But in their day-to-day professional life, psychiatrists and psychoanalysts also use *affect* to signify the particular emotion that the patient or consultee is exhibiting, through intonation of speech and through his gestures, at the very moment of the interview. *Affect*, in this context, is something the interviewer intuits, relying on his own empathic machinery and upon his memory for the meaning of similar intonations and gestures in his or her past. Many times a consultant or therapist will be quite convinced he or she has perceived the patient's affect correctly, even though a statement to this effect maybe vigorously denied by the patient. Thus a patient may make contemptuous remarks about the members of his family, with extremely tense facial musculature throughout this rehearsal, eyes unblinking and pupils narrowed—all of which telegraph to the interviewer the affect of *hatred* or perhaps, even more specifically, of *scorn*. Here *affect* is the conclusion reached by the *observer* about the transitory emotional state of another person.

Overlapping in some respects with *affect* is the notion of *mood*. Mood also implies transitoriness, but it need not always be (although it usually is) readable by an observer. Mood has a greater *subjective* component than does the technical or abstract "affect." Someone could, for example, be in a "bad mood" without necessarily displaying a depressive affect (namely glum face, slowed movements) which others could readily detect. Often sufficient facial and other cues allow one's subjective "mood" to be interpreted correctly by an outsider (who might remark, "you seem to be in a happy mood"). Because it is more often colloquial than technical, "mood" is only occasionally used in scientific writing, as when one refers to the manic-depressive illnesses as "disorders of mood" (inappropriate elation or depression being their chief characteristics). Although a particular mood may remain for some extended period of time, the term is generally reserved for those aspects of emotional state most susceptible to fluctuation. The most predictable, least varying, and seemingly inborn aspects of one's emotional state (placidity, chronic irritability, intensity, fidgetiness, for example) come under the heading of *temperament*. Some overlap with affect will occur in certain persons, especially those with constitutional predisposition to depression—those whose "affect" is habitually sad, morose, resentful, worried, but whose *temperament*, from birth onward, will contain such similar elements as low pleasure capacity, sluggishness, pessimism.[4]

The study of *temperament* is relevant to the broad concept of affect, inasmuch as one's inborn temperament is important in determining one's predisposition to experience particular affects. The individual with manic temperament,[3,4] for example, will tend to feel optimistic and elated more often than others; the schizoid person will be exaggeratedly prone to embarrassment, shame, aversion (of other people). Still others will experience more than their share of hostility, scorn, jealousy (the "paranoid" personality, some instances of which appear to be founded on special genetic/constitutional vulnerability). Some temperaments outlined by Kraepelin—depressive, irritable, manic—correspond closely to the ancient taxonomy of *melancholic, choleric, sanguine*, respectively. These latter terms, along with the *phlegmatic* (corresponding to the sluggish or passive personality), were in common use from the time of the ancient Greek philosophers through the medieval period and into the mid-nineteenth century. The ancient writers ascribed these temperaments to excesses of one of the four elements—Earth, Air, Fire, or Water—of which our bodies were supposedly composed.[5]

Historically, the terms *affect* and *emotion* were preceded by the concept of *passion*, which had not yet evolved into the narrower usage, as we know it currently, for feelings of extreme intensity (most often of a sexual but, in other contexts, of a hostile nature). Descartes,[6] for example, spoke of the *passions* in their etymological sense of passive (*passio*) reactions on the part of the soul provoked by various *actions* in the body (or by various perceptions by the sense organs). Catching sight, for example, of a rapidly approaching and angry-appearing dog would lead, quickly and involuntarily, to the *passio* of fear.

Our mention of Descartes will prepare us for the examination of some important theories of emotion and affect, of which Descartes' monograph serves as the forerunner.

AFFECT AND EMOTION: SOME THEORETICAL APPROACHES

Descartes' view of the emotions represented a major advance over the Galenic notions, emphasizing the "four temperaments," which had held sway for a millenium and a half before Descartes' time. Already clearly in his 1650 essay, *Passiones Animae*, Descartes made the distinction between perceptions related to the body and those related more to mental states or the "soul." The former constituted what are now called the *drives*, such as hunger, thirst, or the need for sex, sleep, or physical comfort (warmth, freedom from pain). Those related to the soul are what we now call the emotions: joy, anger, and the other "sentiments" evoked in the soul by events, both external and internal. An external event could come as a nurturing action by a loved one, leading to the *passio* of contentment; an internal event would include sudden worries that could induce sadness. In Descartes' theory, emotions are regarded as intensified—or amplified—perceptions (along with the immediate inner consequences of those perceptions), whose effects are more widespread than are perceptions of things or people who do not interest, attract, or menace us. Descartes' work also embodies a *pain/pleasure principle*, similar to that of Freud and the psychoanalysts who came after him. Affect, in other words, is an intrinsic part of our mechanism for avoiding what would be harmful in any way, or of moving closer (physically or spiritually) to what would be of benefit.

Though *mind* (soul) and *body* were separable for Descartes, this famous "Cartesian dualism" did not preclude a close cooperation between the two agencies, such that the *passions* excited by actions on and in the body (including its special sense organs) stimulated immediate actions within the soul, namely, our *desires*.[4] Collectively, our desires constitute the will, although *desire* in the abstract was also understood as one of the primary "passions." Descartes felt all simple and complex feeling-states could be understood as expressions or as derivatives of six fundamental passions: *admiration, love, hate, desire, joy,* and *sorrow.* "Desire" was used in a manner that was conceptually very sophisticated, though it would strike us now as somewhat paradoxical. We tend to think of desire as designating a positive state—looking forward to something; in Descartes' usage *desire* was not unidirectional. A menacing situation, for example, could induce in us the *desire* to flee. Flight, then, was the form desire took in *aversive* situations.

Following Descartes, whose work in this area was largely ignored until recently,[7] few theoreticians addressed the issues of affect or emotion until the pioneering psychologists of the nineteenth century. Darwin also wrote on emotion,[8] but primarily as a biologist interested in evolutionary chain between man and the "lower" animals. He focused upon the various *actions* taken by the organism, following an emotion engendered by some change in the environment.

In the work of John Dewey,[9] we encounter concepts reminiscent of those expressed by Descartes. Describing "sensuous feeling," he wrote that the first and simplest form in which the soul puts forth its activity is through the physical organism. Feeling is the internal or individual side of all activity . . . if the eye sees, the whole organism feels the experience. . . . A sensation is itself an intrinsic affection of the soul, possessing a peculiar emotive quality of its own" (p. 250).

Further on, Dewey provides a rudimentary catalog of affects and feelings, compartmentalized into such subdivisions as feelings of "novelty" (similar to Descartes' *admiration*), which may be associated with either pleasure (and lead to *buoyancy*) or pain (and cause *terror*); feelings of transition (from one emotional state to another), which can include melancholy and gladness; or feelings "directed toward the future," such as anxiety and hope.

The theory of affect enunciated not long after Dewey's work by William James[10] was largely mechanistic. Emotions, for James, constituted a type of subjective awareness of one's physiological responses. One was *angry*, for example, because one became aware of the increased heart-rate and heightened muscle tension accompanying some change in one's personal environment. From a neurological standpoint, James saw no reason to hypothesize a particular region in the brain which might subserve "emotions"; rather he believed that the cerebrum was merely a surface upon which every sensitive spot and every muscle in the body had its projection.

In the early years of this century, psychologists and neurophysiologists were intrigued with stimulus-response mechanisms, behavioral theories,[11] and operant conditioning. For Cannon,[12] the quality of the experienced emotion depended upon the way in which the thalamus was activated. Central to Cannon's theory is a pleasure-pain principle, and in relation to that, an emergency-oriented psychology, built on the premise that we (or, indeed, any organism) will repeat a pleasurable activity and avoid one that causes pain. One set of affects may be lined up on the side of pleasure; another integrated into our emergency reactions in the face of physical or mental pain.

This theme finds expression in most psychoanalytic theories, especially that of Rado (see below). The neurophysiologist Papez[13] emphasized the role of the hypothalamus in affective states, the various emotions representing specific actions and subjective feelings and depending on neural connections between hypothalamus and the cerebral hemispheres. His work has been carried further by MacLean,[14] who elaborated a generalized theory of emotions, a central element of which was the functions of the *limbic system* (amygdala, hippocampus, fornix). The close connection between the limbic system and nerve tracts subserving the sense of smell underline the importance, particularly in lower animals, of olfactory functions in a wide range of emotional states. Rage, fear, sexual arousal—i.e., self-preservative as well as species-preservative affects—are thus mediated by the olfactory/limbic systems. MacLean[15] particularized his view of the central nervous system as composed of (a) the evolutionarily most primitive hypothalamic brain, concerned with pleasure/pain, (b) the limbic brain, housing "affective" memory, and (c) the neocortex, relating to higher cognitive functions.[16]

We have noted earlier that affect in its commonest usage in psychiatry refers to the emotional state of another person, as inferred by an observer, according to various visible behavioral cues. Izard[17] has given this aspect of affect a central position in his theory. Affect, in his claim, can be understood fully only by visualizing *personality* as a process of social communication. Facial expressions play a prominent role in this process and can telegraph such emotional states, usually with a high rate of "readability," as excitement, joy, surprise, distress, disgust, anger, shame, and fear.

How "affect," here in the sense of prevailing emotional state, is labeled by the subject appears to be influenced by preexisting expectations (usually known by the term "mental set"). As an example, the mental set of someone attending a film billed as "romantic" would be dominated by the expectation of love-scenes and an atmosphere of tenderness. If, in that situation, grotesque scenes of violence were shown, one's affect—of shock or revulsion—would tend to be much more intense than if one had witnessed the same sequences with the prior "set" of expecting to see a horror film. In the latter situation, the viewer might actually register titillation—a totally different affect—rather than revulsion, especially if the horror scenes were artistically or cleverly executed. Recently investigators, including Schacter,[18] Lazarus,[19] and Skinner,[20] have drawn attention to these seemingly paradoxical phenomena. Becker,[21] in this connection, noted how novice marijuana smokers had to be taught by experienced users how to label as a "high" the various physiological symptoms that would begin to manifest themselves. In other contexts, physiological changes, such as increase in blood pressure or heart rate, can be induced by noxious memories, by certain moment-to-moment shifts in ideation,[22] for example.

According to cognitive psychologists, the resultant affect in any novel situation is an expression of another modifying influence: "appraisal."[23] Cognitive appraisal, occurring almost instantaneously with perception, involves comparison with the memory bank of past experiences and with the affects associated with those experiences. To be yelled at by one's boss ordinarily provokes the affect of anger. This will be all the keener if one needs the job and has no options. The same event, should one have just received a better job offer elsewhere, may provoke something quite different: less anger, perhaps, or mere contempt (without any concomitant feelings of helplessness or bitterness). In the second, safer situation, the employee might feel emboldened to talk back; in the first, he might elect to suffer in silence.

Affect has also been considered from the vantage point of the ethologist. The communication of emotion in animals has been studied by Eibl-Eibesfeldt,[24] who focused on courtship behavior, gestures of submission, and facial expressions signaling warning of impending danger or readiness for attack. Ethologists assume certain instinctive patterns for emotional communication existing in man and also patterns that would manifest themselves even in the absence of opportunities for learning gestures from a social group. Certain affects may accompany, and be a part of, built-in behavioral patterns connected with learning social cues of high survival value to the individual. Human infants, beside having an instinctive predisposition to smile at mother, maternal surrogates, or even at a "happy face" (oval with two "eyes" and up-turned lips), soon recognize mother's smile, along with its psychological meanings (all is well, I love you, all right to go ahead). If mother *smiles* as she holds a cookie, she will likely offer it; if she wears a *frown*, she will likely withhold it.

At a later stage of development, a child is able to grasp through words alone the *affective experience* of another, complete with its physiological concomitants. Imagine two children, one of whose fathers related an incident where he was once pushed into the water at camp, but, after his initial fright, treaded water, and learned to swim. The other father, relating a similar experience, mentions that he nearly drowned and has avoided the water ever since. We could predict (with a good degree of accuracy) that the first child would be relatively unafraid of the water and would learn to swim without much difficulty. The second, having registered the panicky affect implicit in the story, might well identify with his father's apprehension and become phobic in turn.

Freud, from the beginning, dwelt more on the abstract nature of affect than on the particular varieties we commonly recognize. *Affect* was distinguished from the ideational *content* that might otherwise adhere to it. There was, in mental functions, "a quota of affect, capable of increase, diminution, displacement and discharge." This wave of affect was then pictured by Freud, in the neurophysiological model of his day, as "spreading over the memory-traces of ideas as an electric charge is spread over the body."[25] It was a cornerstone in Freud's metapsychology that an increase in affective "tension" led to pain ("unpleasure") and a decrease to pleasure or, at least, a lowering of unpleasure, until a state of neutrality or homeostasis was achieved.* Elsewhere he wrote: "An affect includes . . . particular motor innovations . . . and secondly, certain feelings; the later are of two kinds—perceptions of the motor actions** that have occurred and the direct feelings of pleasure or unpleasure which . . . give the affect its keynote."[27]

A similar closed-system theory of affect was elaborated by Rapaport,[28] for whom percepts stemming from the environment initiated an "unconscious process," which then mobilized "unconscious instinctual energies." *Conflict* was understood as the outcome of a situation where (again, in highly mechanistic terms) no free pathway to voluntary motion was open for these energies. The result of this blockade was a spillover of energy into *emotion*.

Sandor Rado, the founder of the adaptational school of psychoanalytic thought, made several important contributions to affect theory. He made a practical division of the more common affective states into "welfare" emotions (love, joy, pride, pleasurable desire) and the "emergency"

---

*Later, Edith Jacobson[26] was to point out that certain pleasurable affects can occur "paradoxically" (with respect to Freud's tenet), under conditions of *increased* tension, as in the case of sexual orgasm.
**Cf. William James' theory, cited above.

emotions (fear, rage, guilty fear, guilty rage).[29] Recognizing the survival value of the latter in true emergencies, Rado also dwelt on how often these affects are engendered in neurotic individuals under circumstances where danger is not present realistically, but merely misconstrued as being present.

As for the welfare emotions, many are now understood as derivatives of favorable interaction between mother and infant; to promote this interaction the infant has an instinctive repertoire of behavior patterns. These comprise crying, clinging, sucking, following with the eyes, and smiling.[30] The innate attachment mechanisms elicit nurturing and loving responses from mother and other persons important in the environment and underlie the most intense of the pleasurable *affects* (joy, contentment) we recognize. Not related to body contact or intimacy appear to be another set of pleasurable affects, namely, those resulting from innate drives toward mastery of the environment. Piaget[31] has delineated these joys-of-action: seeking, learning, competing, creating.

Later, Rado,[32] in writing on persons who exhibited various clinical forms (collectively known as the *schizotype*) of the schizophrenic genotype, emphasized the crucial role in their condition played by *anhedonia* (the inborn deficiency in the capacity for pleasure). In Rado's view this constitutional defect undermined the schizotype's efforts to live a normal life among people by lowering self-confidence, by weakening the counterbalancing effects that the welfare emotions ordinarily exert over fear, by inhibiting sexual function, and by limiting the capacity for appropriate enjoyment of life activities. The clinical vignette at the end of this chapter will illustrate many of these points.

With respect to the mind-body dualism so prominent in Western thought, the concept of *affect* clearly cuts across both lines. In the same way that it sometimes makes more sense to speak of light as corpuscular and in other contexts as wave-like, some aspects of affect will seem predominantly mental, others somatic. The balance between these "components" is itself dependent upon the particular affect under discussion. *Shame*, for example, is often accompanied by blushing, a lowering of the head, and a quickening of the heart rate—over and above its well-known psychological features. Shame envelops the whole person in this sense: Mind and body are both involved as near-equal partners. The affect of *mockery*, however, ordinarily has fewer somatic accompaniments. Apart from some change in facial expression, this affect is largely "mental."

If mind and body are both separable and integrated, depending on one's area of interest, some psychoanalytic theoreticians have, in accordance with their special interests, dwelt on one or the other aspect of emotional phenomena. Some have dwelt upon both at once. Franz Alexander's approach was *integrative*. Because, in his view, such processes as facial flush in anger, sobbing after news of a loved-one's death, etc., are perceived subjectively as emotions and then observed objectively as changes in bodily functions,[33] Alexander preferred to think of affect as a *psychosomatic* phenomenon. He advocated simultaneous study of psychological and physiological events in carrying out research on emotional states. Brenner[34] also adopted an integrative view, having defined *affect* as a complex mental phenomenon that includes both *ideas* (namely, thoughts, memories, wishes, fears) and *sensations* (of pleasure, unpleasure, or mixtures of the two).

Reexamining affect from an object-relations perspective, Kernberg[35] has stressed the survival value of emotion. Affects have a particular *raison d'être* for the individual, because they serve to "increase the perception of external and internal stimuli," which then promotes the fixation of memory traces for those particular events critical to the welfare of the individual.

Peter Knapp[36] has recently drawn our attention to some aspects of affect about which less has been written. He mentions, for example, the *immediacy* of the emotional experience, its urgency or *imperiousness* (riveting our attention and blocking out awareness of other stimuli), the quantitative *range* of emotions (from faint to massive and overwhelming), and the relatively stereotyped *expressive patterns* connected with each important species of affect (many of which are shared with other animals).

SYSTEMS-ORIENTED APPROACHES TO AFFECT

A number of psychologists and psychiatrists have attempted, during the past 15 years, to develop a rational and systematic taxonomy of affective states. These investigators have prepared extensive lists of all commonly recognized emotions as a first step in reaching higher abstraction in the psychology of affect. Each has searched for factors common to several otherwise distinguishable emotions, in the hopes of establishing a small and more manageable set of fundamental affective building blocks, analogous to the periodic table of elements in chemistry.

Davitz[37] compiled a list of 400 emotional terms. Many were not readily classifiable in a reliable way among the reviewers to whom he submitted his catalog, but in about 140 instances the connotations were sufficiently similar in the minds of the reviewers to warrant further analysis. Davitz felt that these remaining emotion-words could best be regrouped in accordance with four factors, each existing in three states.

The four factors were: (a) level of activation (which could be normally-, hypo-, or hyper-active), (b) relatedness (moving toward, away, or against), (c) hedonic tone (or degree of joy, gladness)—where comfort, discomfort, or tension might be encountered, and (d) competence (namely, degree of vitality, energy), divisible along lines of enhancement (trying, competing), incompetence, or inadequacy.

Davitz was interested in the process by which we come to label various affective states. He acknowledged that the language of emotion reflected actual experiences, but was also conditioned by linguistical considerations: People *learn* to label their emotions, and this learning is not achieved with uniform success or results by all members of a culture (see below the condition of "alexithymia").

More recently, De Rivera,[2] Hartvig Dahl,[38] and Dahl and Stengel,[39] have made significant contributions toward a systematic theory of emotions. I have elaborated on their models in a previous paper.[7] Dahl and Stengel have constructed a three-dimensional classificatory tree, in which each of three variables exists in two states. This schema generates 2^3 or 8 fundamental emotions. First, affects can be related either to the *self* or to *other persons* (designated ME- and IT-emotions, respectively). Second, emotions can be characterized by *attraction* or *repulsion* (analogous to Davitz's moving toward or moving away) or, in the case of the ME-emotions, positive or negative. Finally, the IT-emotions can be directed *to* or derived *from* external sources (in the case of the ME-emotions, a division into *passive* or *active* is possible). The four fundamental IT-emotions are love (attraction *to* an object) surprise (attracted by an object or event), anger (repulsion or hostility toward an object), and fear (repulsion or flight *from* an object). The four ME-emotions are contentment (passive, positive "me"), joy (active, positive "me"), depression (passive, negative "me"), and anxiety (active, negative "me").

Dahl presents a convincing teleological argument, comparable to Rado's, that powerful survival advantages would accrue to those persons (or members of animal species) that best knew when to be attracted, when to be repulsed, when to relate to some external "object" (including other persons), or when to attend to its own internal messages. A fascinating observation to emerge from Dahl's work[38] is that certain positive ME-emotions (love, in particular) are essential to life, yet cannot be satisfied by a consummatory act that the individual could initiate (in the manner that eating is a "consummatory act" that can satisfy hunger). An infant cannot survive unless it becomes the object of someone else's love (or more specifically, of someone else's "appetite" of or need to be loving toward another human being); yet, as Dahl points out, there is no special act the infant can perform to *insure* that he will receive this essential nurturing emotion from another. The poignancy surrounding this situation, the awful consequences when enough love has not been received in one's formative years, and the unusual mechanisms that may be resorted to by those who have suffered affective deprivation of this sort will, I hope, come alive in the clinical vignette offered in the next section.

The close correspondences between the elegant model of Dahl for systematizing emotions, and that of Descartes in his 1650 monograph have been touched on elsewhere.[7] Those interested in reading some classical psychoanalytic papers on affect theory and on such particular affective states as pouting, arrogance, anxiety, boredom, querulousness, etc., should consult the recent book of Socarides,[40] in which these papers have been gathered.

FINAL REMARKS AND ILLUSTRATIVE CLINICAL VIGNETTE

Though the capacity for pleasure is inborn, it may in certain persons be impaired or drastically deficient. This is particularly true of those with high genetic vulnerability to schizophrenia. These persons exhibit the anhedonia, which Rado felt was a key symptom in the "schizotype" (see above). It now appears that abnormalities of chemical neurotransmitters in the limbic system may underlie this anhedonia.[41] The incapacity for pleasure in such persons is thus largely constitutional, and not the by-product of faulty rearing, orphanage, or other forms of adverse environment.

Some patients with anhedonia and a few others who retain the capacity for experiencing pleasure nevertheless exhibit another peculiarity in the realm of affect: an inability to identify and to label properly their moment-to-moment feelings. This situation has been described[42] by a word of mixed Latin and Greek parentage: *"alexithymia"* (literally, not-to-read-the-passions). Certain psychosomatic patients, epileptics, schizophrenics, manics, and victims of organic brain damage demonstrate this incapacity. Persons with this trait are constantly getting into trouble in intimate relationships, because, for example, they do not know they are angry when (as is clear to any onlooker) they are actually seething with hostility. For people with alexithymia, of course, their emotions are in effect cut off from their cognition. *Affect* no longer serves as a reliable signaling or alerting system regarding sources of pleasure or danger stemming from those around them or from the environment in general.

In my clinical work, the functions of affect as alerting device and as catalyst to action (appropriate action in the normal person; woefully inappropriate action, all too often, in the neurotic) have never stood out with such clarity for me as they have in the case of a young man with whom I had been working, during a three-year span, some five years ago.

This man sought help at age 26 because of difficulty overcoming the kind of depression, lack of self-confidence, and suicidal ruminations that had caused him a little earlier to withdraw from a promising legal clerkship. He was quite good-looking in a conventional masculine way; he dressed meticulously, spoke in a refined manner using an excellent vocabulary, was highly cultivated in the areas of music and literature, and presented no eccentricities of comportment or gesture such as might appear odd or unpleasant in the eyes of strangers. Despite this agreeable façade, he gave evidence of the most withering self-hatred. He saw himself almost literally as a roach or alley rat slinking along the sideboards below the level of ordinary folk; he was convinced their gaze reflected contempt for him, as though he were either a worthless subhuman—like the huge bug that Kafka's Gregor Samsa awoke one fine morning to find himself transformed into—or else a homosexual.

As one may imagine from this description, he was painfully shy, a habitual loner, the kind of patient that vitally illustrates the nineteenth-century term for the mentally ill: *alienated*. Wherever he was—in his home, in his home town, in his job, in his dormitory at school—he was always the *alien*. But what was most striking about this otherwise personable and—to the extent that he persevered in the face of his self-hatred—courageous young man was the *near absence of pleasurable affect*. Apart from Chopin and the dancing of a Melissa Haydee or a Natalia Makarova, nothing moved him to pleasure. And when he was in a particularly bad mood, he would even rip up his concert or ballet tickets hours before the performance, as though someone as unworthy as himself had no business infecting public places with his presence. The few times he dared approach girls for dates, he experienced even the slightest hesitation, the most exiguous sign of unfriendliness on the girl's part, as a quite literal castration. He actually fantasized she were about to unman him with some stiletto secreted about her person, were he to move an inch closer.

While he would be telling me of these fantasies—which at times amounted to transitory delusional episodes—he would regularly fantasize that I too meant to attack him in a similar fashion. This would cause him to cross his legs in self-defense and to glower at me with the most intimidating look of hatred I had ever experienced from a patient. He felt mortally frightened of me, who meant him no harm (so grossly did he misread *my* affect), meantime scaring me as no patient had ever done before, to the point where for several sessions I took to carrying an open knife in my pocket lest he attack me and to stationing, unbeknownst to him, a rather hefty acquaintance in the anteroom during the hour set aside for our meeting, so that I could summon help in an emergency. Thus armed, I grew more relaxed and was able with some composure to interpret to him how intimida*ting* he truly became, whenever he felt intimida*ted* over realistically harmless gestures or facial expressions in his personal environment.

I shall not detail here the many steps and many months of work necessary to reduce this man's anxiety to livable levels. What is of interest for our purposes is to understand how his disorder of *affect* highlighted the chief functions of affect, one of which had never been so clear to me before.

Specifically because he had so little constitutional capacity for pleasure, human intimacy—instead of a potentially joyful togetherness, the happiness from which could far outweigh the moments of anguish, dislike, and disharmony—became for him a crowded minefield through which he dared not walk, because in his eyes there were explosions at every step and nothing better than hardtack and stale water at the other end. Why, therefore, get close? How much better to avoid people altogether and relate instead to his cat, the only creature he could envision capable of sustained love free of castrating hatred. This man had several close relatives with outright schizophrenia—whereas his condition was a less-serious schizoid personality disorder, in the penumbra, as it were, of full-blown schizophrenia. But the type of affect disturbance he showed, rendering him exquisitely sensitive to other people's negative feelings and completely blind to their warmth and acceptance, made comprehensible to me for the first time why schizophrenics and their less drastically ill schizoid cousins avoid intimacy and become "alienated."

The other chief function of affect also becomes clear through its absence in this clinical vignette.

The correct reading of *other* people's affect, through appropriate enregistration of tone of voice, facial expression, bodily gesture—and through appropriate comparison (unconscious and instantaneous) in our memory bank with all previously enregistered tones of voice—permits us, while still at a safe distance from the other or others in our interpersonal field, to shift our own behavior in keeping with the message that is being transmitted. This subtle, largely unconscious process enables a courting couple, with few words being spoken, to understand how far it is all right to go in their moves toward sexual union, enables a young person to know which parent and at what moment he might most propitiously ask for the car keys, and so forth.

The young man in my example never learned the vocabulary of tender feelings or of joy, partly because neurophysiologically he seemed to have been born with something missing—something which left him improperly equipped in the whole domain of pleasure, much as though he possessed a crazy radio tuned only to cacophony and unable to transmit Mozart. He could only pick up other people's rage, indifference, boredom, disaffection, and furthermore magnified small signals of those affects to such a degree he could scarcely distinguish those who befriended him from those whose ill-will approximated his worst fears.

There appeared, however, to be another component to his anhedonia, one that was psychological rather than biological in origin. When working with an adult patient, reconstructing the prevailing emotional atmosphere at home during the childhood years is difficult. One seldom has access to the patient's relatives, and many of their accounts would be hazy, distorted, or otherwise unreliable. The patient's own recollections are necessarily subjective and prone to distortions and inaccuracies. Those with unresolved hostility toward parents, or with the anhedonia of the schizotype, may have no ability to recall having been loved, even when one or both parents were adequately warm and nurturing.

With this caveat, I feel it nevertheless justifiable to express the opinion, as well as my clinical intuition and my reconstruction of his memories would permit me, that the family of the man in our vignette was singularly lacking in empathy for his feelings or in demonstrativeness of whatever warm feelings they may ever have held toward him. The father seemed consistently aloof and hostile; an older sibling was sadistic until the patient was nearly fully grown; the mother showed tenderness and concern on occasion, but seldom rallied to her son's defense and often suppressed what warm feelings she may have harbored, in keeping with certain fundamentalist religious prohibitions against showing love—a tradition in which she was raised and which she perpetuated in her own household. In summary, the emotional aridity of this man's early environment afforded him little love or warmth that was in any way visible to him and made love seem either totally inaccessible because "no one" (in his view) loved anyone else, or, at best, like something one encountered in poetry or in other people's homes. He grew to feel he was simply not destined ever to be the object of another's love. All his experience in life told him love did not exist; there were no joyful memories from his past to bolster his spirits during moments of adversity. The whole spectrum of warm emotions was absent, through experience, from his psychological palette, leaving him only the grays and the blacks. He was, in other words, "taught" to have no sense of pleasure; hence he became anhedonic for environmental as well as for constitutional reasons.

Life would be insupportable unless one could feel lovable at least to some degree, but since, as we noted in our review of Dahl's theories, one cannot compel love from another person, the patient in our example found himself in perilous circumstances. The device he intially chose for coping with this otherwise universal lovelessness was at once adaptive and immensely sorrowful. He turned his cat into a creature he could endow with the whole range of loving feelings to which in "real" (i.e., interpersonal) life he remained a stranger. Mostly she "loved" him; sometimes she was "disappointed" in him; at other times, she considered him wonderful or gallant. In a word, he created, through fantasies at times so intense as to border on the delusional, the love of which he had for so long felt himself deprived. To be sure, the cat was reasonably friendly, though he mostly knew, intellectually, this love was a figment of his own imagination. But this make-believe love sustained this man. His capacity to invest his pet with this emotion is a tribute to his resourcefulness and may well have protected him against suicide. Unfortunately, vicarious experiences of this kind cannot substitute fully for the genuine love from another person. The hope would be that the relationship with the pet might tide over such a patient, until such time as the human relationship—with the analyst or psychotherapist—begins to teach the patient that love, nurture, and warm regard are not phantom emotions detectable only in fiction. With schizotypal patients, in particular, this process requires many years.

*****

Those of us who fare better in the interpersonal world to do so clearly because (1) we have a better capacity for pleasurable affect and (2) we have the equipment to read others' affects with some accuracy, with regard to both their specific nature and their intensity.

In conclusion, the mechanisms for reading affect are themselves becoming clearer, thanks to some recent methodological breakthroughs. Work with split-brain preparations and with testing capable of isolating the two cerebral hemispheres has begun to teach us that the correct appreciation of the *emotional* meaning of sounds and sights around us is mediated chiefly by the cerebral hemisphere which is nondominant for logical speech.[43] Usually this is the right hemisphere, even in many left-handed persons. The appropriateness or inappropriateness of our behavior, in relation to the affects expressed by others, is the product of an interplay between the nondominant hemisphere *identification* of affect and the dominant hemisphere mediated selection of the *most reasonable strategy* for responding to the just-processed affective signals. This enables us to run *from* the tiger and *toward* our loved ones with an efficiency that is highly favorable to survival, and without which gratifying interpersonal life or life itself would become impossible. Thus reason and emotion, the rational and the irrational, help each other to guide our lives.

Normally, a mother loves her child simply because it is *hers*, and irrespective of the fact other children might be found who were smarter, prettier, neater, kinder, and more talented than her own. As far as she is concerned, her baby is the best. This is, from a purely logical point of view, wholly irrational. But this very pervasive, all-encompassing, blind, and irrational love serves as the wellspring for the growing child's self-image as a lovable human being. This, too, takes on an "irrational" quality. The once sufficiently loved youngster matures into an adult who will continue to feel worthy (unless he does something truly monstrous) even in the teeth of scorn, disappointment, criticism, or abandonment. Love fosters the normal component of our narcissism. Life itself, under optimal circumstances, thus depends on the proper balance between realism and the appropriate sort of life-enhancing "irrationality." Probably the incorporation of the abundant love of a good mother permitted Freud to persevere—against the wholesale criticism of the orthodox psychiatric community of his day—in laying the groundwork for the theories of affect which we have examined here.

NOTES

[1] R. Bacon (1640). *The Advancement and Proficiency of Learning*. Oxford: L. Lichfield.

[2] J. De Rivera, (1977). "A Structural Theory of Emotions. *Psychol. Issues: Monograph* 40. International Universities Press, New York.

[3] E. Kraepelin, (1921). *Manic-Depressive Insanity and Paranoia*. Edinburgh: E. and S. Livingstone.

[4] M. H. Stone, (1980a). *The Borderline Syndromes: Constitution, Personality and Adaptation*. New York: McGraw-Hill.

[5] J. Huarte y Navarro, (1603). *Examen de Ingenios para las Sciencias*. Plantiniana.

[6] R. Descartes, (1650). *De Passionibus Animae*. Amsterdam: L. Elsevir.

[7] M. H. Stone, (1980b). "Modern Concepts of Emotion as Prefigured in Descartes' *Passions of the Soul*." Presented at Payne Whitney Clinic, Seminar on History of Psychiatry, New York, March 14, 1979. *Journal Amer. Acad. Psychoanal.* 8:473-495.

[8]C. Darwin, (1872). *The Expression of Emotions in Man and Animal.* New York: Philosophical Library, 1955.

[9]J. Dewey, (1887). *Psychology.* New York: Harper and Bros.

[10]W. James, (1890). *The Principles of Psychology* (2 vols.). New York: Henry Holt, p. 473.

[11]See J. B. Watson, *Behaviorism.* New York: W.W. Norton, 1970.

[12]W. B. Cannon, (1915). *Bodily Changes in Panic, Hunger, Fear and Rage.* New York: Appleton-Century-Crofts; (1927). "The James-Lange Theory of Emotion: A Critical Examination and an Alternative Theory." *Amer. Journal Psychol.* 39:106-124.

[13]J. W. Papez, (1937). "A Proposed Mechanism of Emotions." *Arch. Neurol. Psychiat.* 38:725-743.

[14]P. D. MacLean, (1945). "The Limbic System and Its Hippocampal Formation: Studies in Animals and Their Possible Application to Man." *Journal Neurosurg.* 2:29-44.

[15]P. D. MacLean, (1967). The Brain in Relation to Empathy and Medical Education." *Journal Nerv. Ment. Dis.* 144:374-382.

[16]See also O. F. Kernberg, (1967). "Borderline Personality Organization." *Journal Amer. Psychoanal. Assoc.* 15:641-685, p. 87.

[17]C. E. Izard, (1972). *The Face of Emotion.* New York: Appleton-Century-Crofts.

[18]S. Schacter, (1964). "The Interaction of Cognitive and Physiological Determinants of Emotional State." In Berkowitz, L. (ed.). *Advances in Experimental Social Psychology,* vol. 1. New York: Academic Press. Pp. 49-80; (1970). "The Assumption of Identity and Peripherilist-Centralist Controversies in Motivation and Emotion." In Arnold, M. B. (ed.). *Feelings and Emotion: The Loyola Symposium.* New York: Academic Press.

[19]R. S. Lazarus, (1968). "Emotions and Adaptation: Conceptual and Empirical Relations." In Arnold, W. J. (ed.). *Nebraska Symposium on Motivation.* Lincoln: Univ. of Nebraska Press.

[20]B. F. Skinner, (1957). *Verbal Behavior.* New York: Appleton-Century-Crofts.

[21]H. S. Becker, (1953). "Becoming a Marijuana User." *Amer. Journal Sociol.* 59:235-242.

[22]H. Leventhal, (1974). "Emotions: A Basic Problem for Social Psychology." In Nemeth, C. (ed.). *Social Psychology: Classic and Contemporary Intergrations.* Chicago: Rand-McNally, Pp. 1-51.

[23]M. B. Arnold, (1960). *Emotion and Personality* (2 vols.). New York: Columbia Univ. Press.

[24]I. Eibl-Eibesfeldt, (1970). *Ethology: The Biology of Behavior.* New York: Holt, Rinehart and Winston.

[25]S. Freud, (1894). "The Neuro-Psychoses of Defense." *SE* vol. 3, 60.

[26]E. Jacobson, (1953). "The Affects and Their Pleasure-Unpleasure Qualities in Relation to Psychic Discharge Processes." In Loewenstein, K. M. (ed.). *Drives, Affects and Behavior.* New York: International Universities Press.

[27]S. Freud, (1916). "Introductory Lectures on Psychoanalysis." *SE* vol. 20, 395.

[28]D. Rapaport, (1942). *Emotions and Memory.* Baltimore: Williams & Wilkins, p. 37.

[29]S. Rado, (1956). *Psychoanalysis of Behavior.* New York: Grune and Stratton.

[30]J. Bowlby, (1969). *Attachment and Loss* (Vol. 1). New York: Basic Books; (1973). *Attachment and Loss* (Vol. 2). New York: Basic Books.

[31]J. Piaget, (1954). *The Construction of Reality in the Child.* New York: Basic Books.

[32]S. Rado, (1962). "Schizotypal Organization." In *Psychoanalysis of Behavior,* vol. 2. New York: Grune and Stratton, p. 2.

[33]F. G. Alexander, and Selesnick, S. T. (1966). *The History of Psychiatry.* New York: Harper and Row, p. 389.

[34]C. Brenner, (1974). "On the Nature and Development of Affects: A Unified Theory." *Psychoanal. Quart.* 43:532-566.

[35]O. F. Kernberg, (1976). *Object-Relations Theory and Clinical Psychoanalysis.* New York: Jason Aronson, p. 109.

[36]P. H. Knapp, (1979). "Core Processes in the Organization of Emotions." Presented at the December meeting of the American Academy of Psychoanalysis, New York.

[37]J. R. Davitz, (1969). *The Language of Emotion.* New York: Academic Press.

[38]H. Dahl, (1978). "A New Psychoanalytic Model of Motivation." *Psychoanal. Contemp. Thought* 1:373-408.

[39]H. Dahl, and Stengel, B. (1978). "A Classification of Emotion Words." *Psychoanal. Contemp. Thought* 1:269-312.

[40]C. W. Socarides, (1977). *The World of Emotions*. New York: International Universities Press.

[41]C. D. Wise, and Stein, L. (1969). "Facilitation of Brain Self-Stimulation by Central Administration of Norepinephrine." *Science* 163:299-301.

[42]P. E. Sifneos, (1973). "The Prevalence of 'Alexithymic' Characteristics in Psychosomatic Patients." *Psychother. Psychosom.* 22:255-262.

[43]R. E. Gur, Levy, J., and Gur, R. C. (1977). "Clinical Studies of Brain Organization and Behavior." In Frazer, A., and Winokur, A. (eds.). *Biological Bases of Psychiatric Disorders*. New York: Spectrum Publications, p. 135.

ACKNOWLEDGMENT

The author wishes to acknowledge with gratitude the help of Dr. Clarice J. Kestenbaum in the preparation of this manuscript, particularly in relation to the history of affect psychology.

Chapter 4

The Structure of
Freud's Dream Theory

Marianne Horney Eckardt

Why do we dream? To Freud, the answer was a key element in his theory about dreaming: A dream is always the fulfillment of an unconscious wish arising from the drama of infantile sexuality. This he called the essential nature of dreaming. A momentous accidental discovery in 1953[1] demanded a new perspective. Dreams were found to be a characteristic of a distinct state of sleep evidenced by physiological and neurophysiological changes which recur in phasic regularity, were common to the mammalian species, occurred in greater frequency in infants, and decreased with age. We still do not know why we dream, but the very regularity makes the act of dreaming, but not the content, an event independent of psychological happenings.

But we cannot sidestep Freud's theory about dreaming. The conceptual giants of our civilization stand above the right or wrong of key elements of their theoretical structures. The structures hold together a wealth of observations which have given food for thought to centuries of men. There is no new dream approach which does not have to argue with Freudian doctrine. No less important is the fact that the systematic approach to dream understanding was Freud's creation and that the various phenomena of dreaming were given his terminology, his conceptual signature.

The dilemma posed by the stimulating wealth of Freud's observations and ideas and the disconcerting limitations of his theoretical structure can be met by an attempt to gain conceptual clarity about the basic theoretical structure. This paper will emphasize the theoretical structure, rather than the observations and will also sketch only briefly present concepts. This endeavor has its difficulties:

> (1) Freud's *The Interpretation of Dreams*,[2] the publication of which in 1900 was an event without equal in the history of dreams, is his first elaborate attempt to explain his new discovery, "psychoanalysis." Dream analysis permitted glimpses into the unconscious. The study of dreams was a most suitable vehicle to express the rich tapestry of Freud's thoughts and designs about psychoanalysis. The book is about psychoanalysis, not primarily about dreams.
> (2) An unencumbered historical approach to dream theory is as yet impossible. Freud's theories are still vested in larger systems of belief and nonbelief.
> (3) There is no way we can do justice to Freud by embarking on a basically prosaic task of schematizing his theoretical structure.

"By general consensus," Ernest Jones wrote in his biography of Freud, "*The Interpretation of Dreams* was Freud's major work."[3] It was major because it was his first elaborated statement about the basic principles of his epoch-making creation, to which he gave the name "psychoanalysis." This psychoanalysis is least of all a psychotherapeutic method. It is a psychology of the human mind. Freud may talk about insignificant events like slips of the tongue, but his mind always aimed at a universally valid design. Already in 1895, a month before the publication of *Studies in Hysteria*, Freud spoke about his dominant passion in the service of which he knew no moderation. He wrote:

> A man like myself cannot live without a hobby horse, without a dominant passion; in fact, without a tyrant, to use Schiller's expression, and that is what it has become. For in its service I know no moderation. It is psychology which has been the goal beckoning me from afar, and now that I have come in contact with neuroses, the goal has drawn much nearer. Two aims plague me: to see how the theory of mental functions would shape itself if one introduced quantitative considerations, a sort of economics of nervous energy;

secondly, to extract what psychopathology has to yield for normal psychology.[4]

Understanding this daring grand dominant passion is important for the understanding of Freud's theories. In 1895 Freud had begun the writing of his "Project for a Scientific Psychology."[5] He wrote it in two weeks in a spirit of great excitement, complete preoccupation, and immersion. A letter written less than two weeks after finishing the "Project" gives a flavor of the incredible richness and reach of his mind. He wrote:

> One evening last week when I was hard at work, tormented with just that amount of pain that seems to be the best state to make my brain function, the barriers were suddenly lifted, the veil drawn aside, and I had a clear vision from the details of the neuroses to the conditions that make consciousness possible. Everything seemed to connect up, the whole worked well together, and one had the impression that the thing was now really a machine and would soon go by itself. The three systems of neuroses, the free and bound state of quantity (energy), the primary and secondary processes, the main tendency, and the compromise tendency of the nervous system, the two biological laws of attention and defense, the indications of quality, reality, and thought, the particular position of the psychosexual group, the sexual determinant of repression, and finally the necessary conditions for consciousness as a function of perception; all that was perfectly clear, and still is. Naturally I do not know how to contain my pleasure.[3]

A month later Freud dropped this vision. Yet this brilliant tour de force contains most of the essential ideas Freud incorporated into his psychoanalytic system a few years later and thus into *The Interpretation of Dreams*.

THE DREAM THEORY—THE BASIC PRINCIPLES

Freud's writing reflects a hierarchy of theoretical principles: (1) general principles belonging to the science of his time; (2) major principles of mental functioning; (3) secondary principles of this psychology.

One general principle belonging to the scientific beliefs of the time is Freud's belief in the law-abiding determinism of all events, and specifically the totally determined meaningfulness of even the most obscure arbitrary phenomenon. These laws had to be universal. Psychopathology would point to psychology of the normal and to universals. In this sense Freud was not interested in unique individual phenomena, be they the parent's personality, individual stresses, or cultural impingements, unless they demonstrated universal laws. Freud also embraced the then current notions of laws of physics, those of energy in particular. Processes of the mind ultimately had to be measurable in terms of force and quantity, this meaning energy. Freud believed that psychical processes do not occur without physiological ones, and that the physical must precede the psychical processes.

The foremost principle of the psychology of mind is the pleasure-pain principle. The mental apparatus tends to get rid of any excess quantity of excitation. An increase in excitation produces pain or unpleasure, and pleasure is the discharge of this excitation. The pleasure-pain principle is the regulatory principle. The mind is separated into three regions—the conscious, preconscious, and unconscious. The unconscious and the conscious function according to different rules, the primary and secondary processes respectively. The concept of the primary and secondary processes is basic to the theory of dreams; thus a brief outline is important.

The energy in the primary process can be freely displaced or transferred from one idea to another. The unconscious does not heed contradiction, has no sense of time or reality. A wish produces an uninhibited flow of excitement which may lead to imaginary wish fulfillment if the wish cannot be gratified by direct motor action.

The secondary processes are characteristic of ego function. They bind and store energy for considered and delayed action. The secondary process is sensitive to the pain or unpleasure which develops when an unconscious wish trespasses into the realm of the civilized world. Thus undesirable wishes, by virtue of the unpleasure they create in the ego, are banished to the unconscious or modified in such a way that they are acceptable to the ego. The all-important preconscious is the domain where the censorship offices are located as agents of the ego government. Like secret services anywhere, they are largely secret.

Just a brief word about the libido theory. Freud's concept of the libido theory, that is, the role of the sexual instinct as motivating force of the mental apparatus, developed only slowly. The libido theory, and especially the Oedipus complex, which I shall explain later, is absolutely essential to Freud's elaborate conceptual mental engine. Freud needed a source of energy, of excitation, which was universal and which was in basic conflict, again universally valid, with conscious functioning. Freud needed a wish which would arouse disgust, displeasure, and conflict with societal functioning. Infantile sexuality represented for him such a force of excitation which would be disapproved of. Even more abhorrent was the notion of incestual desire. Freud's early seduction theory, that is, of sexual trauma induced in children because they were seduced at an early age by nursemaids, parents, or others—traumas which were then revived in adolescence and initiated symptoms of hysteria—would never have served Freud's aim for a total theory. The shift to the idea of infantile sexuality was essential. It provided him with the keystone for his theoretical building. Freud's ideas gained their significance from their place in his total system. He modified some ideas, but never those that belonged to the essential structure of the system.

THE DREAM THEORY—THE GRAND DESIGN

Freud's concept of human mental functioning reflected in dreaming is a continuous engagement of opposing forces which are subject to the rules of the species. Dreams are special episodes in this engagement. I shall first outline the grand design underlying this act of dreaming and then detail Freud's argumentation.

All dreams arise from wishes and are, in the form of imagery, the fulfillment of these wishes. The dream as told cannot be recognized as a wish fulfillment. Yet when approached by the psychoanalytic techniques and interpretations of psychoanalysis, the dream reveals wishes that are unwelcome to the conscious mind. At first glance these concern wishes of revenge, or wishes to see someone dead, but the final penetration of all-distorting obstacles shows the source of the wish to be the ever-present energized strata of suppressed infantile sexuality. These universal sexual wishes, especially those of incest, occur in the early period of childhood amnesia. These wishes are permanently retained as underground forces always pushing for eruption, and their energy cathexis attaches itself to any suitable wish vehicle that may come along, arising from later perturbations of life. These earlier and later wishes are invariably abhorrent to the censor, which guards consciousness. Sleep prevents discharge of these wishes in active waking form, but the charge reverts, that is, it regresses back to the more primitive preceptual or imaginary mode in us. As it regresses, it touches on memory traces all along the line of the life we have lived. For these wishes to express themselves in hallucinatory wish fulfillment and yet not to disturb our sleep, the dream thoughts or wishes have to be disguised. The effort that goes into disguising dreams is called dream work. The main tools of dream work are condensation, displacement, symbolism, and secondary elaboration.

To decipher a dream, the dreamer engages in free association concerning its various separate elements, not concerning the dream as a whole. Freud evolved the method of free association in his work with psychoneurotics. The dreamer attends to one image, then says without sifting or censoring whatever comes to mind. The chain of free associations provides many times more material than is contained in the manifest dream. The free flow of associations has an unconscious directing thrust that will lead to relevant but disturbing recollections. The thoughts revealed by this method, when investigating dreams, are called dream thoughts. They are part of the latent content, in contrast to the manifest content, of the dream as reported. The manifest dream uses recent occurrences, often from the previous day, to invent its apparent story.

THE DREAM THEORY—THE PROPOSITIONS OF WISH FULFILLMENT AND INFANTILE SEXUALITY

In all of his expositions of his dream theory, Freud eases us gently into a demonstration that dreams invariably are special wish fulfillments. I have mentioned before Freud's effective style or strategy of writing which engages the reader's mind with all-too-human, often humorous examples of everyday life, only to take him, without letting him know beforehand, into his grand design. Thus Freud moves from dreams, which rather readily reveal ordinary wishes, to wishes about someone dear to us being dead, to the wishes arising out of the strata of infantile sexuality.

For the sake of brevity, I shall illustrate this gentle first step by a simple illustrative speculation. Freud writes:

> I have ventured to interpret without any analysis, but only by a guess, a small episode which occurred to a friend of mine who was in the same class as I was all through our career at secondary school. One day he listened to a lecture which I gave before a small audience on the novel idea that dreams were wish-fulfillments. He went home and dreamt that he had lost all his cases (he was a barrister) and afterwards arraigned me on the subject. I evaded the issue by telling him that after all one can't win all one's cases. But to myself I thought: "Considering that for eight whole years I sat on the front bench as top of the class while he drifted about somewhere in the middle, he can hardly fail to nourish a wish left over

from his school-days, that some day or other I may come a complete cropper" (*SE* vol. 4, 152).

Freud's main elaborate and extensive illustration of the wish-fulfillment character of dreams is his account of his own dream, the Irma dream, and of his own associations to this dream. He discovered wishes of hurt pride conjuring up a whole assortment of retaliatory wishes.

Dreams containing dream thoughts of wishing the death of a parent, usually the parent of the same sex as the dreamer, provided Freud with the needed transition to his central ideas about childhood sexuality, in particular to the replica of the Oedipus legend in all of us. We must look, he says, for the origin of a death wish of a parent in our earliest childhood. The work with psychoneurotics gave him the "proof." He writes: "We learn from them [psychoneurotics] that a child's sexual wishes awaken very early, and that a girl's first affection is for her father and a boy's first childish desires are for his mother. Accordingly, the father becomes a disturbing rival to the boy and the mother to the girl; and I have already shown in the case of brothers and sisters how easily such feelings can lead to a death wish" (*SE* vol. 4, 257).

Freud continues:

> Being in love with the one parent, and hating the other are among the essential constituents of the stock of psychical impulses which is formed at that time and which is of such importance in determining the symptoms of the later neurosis. It is not my belief, however, that psychoneurotics differ sharply in this respect from other human beings who remain normal—that they are able, that is, to create something absolutely new and peculiar to themselves. It is far more probable that they are only distinguished by exhibiting on a magnified scale feelings of love and hatred to their parents which occur less obviously and less intensely in the minds of most children.
>
> This discovery is confirmed by a legend that has come down to us from classical antiquity; a legend whose profound and universal power to move can only be understood if the hypothesis I have put forward in regard to the psychology of children has an equally universal validity (*SE* vol. 4, 260).

Freud describes the well-known legend of Oedipus. He then continues:

> If Oedipus Rex moves a modern audience no less than it did the

contemporary Greek one, the explanation can only be that its effect does not lie in the contrast between destiny and human will, but is to be looked for in the particular nature of the material on which that contrast is exemplified. . . . His destiny moves us only because it might have been ours—because the oracle laid the same curse upon us before our birth as upon him. It is the fate of all of us, perhaps, to direct our first sexual impulses towards our mother and our first hatred and our first murderous wish against our father. Our dreams convince us that this is so. . . . Like Oedipus we live in ignorance of these wishes, repugnant to morality, the desires that nature has forced upon us, and after their unveiling we may prefer to avert our gaze from the scenes of our childhood (*SE* vol. 4, 262).

Two aspects of these early wishes are important in the Freudian scheme: First, Freud believed that these unconscious wishes are always active and ready to express themselves whenever they can ally themselves with an impulse from consciousness and transfer their own greater intensity (read energy) to the lesser intensity of the latter. These ever-active and, as it were, immortal wishes of our unconscious Freud likened to the legendary Titans, who, from time immemorial, have been buried under the mountains that were once hurled upon them by the victorious gods and that even now quiver from time to time at the convulsions of their mighty limbs.

Second, these wishes necessarily become painful or cause abhorrence or disgust in the conscious mind. At one point Freud states that the sexual impulse is the one most immediately tied to disgust. This pain/abhorrence is an essential element in the mental apparatus as it functions on the pleasure-pain principle. The unconscious governed by the primary processes is capable of only wishing. But the endopsychic censor, which not only guards sleep but also is essential for our civilized or secondary process mode of thinking and feeling while awake, is activated by pain or displeasure to any thought or feeling we consciously abhor. This is important because being able to arouse universal abhorrence made sexual incestuous desires such a key element in Freud's mental dynamic apparatus.

I shall emphasize this with one more quote from Freud[6]:

The ego, freed from all ethical bonds, also finds itself at one with all the demands of sexual desire, even those which have long been condemned by our aesthetic upbringing and those which contradict all the requirements of moral restraint. The desire for pleasure—the libido, as we call it—chooses its objects without inhibition, and by preference, indeed, the forbidden ones; not only other men's wives, but above all incestuous objects, objects sanctified by the common agreement of mankind, a man's mother and sister, a woman's father and brother. . . . Hatred too rages without restraint. . . . These censored wishes appear to rise up out of a positive Hell; after they have been interpreted when we are awake, no censorship of them seems too severe (*SE* vol. 15, 142).

Freud then continues to reassure the reader that dreams really are not depraved, as these impulses from early childhood are universal and that after all dream distortion also leads us to the important function of censorship which arises from what is noble in human nature.

Freud's thoughts here are similar to religious beliefs that man is born in sin and that this original fallenness in its turn creates the striving and mental forces that produce culture and civilized man.

THE DREAM THEORY—THE DREAM WORK

I shall only briefly describe the means used by the endopsychic censor or the preconscious to disguise dreams. These means are called the dream work. The dream work employs the primary process, which uses its energy with much artistic license, condenses several features into one, attaches itself rather freely to any idea without regard to time, contradiction, and reality. Condensation is an important tool of dream work. The dream condenses by omission, by presenting a fragment for a whole, by melding diversified ideas into one image. A person in a dream may resemble A in appearance, his dress recalls B, his occupation is that of C, and yet the dreamer calls him D. Another tool is displacement. An important latent dream element may be replaced by a more innocuous one. The dream may place the accent on an insignificant aspect of the dream and divert the focus from the more important elements. An ever-present form of disguise is the dream's use of symbols or metaphors. The dreamer may use symbols uniquely his own, but dream language employs many universally valid symbols pertaining to sexual matters. The male genitals can be represented symbolically by the number three. Phallic symbols abound, be they sticks, umbrellas, poles, knives, such waterflowing objects as taps, and the like. Female genitalia may be represented by enclosed spaces, such as pits, hollows, caves, boxes, and houses. Breasts may be represented as apples and peaches, pubic hair by woods and thickets. The list is endless; it is not too helpful, as invariably the symbol may also mean something else.

Freud's lively style often uses a dialogic form. He poses imaginary questions or objections and then argues his case. This abbreviated exposition of Freud's theory of dreams will conclude with such a hypothetical objection and answer.

The question posed is: "Granted that dreams always have a sense, and that that sense can be discovered by the technique of psychoanalysis, why must that sense, all evidence to the contrary, be invariably pushed into the formula of wish fulfillment? Why should not the sense of this nightly thinking be as diversified as that of daytime thinking? Why, that is, should not a dream correspond sometimes to a fulfilled wish, sometimes, as you yourself say, to the opposite of that or to a realized fear, or sometimes express an intention, a warning, a reflection with its pros and cons, or a reproach, a scruple of conscience, an attempt at preparing for a coming task, and so on?"

Freud's first answer is: "I don't know why they shouldn't . . . but that it isn't so in reality" (SE vol. 15, 222). Freud points to the confusion that arises when dream thoughts are not differentiated from the essential nature of dreams. The latent dream thoughts are the material that is transformed by the dream work into the manifest dream. Analytic observation shows that the dream work never consists merely of translating the latent thoughts into the archaic or regressive forms of expression. Invariably, the actual motive force in dream formation is added. This is the unconscious wish. Insofar as only the dream thoughts are being considered, they indeed can be any conceivable thing—a warning, a resolve, a preparation. To Freud the essential nature of dreams rests with the empowering unconscious wish that has its roots in the infantile period and that motivates the elaborate disguising dream work. Freud emphasizes that any misunderstanding of this essential nature of dreaming imperils the value of dream interpretation for the understanding of neuroses.

1953: A NEW PERSPECTIVE

I hope I have made it abundantly clear that Freud opened the door and created the guiding roads into the uncharted territory of dreamland. His wealth of contributions is not affected by a challenge to the key elements of his theoretical substructure, which was vitally important to him not because of his interest in dreams but because of his theory of psychoanalysis, the theory of mental functioning of all of mankind.

The challenge to his ideas of the "essential nature of dreams" came in 1953. Aserinsky and Kleitman[1] noted by direct observation in the course of studying sleep characteristics of infants that eye movements recurred at regular intervals during sleep. This lead to similar observations in the sleep of adults. Aserinsky and Kleitman further discovered that these eye movements coincided with characteristic changes in the electroencephalogram, in rates of pulse or respiration and of blood pressure, in skin temperature, and with other signs of changes in autonomic activity, such as penile erections. These changes suggested the possibility of some sort of emotional happening, possibly a dream. Reports of dreams during these periods of eye movement sleep were compared with reports of dreams during other periods of sleep. Dreams were reported by a high percentage of subjects when they were awakened out of the rapid eye movement state of sleep. Far fewer dreams were reported on arousal from the other states of sleep.

The sleep accompanied by rapid eye movements came to be called REM sleep or the D-state of sleep. Other states were called non-REM sleep. The D-state is also found in animals and is a basic biological characteristic of mammalian life. Age is a factor. As we get older, the amount of time we spend in D-state sleep becomes less. The newborn spends 50 percent of his sleep in this D-state. At age two the percentage is 40 percent, at age five 25 percent, during adolescence and adulthood 20 percent, and at age sixty 15 percent. D-state cycles recur at 90-minute intervals. In the beginning of the night the REM period is short, lasting about five to ten minutes. The periods become longer as the night advances, the early morning period lasting up to 40 minutes. A fascinating observation was made when the subjects were deprived of their REM sleep by arousal whenever the REM period occurred. The following nights many more periods of REM states were observed, as if the body had to recover from the state of deprivation, establishing that a physiological need existed, not for dreaming, but for the physiological activity of this state. Schizophrenic patients did not differ from normal subjects in their phase regularity.

Thus dream activity was shown to be a regular component of a neurophysiological state which recurs with regularity, which is not influenced by emotional disturbances, and which belongs to the mammalian species. Thus Freud's vision of the essential nature of dreams had to give way to new scientific discovery. But, as mentioned, our indebtedness to Freud is unquestioned. There remains his conviction about the invariable meaningfulness of dreams, his method of free association to make meaningful connections to prevailing stresses, thoughts, emotions, and past memories. Dreams have remained a fascinating partner in our inner dialogue with ourselves about ourselves and the world. We have gained increasing respect for this partner, for its range of interest, for its sensitivities, for its artistry, and for its wisdom.

Is there a new theory of dreaming? No, no new theory exists. We approach dreams, however, with a few general assumptions which are less complicated than Freud's but not less valuable. Richard Jones, in his book *The New Psychology of Dreaming*,[7] defines dreaming as the "augmentative response of the human psyche to the distinctive neurophysiological conditions of the mammalian D-state." This proposition "leaves conceptual space for assigning psychological functions to the D-state over and above its neurophysiological functions, by presuming that whatever psychological functions dreaming may serve have been exploitative of more fundamental organismic conditions characteristic of the species." Dreaming uses a capacity we all possess, the ability to translate impressions into symbols, metaphors, and stories. This basic function is in us and goes on all the time. Sometimes we are aware of it; sometimes we are not. Dreams give us the raw material out of which rational thought or conscious perspective may arise. The dream is not meant for public communication, so it is free to use idiosyncratic symbols, and these are free to meander and intersect without pressure to organize themselves into forms. Yet dreams also can create very well written stories if the spirit so moves them.

Susanne Langer, in 1942, gave the first classic description to the idea and her belief that the symbol-making function was a primary need in man. She writes:

> Symbolization is the essential act of mind; and mind takes in more than what is commonly called thought. Only certain products of the symbol-making brain can be used according to canons of discursive reasoning. In every mind there is an enormous store of other symbolic material, which is put to different uses or perhaps even to no use at all—a mere result of spontaneous brain activity, a reserve fund of conceptions, a surplus of mental wealth.[8]

I like Langer's term "surplus of mental wealth." It is from this surplus of mental wealth that dreams spin their stories and throw up their imagery, and digest perceptions, thoughts, and experiences that have passed through the brain. It indeed seems as if dreaming serves the function of giving form to affective experiences and thus generates expressions of individual truth. It has been suggested that dreaming in adulthood can perform the same functional role that symbolic play does in childhood. Richard Jones suggests that the child's symbolic play serves to extend his understanding and comprehension of the world by means of his acting upon it and making it part of himself by transforming it in terms of his own wants and needs.

Dreams may reflect an ongoing unconscious activity, which day or night mulls over experiences, reflects upon them, reacts to them, and recasts them, creating meaning and patterns that find a place in the unique personal vision of the world. We must compose and recompose our world in order to function, act, and think in it.

The glimpses of this activity, which dreaming grants us, have led to a profound respect for its quality of outer and inner perceptiveness and fundamental wisdom.

How do we approach the task of dream interpretation without Freud's concept of dream work?

(1) We do not approach the manifest dream as disguised by any censor. The manifest dream is the dream story the dreamer wanted to write. If the dream tells a coherent story, then we contemplate the theme of the whole story, as well as its parts.

(2) Freud's stress on condensation and displacement still is pertinent, as they are inherent qualities of imagery and metaphors as seen in art, poetry, drama, and paintings. The artist, however, will use metaphors or imagery which can be accessible to others. The dream is produced without thought of audience.

(3) As the symbols, as well as the experiences alluded to, belong to the mental wealth of the dreamer, only he can lead us to the meaning. His spontaneous comments and associations count.

(4) We are not concerned with interpreting the dream. We are interested in the additional dimensions of the patient's experiences to which the dream may point. These dimensions may point to affect, conflicts, problem-solving, hopes, wishes, modes of being-in-the-world, modes of seeing oneself in relation to others, apprehensions and fears. Patients who have the world of poetry at their mental fingertips will provide similar dimensions by spontaneously remembered lines of poetry, lines of songs, or a vignette of a drama or movie.

SUMMARY

Freud was the father of this exciting child—our working with dreams. But this child has grown into a fundamentally different world; it has changed scientific principles, changed culture, and gained much new experience. Freud would have to disown this emancipated child. Yet dream approach will for a long time to come carry Freud's signature. Theory and practice are worlds apart. For this reason a clear concept of Freud's original theory is important for the present student of dreams. With the challenge to Freud's concept of the essential nature of dreaming, much of the wealth of his own observation can now be seen in a new light. Probably the most basic difference between our approach to dream meaning and that of Freud lies in his interest in and search for universal significance and validity, while we tend to view dreams as an expression of that part of our world which transforms experiences into the most private and uniquely personal ongoing comments on life's events in and about us.

NOTES

[1]E. Aserinsky and N. Kleitman (1953). "Regularly Occurring Periods of Eye Motility and Concomitant Phenomena during Sleep," *Science* 118, 273-274. See also W. Dement and N. Kleitman (1957). "The Relation of Eye Movements during Sleep to Dream Activity: An Objective Method for the Study of Dreaming," *Journal of Experimental Psychology* 53, 339-346.

[2]Sigmund Freud (1900). "The Interpretation of Dreams," *SE* vol. 4.

[3]Ernest Jones (1953). *The Life and Work of Sigmund Freud.* Vol. 1. New York: H. Wolff.

[4]Sigmund Freud (1954). *The Origins of Psychoanalysis. Letters to Wilhelm Fliess.* New York: Basic Books.

[5]Sigmund Freud (1895). "Project for a Scientific Psychology," *SE* vol. 1, 281-397.

[6]Sigmund Freud (1916-17). "Introductory Lectures in Psychoanalysis," *SE* vol. 15.

[7]Richard M. Jones (1970). *The New Psychology of Dreaming.* New York: Grune & Stratton.

[8]Susanne K. Langer (1942). *Philosophy in a New Key.* New York: Mentor, p. 45.

Chapter 5

Sublimation

Lawrence Friedman

I

Freud's special use of the term sublimation in *Three Essays on the Theory of Sexuality* (1905) determined its role in the history of Western ideas.* In *Three Essays*, Freud tells us that our appreciation of a lovely body is the residue of genital curiosity that has learned shame. In fact, ideals generally—not just beautiful bodies, but beautiful pictures, worthy institutions—all are the result of our building ethically higher interests to take up the zeal originally invested in more animal preoccupations.[1] The public learned from Freud that all man's proud accomplishments are successful efforts to deny his base origins. That is forever the connotation of the now-colloquial word, sublimation.

But this connotation does not exhaust the technical meaning of the word. You may have been intrigued enough by *Three Essays on Sexuality*

---

*Psychoanalytic theory has several aspects, and offers several ways of discussing sublimation. I have chosen to avoid the terminology of psychic energy, instinct de-fusion, neutralization, etc. These terms can only lead to misunderstanding unless they are seen in the context of the developing Freudian theory, to which it is as impossible to do justice within the limits of this paper as it is to discuss the future impact of recent child studies on psychoanalytic theory.

to read further and learn that sublimation not only gives our passions a more dignified object, but also gives our life-style a more ethical form. The alchemical sublimation that turns delight in feces into a love of gold also inspires us to think carefully and searchingly in science and philosophy. Sublimation does not raise just our vision; it raises our being. Through it, we develop what psychoanalysts call "character."

Even in the early *Three Essays*, where sublimation has its popular significance, the term is not a label for some minor trick-of-the-mind or a moral sleight-of-hand for distracting us from the sucking, defecating, voyeuristic lusts of infancy. Almost everything of daily life, except dreams and errors, is explained by psychoanalysis as sublimation: Man's interests, aims, and culture, his sports, politics, and industry, his personality and tastes—in a sense all are sublimations of primitive urges. Even his adult sexuality is a sublimation of his infantile sexuality (though you now realize how much I am exaggerating!).

Obviously, this gross term was not destined to play a major role in so subtle and intricate a theory as psychoanalysis. And you may wonder why I have chosen to deal with it now, when it does not even have any shock value left. There are two answers: (1) Sublimation is the writ by which psychoanalysis summons the rest of human endeavor to its jurisdiction, and (2) human endeavor would do well to examine the extent and limits of its inquisitorial authority.

Yet a more important reason exists for examining the somewhat antique term respectfully, however. The theory proposes to explain a change of meaning within a state of continuity. And if you think about it for a minute, you will see that this is what we are all looking for, as scholars, scientists, and psychotherapists.

Now, what sort of picture do you have when I talk about *change*? No doubt some of you think of a bud developing into a flower or a crawling infant into a gymnast. Others may imagine the rebound of a billiard ball as it snaps in a new direction. The theory of sublimation is a great lesson in the difficulty of deciding whether the continuity that underlies change comes from the unfolding growth of a constant, potential meaning, something like an Aristotelian *entelechy*, or whether it is the giving up of one meaning and its careful replacement by another, according to a fixed principle (as in a reaction formation).

As you must know by now, psychoanalysis is obsessed with mental conflict. How does a term that refers mainly to *change* make sense in a theory of entrenched mental opponents? Those of you with an Hegelian or Marxist turn of mind will have a quick and cogent answer: Sublimation is successful compromise; that is the meaning it had for Freud in *Civi-*

lization and Its Discontents (1929), where he wonders how far cultural successes can be stretched.[2] Speaking roughly, psychoanalysis is an account of more or less successful protections against upsets brought on by wishes. Temporary ways of settling conflicts are called defenses. The permanent and most successful ways of settling upsets are called sublimations: The wishes have changed and the danger is gone for good. There is no longer any dangerous wish, nor any need to protect against danger.

But if we take this as the paradigm—that a wish is countered by a fear, that it is repudiated as unworthy or dangerous, and that it is resolved by substituting a more elevated wish—then apparently there must always be some sublimation before sublimation is possible. We find ourselves asking two difficult questions: (1) How is it possible for conflict to induce a change, unless some general process of change is available—a sublimation more general than any specific conflict? (2) And how is it possible to substitute a more culturally elevated objective unless we already have a notion of higher and lower—itself quite a considerable sublimation of animal energies? A lesser theoretician would have left well enough alone. People do not ordinarily look much closer at their theories than is convenient. But a great theoretician like Freud realized that these further questions were by far the most interesting ones.

II

Let us concentrate on these two questions and look, with Freud, first at the process of change—not conflict, but just change.

One of the earliest changes Freud studied in detail was a patient changing her love of her father into love of her psychoanalyst.[3] Later he called this transference. But strange to say, in what I believe is the first use of the term, Freud refers to this love shift from parent to analyst as sublimation! Now I can assure you that Freud never thought that psychoanalysts are more sublime than parents. Evidently, even though one early image of sublimation was fancy dress for a naked savage, another early connotation concerned development of *new meaning*. In the case of transference, an old fantasy confined by memory was changed into a new affection for the analyst's unique features. The patient's love for the analyst is more sublime than the love for the parent only by virtue of its creativity. (I admit that it also evades the incest barrier.) Even at this early stage, sublimation was associated with the growth of meaning, with the bringing of old, general forms to bear on new, particular situations. Later Freud became even more curious about the growth of meaning. The patient, Dora, to whom I just referred, had a particular fantasy about her father, and changed it to fit Sigmund Freud. That is one kind of creation of new meaning. But how about the very early creations of meaning—how about the forces that bring the *first* kind of definition, focus, and structure? This aspect of sublimation, only occasionally referred to by that term, increasingly absorbed Freud's attention.

How does the rough and shapeless and urgent become well defined and specifically aimed? When Freud wrestled with this question (for example in his paper on *The Unconscious* in 1915[4]), he asked himself: What does the maturation of meaning consist of? Is it a development, or is it a real change? Is it evolution or revolution? Does a primitive meaning gather around it added sophisticated meaning? Or does it develop its sophisticated potential and forever lose its youthful primitiveness?

I do not want to give the impression that Freud asked the question in these terms. It would take us too far afield to go into the extraordinary detail of his early speculation, which centered on the difference between what can and cannot be made conscious. Freud felt that one extremely—uniquely—important type of change has to do with the *breaking up of concrete awareness into relational abstractions*, and that, even as this change progresses, the original concrete awareness remains available and in some way untouched, which suggests simultaneously: that new meaning is latent in old meaning; that it radically transforms the old meaning; and that it can always refind its ancestral home! Here is a startling, self-contradictory, suggestive, poignant, and plausible notion.

After 1927, this growing-up of meaning is represented by the ego: The ego, whatever else it is—and it is a very confused concept—represents a higher organization of the id. It is the mind's first sublimation, so to speak. This fundamental sublimation is defined not by its beauty nor its nobility, but by its level of organization. Before any of the more famous cultural sublimations can get a foothold, the soul must be sublimated into conceptual, organized forms. Before ethical heights can be reached, organizational peaks must be achieved.[5]

This is a far cry from the morality tale of the popular notion. Sublimation in the first place is not ethically mandated; it is a simple requirement of survival and is requisite for the development of any and all of man's potential. Raising ethical standards, then, is only one form of sublimity. Raising logical standards, raising the thoroughness of integration, raising the power to focus, raising the usefulness of potential—these sublimations are more fundamental to a developmental theory of the mind. The advance from genitals to Giotto is nothing compared to the giant step from inchoate, unconscious urge to conscious, conceptual, plain old sexual curiosity.

III

Now let us turn to the second riddle. Sublimation, to begin with, may be a matter of cognitive refinement, but sooner or later it indeed becomes a moral matter. Outright infantile satisfactions are not permitted to civilized man, under penalty of confinement. Where do these internal standards come from, by which we police ourselves for society? What is sublimated to produce those standards that *guide* our sublimations?

At first Freud tried to dodge this question.[6] He seems to have treated the conscience as though it *were* society's standards, and he measured a man's sublimation by how well he lived up to his conscience, which is to say, usually very little. But by the time he wrote *The Ego and the Id* (1923), he had characteristically seen that he had not been asking all the questions to be asked, and the one aspect that marks Freud as a theoretician is that he asked all the questions.

So he asked: How does a man sublimate his animal urges enough to form an image of a higher ideal, let alone measure himself by it or conform to it? (Ricoeur[7] points out that no matter what is made over into an ideal, that which makes it over must have at least the capacity for veneration. In that sense, Ricoeur would argue that a quest for ideals must be planted as a primitive term in Freudian theory, and we shall see how later theorists have picked up on this theme.)

Be that as it may, Freud was quite explicit about the two origins of this first ethical norm: One origin is in primitive incorporation of the caregivers. Little more is said about this incorporation; this root of development is shrouded in mystery, a temptation for such later writers as Kernberg[8] and Kohut.[9] The other origin of our ethical standards was fully discussed by Freud: Infants sublimate their attachment to their caregivers by identifying with them, and they do so in order to be somewhat self-sufficient when they are alone.

I want you to use your imagination on that formula. It is crucial to an understanding of sublimation. An infant models himself on his parents and develops a good feeling about himself, and that good feeling can spread out to all his works—to everything that he feels *for*, to his friends, to his imagination, to what he learns, to the world he builds. By virtue of this early self-regard, he has a vast fund of respect and admiration which can extend far beyond the few people who take care of him.

Whatever specific conflicts, whatever grubby urges, are transformed into the works of civilization, part of the cultural attainment comes from this fund of interest *already* freed up from sexual attachments.

One alchemical sublimation made possible by this first sublimation is the humanization and personalization of the great biological necessities that rule the infant. As a consequence of identifying himself with the people toward whom he feels animal urges, and from whom he feels species-specific prohibitions addressed in reply, Man makes his evolutionary heritage into the private drama of his life, and the lower drives are transformed into the highest ideals.

Let us stand back and look at this picture for a moment: Freud has shown how sophisticated meanings develop out of shapeless urges and how ethical meanings develop out of brutish wishes. In effect, you will see, Freud's theory is an accounting for the very early multiplication of human meanings and motives out of the few original sexual ones.

By the time the great conflict of sexual wishes and fears known as the Oedipus complex comes along, a child already has a vast fund of personal interests (in knowledge, beauty, goodness, respect, power) that can be *directly* satisfied by any compromise with which the sexual wishes have to be *indirectly* satisfied. Indeed, only because he has all these other opportunities is he able to give up his first love and live comfortably with his rival parent.

We must always keep this in mind when we look at major cultural accomplishments as sublimations. These are sublimations only in the sense that in their formation they make use of developed sexual wishes. But they are also direct, unsublimated expressions of aspirations that were sublimated from the sexual so long ago as to now amount to independent strivings.

We could, in fact, spend a very profitable two hours on the relativity of the notion of sublimation. Just like a "defense," a sublimation is always a sublimation only with regard to one field of forces; it is a direct expression with regard to another. Sublimation is always a diversion of one aspiration and at the same time a progression of another. (You will have seen in Ricoeur's commentary that one very early meaning of sublimation is the attaching of a waiting drive onto an opportune but otherwise irrelevant activity—for instance oral erotism is linked with mere eating.) Though it would not be Freud's preferred expression, one might say that sexual conflict is useful because it helps to parley the merely humanizing early sublimations into the later civilizing, ethical ones.

Now you can get a glimpse of how psychoanalysis manages to combine a theory of change with a cynical belief in conservative continuities: New expressions that detour one drive offer a straight highway for another. The new always has something old in it.

IV

A rough overview of psychoanalytic history might appear like this:

In its general spirit, Freudian theory tried to say what transformations of a wish result in an expressive act. Sublimation was a popular term just as long as ethical disguises were thought to be a universal source of meaning change. One could ask precisely about any expression (an artistic expression, for example): *What sort of wish is this a more respectable version of?*

Meantime, however, Freud became involved in transformations of meaning far subtler than the switch from ethically crude to ethically refined. In general, these more pervasive transformations had to do with the movement from unconscious to conscious, from infantile unstructuredness to mature detail, and from momentary reaction to fixed patterns of living—in short, everything concerning the passage from source to outcome.

Some later theorists have felt that to do justice to all those transformations, one must put special emphasis on the *wholeness* which is necessary if a person is to be successful.

Hartmann[10] wanted psychoanalysts to remember that mental developments were expressive not only of single wishes, but also of general human necessities. A myth might be the outcome of Oedipal strivings, but it also is a principle for organizing thoughts and actions.

Such theoreticians as George Klein[11] portray what happens in the mind as an effort to stabilize a concept of the self. On this account, equilibrium becomes an overriding determinant for the transformation of meaning. According to Klein, man has many motivations. Some may be instrumental to others and some subordinate, but the principle that determines their outcome is a cohesive self; thus the *final* expression does not disguise the basic meaning. Quite the contrary, the final expression best reveals the defining character of an aim, because meaning comes from fitting in with the self-organization, and the mature self is the most complete self—the self with the most definition.

Likewise for Kohut[9]: the final, mature forms of human expression are not simply the results of mental processes; in a sense they are themselves the basic material of mental processes. The ambitions and ideals that might once have been called sublimations are now looked on as manifestations of a cohesive self toward which the individual has always groped. Sublimation merely refers to maturity.

These post-Freudians all emphasize that the way man turns out is prefigured in the way he begins, and not only does his end betray his beginnings, but his beginnings are elucidated by his end. As Ricoeur suggests, psychoanalytic theory implies that the human being is born as much to ideals, religion, and culture as to sex and aggression. And if humans were not born to them, they would never acquire them.

Long ago, clinicians lost interest in sublimation chiefly because it did not add much to the notion of a resolved conflict. Conflict resolution, in one degree or another, has too many outcomes to suit a single term. The term sublimation continued to be used, at least implicitly, in applied psychoanalysis—chiefly in the arts. Even after a groundswell of wholism made analysts less apt to reduce a cultural accomplishment to a single, compromised, uglier wish, such a principle was still used by literary critics and art historians. And there is a reason for this, I think, that goes beyond cultural lag: A lot is lost with the new wholism, a principle of dissection, in particular. A whole is a whole, with nothing prior and nothing after, except (trivially) in temporal order.

Sublimation, in its crudest form, gave us a principle of analysis. An elevated expression can be analyzed into a lower meaning plus a higher objection to that meaning. Therefore, if you announce that you are about to show us sublimations, you have also told us your concept of the meaning of a human expression. If, on the other hand, you announce that you will show us, how an artistic expression satisfies a "basic human need," for example, you have not told us anything at all about what you are going to take as its meaning. Indeed, you could fulfill your commitment by looking at the work any way you want and by doing it differently the next time around.

Sublimation is probably a limiting term in psychoanalysis. In it are fused the asymptotically converging themes of stabilized conflict and pure transformation of meaning. Cross the boundary and you have given up psychoanalysis.

If talking about sublimation has become a bore, then the remedy is not to make psychoanalysis say something else that is not in its vocabulary—or rather something that is in everybody's vocabulary and has no need of psychoanalysis. This would result in a presentation of the current cultural scene, cloaked in the pompous authority of a science of the mind.

What then is the answer? Sublimation may be a limiting term for psychoanalysis. But by the same token, it shares a common border with all the humanities, insofar as it deals with the transformation of meaning.

Today we see a great interest among psychoanalysts in the nature of metaphor and in the forms of literature and history. Through the concept of sublimation, psychoanalysis has probably taught as much as it can about civilization. Now instead of trying to teach what other disciplines can do better, perhaps it is time for psychoanalysis to listen.

NOTES

[1]Sigmund Freud, (1905). "Three Essays on the Theory of Sexuality." *SE* vol. 7, 156-157, 178, 238-239.

[2]Sigmund Freud, (1929). "Civilization and Its Discontents." *SE* vol. 21, 57-146.

[3]Sigmund Freud, (1901). "Fragment of an Analysis of a Case of Hysteria." *SE* vol. 7, 116.

[4]Sigmund Freud, (1915). "The Unconscious." *SE* vol. 14, 159-216.

[5]Sigmund Freud, (1923). "The Ego and the Id." *SE* vol. 19, 19-27.

[6]Sigmund Freud, (1914). "On Narcissism: An Introduction." *SE* vol. 14, 94-95.

[7]Paul Ricoeur, (1970). *Freud and Philosophy: An Essay on Interpretation*, trans. Denis Savage. New Haven: Yale University Press.

[8]Otto Kernberg, *Borderline Conditions and Pathological Narcissism*. New York: Aronson, 1975.

[9]Heinz Kohut, *The Analysis of the Self*. New York: International Universities Press, 1971.

[10]Heinz Hartmann, *Ego Psychology and the Problem of Adaptation*, trans. David Rapaport. New York: International Universities Press, 1958.

[11]George Klein, *Psychoanalytic Theory: An Exploration of Essentials*. New York: International Universities Press, 1976.

Chapter 6

Transference

U. H. Peters

INTRODUCTION

Freud wrote in his study, "The Dynamics of Transference," an exploration of the term:

> It must be understood that each individual, through the combined operation of his innate disposition and the influences brought to bear on him during his early years, has acquired a specific method of his own in his conduct of his erotic life—that is, in the preconditions to falling in love which he lays down, in the instincts he satisfies and the aims he sets himself in the course of it. This produces what might be described as a stereotype plate (or several such), which is constantly repeated—constantly reprinted afresh—in the course of the person's life, so far as external circumstances and the nature of the love-objects accessible to him permit, and which is certainly not entirely insusceptible to change in the face of recent experiences. Now, our observations have shown that only a portion of these impulses which determine the course of erotic life have passed through the full process of psychical development. That

This chapter was translated by R. Bean.

77

portion is directed towards reality, is at the disposal of the conscious personality, and forms a part of it. Another portion of the
libidinal impulses has been held up in the course of development;
it has been kept away from the conscious personality and from
reality, and has either been prevented from further expansion except in phantasy or has remained wholly in the unconscious so
that it is unknown to the personality's consciousness. If someone's
need for love is not entirely satisfied by reality, he is bound to
approach every new person whom he meets with libidinal anticipatory ideas; and it is highly probable that both portions of his
libido, the portion that is capable of becoming conscious as well
as the unconscious one, have a share in forming that attitude.

Thus it is a perfectly normal and intelligible thing that the libidinal cathexis of someone who is partly unsatisfied, a cathexis
which is held ready in anticipation, should be directed as well to
the figure of the doctor. It follows from our earlier hypothesis that
this cathexis will have recourse to prototypes, will attach itself to
one of the stereotype plates which are present in the subject; or,
to put the position in another way, the cathexis will introduce the
doctor into one of the psychical "series" which the patient has
already formed. If the "father-image," to use the apt term introduced by Jung,[1] is the decisive factor in bringing this about, the
outcome will tally with the real relations of the subject to his doctor.
But the transference is not tied to this particular prototype: it may
also come about on the lines of the mother-imago or brother-imago.
The peculiarities of the transference to the doctor, thanks to which
it exceeds, both in amount and nature, anything that could be
justified on sensible or rational grounds, are made intelligible if we
bear in mind that this transference has precisely been set up not
only by the *conscious* anticipatory ideas but also by those that have
been held back or are unconscious.[2]

Freud's characterization of the transference is still clear today. Nevertheless, it seems essential to emphasize certain specific points. Among
these is the fact that for those involved the transference *process* remains
unconscious. The *substance* of the transference, on the other hand, is
conscious. Through this process itself, the origin of the transference has
nearly reached consciousness; this is crucial for the psychoanalytic procedure. Bringing the sources of the transference to consciousness—along
with the resistances that obstruct this process—has become an important
part of psychoanalytic therapy. Thus, every transference analysis is at
the same time a resistance analysis as well.

Transference is also linked to regression, however. Here the relations are reciprocal. In the "classic" psychoanalytic technique the patient lies on the couch while the therapist sits upright. This corresponds to the normal attitude of an infant vis-à-vis an adult, so that in this situation transferences connected with the childhood are provoked. The transference situation of psychoanalytic therapy thereby already differs from the transference relationships established in other forms of psychotherapy between therapist and patient, between physician and patient, or between other persons. In this area of therapy, regression is desired, since there sooner than anywhere else affects, repetitions, and unresolved conflicts of infantile neurosis are given expression. Thus, corresponding to the "regression" in attitude there is a "regression" in the therapy as well, which in itself is specifically psychoanalytic.

Once transferences have appeared, a tendency toward acting and living out repressed infantile desires—toward their social realization—becomes observable in the patient, a tendency associated with the compulsion to repeat. This behavior is from the standpoint of the therapy undesirable, since the transferences are thereby placed in the service of the resistance. Their processes should therefore be recognized and put into words, rather than lived out.

Freud described the developments of the transference so clearly that not only psychoanalysts but many others as well have overlooked that similar developments existed already in preanalytic therapy and even in the earliest forms of psychotherapy, and that today, too, there are similar developments outside of psychoanalytic therapy. To use the term "transference" for all of them would mean obscuring the uniqueness of the analytic situation.

DEVELOPMENT AND RECOGNITION OF A SPECIAL PSYCHOTHERAPEUTIC "RELATIONSHIP" IN THE HISTORY OF DYNAMIC PSYCHIATRY

In the psychotherapeutic relationship, memories and feelings are interwoven in a way that is at first difficult for both physician and patient to grasp. It is thus not surprising, on the one hand, that transference first appeared when therapist and patient began to enter into a more intimate relationship with one another, and on the other, that this also went unnoticed by either. The history of these more intimate physician-patient relationships is of interest because it shows particularly clearly that what we generally call transference and countertransference today are not isolated psychoanalytic problems. This history, taken for the most part from Henri Ellenberger,[3] is instructive also because it contains all the manifestations of the contemporary transference and counter-transference in a nutshell.

We can assume that more intimate relationships with a transference character developed in earlier centuries between physician and patient, provided a more protracted relationship and a psychotherapeutic influence were involved. Precise accounts of transference relationships are lacking, however.

The phenomenon of the psychotherapeutic relationship first became intelligible when, with the development of hypnosis and its predecessors, the immaterial relationship between physician and patient became the primary subject of a treatment of disorder. This became evident already with F. A. Mesmer and the early magnetists when, after their initial experiences, Mesmer himself coined the term still used today, *rapport*, which Freud much later said represented the "prototype of the transference"; Freud, moreover, hereby clearly oriented his model of transference and countertransference toward hypnotherapy. Mesmer was, in fact, the first to exploit this psychotherapeutic relationship systematically for treatment, though admittedly still without completely grasping the intricacies of the process.[4]

Mesmer maintained quite explicitly that as a precondition for a magnetic (hypnotic) treatment an (emotional) "accord" (rapport) with the patient must be created. This meant for the moment that between physician and patient the feeling of mutual understanding and trust on a nonverbal level of communication must arise, a reflection that for the medicine of the time was completely novel. Only nearly 150 years later did Eugen Bleuler come to a similar conclusion when he established that he had been able to produce an "affective rapport" through intensive association with schizophrenics, for decades thought unintelligible.[5]

In the subsequent development of animal magnetism it soon became evident that rapport represented the central phenomenon. The influence of the therapist was observed to extend far beyond the magnetic session, and to encompass more than the posthypnotic suggestion first described in 1787. The term *réciprocité magnétique*, first described by Chastenet de Puységur, clearly emphasized the *reciprocal* influence of therapist and patient. In 1841 Burdin and Dubois[6] warned against repeating sessions too frequently or extending them too long. The question of whether the influence of the therapist can be extended so far that the patient would commit immoral acts, however, had already arisen at that time, and to this day fills novels and television shows.

But what then, as now, was little understood—or little considered—is how the hypnotist himself reacts to the hypnosis and to his patient.

Already at that time the repetition of hypnosis exerted a particular attraction on the hypnotist as well as on the patient. Today, too, it can be concluded from the great passion and often the one-sidedness and exclusivity with which many hypnotherapists perform hypnosis that this form of therapy provides them with a satisfaction that they themselves grasp only imperfectly or not at all.

In any event, the magnetic "condition," as the influence of the magnetist on his subject between sessions was designated, soon came to be distinguished from the true rapport during the magnetic session. Schubert pointed out that many patients would only drink what the magnetist had touched, and that some tended to take up medical theories the magnetist had in mind.[7] Gmelin and Heinecken further noted that many patients who had the same magnetist felt drawn to one another, according to Ellenberger, who referred further to an anonymous Scottish author who had observed that such patients gave each other "mesmeric" names and regarded themselves as brothers and sisters.[8] Freud always based his comparisons between hypnosis and the transference solely on the rapport during hypnosis, while in reality the parallels go much further.

At the end of the nineteenth century Pierre Janet offered a penetrating illumination and further elucidation of the therapist-patient relationship in hypnosis. He worked out his views on the hypnotherapeutic relationship most extensively in a lecture held in Munich in 1896.[9]

Janet divided the period of "influence" (of the therapist-patient relationship)—beyond the hypnotic sessions and seen over the course of a long treatment of hysteria—into two phases. In the *first* phase, according to Janet, a significant recovery "apparently" takes place, in that the patient loses part of his symptoms. The patient feels happier, more intelligent, more active; he seldom thinks of his hypnotist. Transferred onto an equivalent psychoanalytic treatment situation, today this still means that the patient momentarily remits part of his symptoms to please the therapist. Janet observed that in the first phase the susceptibility of the patient to posthypnotic suggestions was at its greatest.

Janet called the *second* phase "somnambulistic enthusiasm" (Janet used the term "somnambulistic" in its old sense—here akin to "under the spell of hypnosis" or "under the spell of the hypnotist"). In this second phase the patient feels the increased need to seek out the hypnotist and develops intense affections in the form of fervent love, jealousy, superstitious fear, and deep respect. This stage is accompanied by the feeling of being accepted or rejected. The same phase, transferred onto the psychoanalytic situation, is often referred to as the "honeymoon" of the therapy: The patient sees in his therapist an extraordinary human being and often regards him as omnipotent; he observes in him qualities that he does not possess in the opinion of others (later termed *acte d'adaptation*, the act of acceptance, by Janet). Or else the therapy is broken off due to equally powerful but negative emotions.

Janet's later observations went still further, in that it was established that the feelings directed toward the therapist in the second phase contain elements of erotic passion, childlike or motherly love, wherein at any given time a specific form of love is contained. Herein, too, the reader will recognize without difficulty individual aspects of Freud's description of the conditions of the transference. But Janet appended yet another factor, which he termed *besoin de direction*, the need to be led. Today this phenomenon is referred to as the need to be dependent.

In order to control this situation Janet made recommendations on technique: The therapist must (in the therapeutic phase) take complete command of the patient, but later teach him to get along without him. This is accomplished by gradually lengthening the interval between sessions and by making the patient conscious of his feelings (vis-à-vis the therapist). Every therapist today knows that this dissociation of the patient from the therapist (often called "cutting the umbilical cord," *the parting of mother and child*) has remained one of the most difficult phases.

In the course of the hypnotherapeutic epoch of psychotherapy most details of the psychotherapeutic relationship called the transference and countertransference today were already worked out. The reciprocal relationship of the hypnotherapist and patient was recognized not only in the hypnotic session and in the posthypnotic suggestion, but beyond them, for the entire duration of the already at that time protracted therapy, and even beyond that. The influence of mother and father imagoes and of the erotic element, the need to be dependent, and the various developmental stages of this relationship had become known and were consciously employed therapeutically. Even the ultimate dissociation of the patient from the therapist was recognized as a problem; techniques for accomplishing it suggested by Janet were later again taken up by C. G. Jung.

Freud, in fact, repeatedly claimed that the introduction of psychoanalytic therapy had been necessary precisely because hypnosis had always led to the lifelong dependence of the patient on the therapist. This reasoning, which can thus be predicated only on the generally inexpertly handled technique of dissociation from hypnosis, is in its basis unsound, however. From today's perspective, psychoanalytic therapy admittedly no longer needs a rationale such as this, which appeared necessary at the beginning.

Anna O. is first mentioned by Freud in a letter to his fiancée written on July 13, 1883, at two in the morning. The treatment, which had been carried out in the years 1880-1882, now already was some time past.

> Today was the hottest, most excruciating day of the whole season, I was really almost crazy with exhaustion. Realising that I was badly in need of refreshment, I went to see Breuer, from whom I have just returned, rather late. He had a headache, the poor man, and was taking salicyl. The first thing he did was to chase me into the bath tub, which I left rejuvenated. My first thought on accepting this wet hospitality was: If Marty were here, she would say: this is just what we must have, too. Of course, my girl, and no matter how many years it will take, we shall have it, but the only miracle I am counting on is that you will love me as long as that.—Then we had supper upstairs in our shirtsleeves (at the moment I am writing in a somewhat more advanced négligé), and then came a lengthy medical conversation on moral insanity[10] and nervous diseases and strange case-histories—your friend Bertha Pappenheim also cropped up again—and then we became rather personal and very intimate and he told me a number of things about his wife and children and asked me to repeat what he had said only "after you are married to Martha."[11]

Freud's formulation "your friend Bertha Pappenheim [Anna O.] also cropped up," suggests not only that she had already been discussed frequently, but that her frequent mention had engendered a certain ennui. The passage from this letter further implies that Freud's fiancée knew everything, or at least quite a bit, about her friend Bertha Pappenheim and her relationship to Breuer. Finally the somewhat offhand formulation "also cropped up" for "was discussed" signals not only an ironic distancing on Freud's part, but also a not yet concluded assimilation on the part of Breuer, who already appeared somewhat bored with this account of his situation. The rest of Freud's sentence then also clearly thematizes the sexual context of the Breuer-Pappenheim association: Breuer and Freud now become "rather personal" and "very intimate"; Breuer tells him things about his wife and children that Freud should only tell his fiancée after he is married to her, since it is improper to discuss sexual matters with a young unmarried girl.

There are further indications that already at this early stage Freud grasped both the universal and the particular aspects of Breuer's relationship to Bertha Pappenheim, although he always avoided a public examination of it. But the position of a nonparticipating observer gave Freud a particularly good opportunity to follow the development of the transference, here transference love, that he perhaps only later experienced personally. Léon Chertok has traced Freud's "discovery" of the transference back to a hypnosis session in 1892 in which a female patient thrust herself upon him and he little by little established that the erotic manifestations were not directed at him personally.[12] Ignoring the fact that there could understandably be no question of a "discovery" in the sense of the natural sciences, and also that the Breuer-Anna O. relationship already belonged to the past, Freud's experience in 1892 was common among hypnotists and thus also familiar to him.

In Freud's scientific work references to the psychotherapeutic relationship, just as to the word "transference," appear for the first time in his theoretical section of the *Studies on Hysteria*, published jointly with Breuer.

> With others, who have decided to put themselves in his hands and place their confidence in him—a step which in other such situations is only taken voluntarily and never at the doctor's request—with these other patients, I say, it is almost inevitable that their personal relation to him will force itself, for a time at least, unduly into the foreground. It seems, indeed, as though an influence of this kind on the part of the doctor is a *sine qua non* to a solution of the problem. I do not think any essential difference is made in this respect whether hypnosis can be used or whether it has to be bypassed and replaced by something else. But reason demands that we should emphasize the fact that these drawbacks, though they are inseparable from our procedure, cannot be laid at its door. On the contrary, it is quite clear that they are based on the predetermining conditions of the neuroses that are to be cured and that they must attach to any medical activity which involves intense preoccupation with the patient and leads to a psychical change in him.[13]

The term "transference" is used a few pages later without expressly having been introduced as a technical term, as is often the case with

Freud, although here likely because he assumes the matter itself to be familiar to the reader.[14] At two additional points, however, are carefully formulated indications of Freud's opinion of Breuer's conduct. The first is in his essay "On the History of the Psycho-Analytic Movement":

> Anyone who reads the history of Breuer's case now in the light of the knowledge gained in the last twenty years will at once perceive the symbolism in it—the snakes, the stiffening, the paralysis of the arm—and, on taking into account the situation at the bedside of the young woman's sick father, will easily guess the real interpretation of her symptoms; his opinion of the part played by sexuality in her mental life will therefore be very different from that of her doctor. In his treatment of her case, Breuer was able to make use of a very intense suggestive *rapport* with the patient, which may serve us as a complete prototype of what we call "transference" to-day. Now I have strong reasons for suspecting that after all her symptoms had been relieved Breuer must have discovered from further indications the sexual motivation of this transference, but that the universal nature of this unexpected phenomenon escaped him, with the result that, as though confronted by an "untoward event," he broke off all further investigation. He never said this to me in so many words, but he told me enough at different times to justify this reconstruction of what happened. When I later began more and more resolutely to put forward the significance of sexuality in the aetiology of neuroses, he was the first to show the reaction of distaste and repudiation which was later to become so familiar to me, but which at that time I had not yet learnt to recognize as my inevitable fate.[15]

In spite of its apparent frankness and criticism of Breuer, Freud's argument in this passage moves in the theoretical realm. Breuer did, in fact, see himself confronted with the sexual desires of Bertha Pappenheim, but he did not recognize the universal nature of these desires, which were thus not directed at him personally. Breuer therefore became alarmed at the sexual desires of Anna O. toward him, since he possessed similar desires toward her.

In his memorial address on Breuer, who died in 1925 at the age of 84, Freud once again alluded to this situation; on Breuer's refusal to continue the treatment of hysterical female patients he remarked:

> I found reason later to suppose that a purely emotional factor, too, had given him an aversion to further work on the elucidation of the neuroses. He had come up against something that is never

absent—his patient's transference on to her physician, and he had not grasped the impersonal character of the process.[16]

Freud thus thought Breuer ought not to have taken these sexual desires personally, but he did not here elaborate the reason for this, namely Breuer's countertransference love. Freud elsewhere repeatedly expressed his opinion on Breuer's refusal under any circumstances to acknowledge the sexual origin or basis of the transference, but there, too, he offered no analysis of the reasons Breuer might have been prevented from doing so.

Our acquaintance with the further course of the Breuer-Anna O. relationship goes back to Ernest Jones, who was able to rely not only on Freud's verbal account, but also on several of Freud's letters to his fiancée which were not included in the published version of the *Brautbriefe*.[17] According to Jones, Breuer appeared during the period of the treatment of Anna O.

> . . . so engrossed that his wife became bored at listening to no other topic, and before long jealous. She did not display this openly, but became unhappy and morose. It was a long time before Breuer, with his thoughts elsewhere, divined the meaning of her state of mind. It provoked a violent reaction in him, perhaps compounded of love and guilt, and he decided to bring the treatment to an end. He announced this to Anna O., who was by now much better, and bade her good-by. But that evening he was fetched back to find her in a greatly excited state, apparently as ill as ever. The patient, who according to him had appeared to be an asexual being and had never made any allusion to such a forbidden topic throughout the treatment, was now in the throes of an hysterical childbirth (pseudocyesis), the logical termination of a phantom pregnancy that had been invisibly developing in response to Breuer's ministrations. Though profoundly shocked, he managed to calm her down by hypnotizing her, and then fled the house in a cold sweat. The next day he and his wife left for Venice to spend a second honeymoon, which resulted in the conception of a daughter; the girl born in these curious circumstances was nearly sixty years later to commit suicide in New York.
>
> Confirmation of this account may be found in a contemporary letter Freud wrote to Martha, which contains substantially the same story. She at once identified herself with Breuer's wife, and hoped the same thing would not ever happen to her, whereupon Freud reproved her vanity in supposing that other women would fall in love with *her* husband: "for that to happen one has to be a Breuer."[18]

The last sentence intimates that Freud recognized the phenomenon of transference and countertransference clearly in Breuer's case, but that out of discretion he did not mention it directly by name. The conduct of Breuer—who abruptly broke off the therapy with Anna O., which had gone on for years, fled with his wife to Venice and there fathered a child, and later would have nothing whatsoever to do with either Anna O. or the treatment of hysterics—can best be understood in terms of the phenomenon of countertransference. He seemed never to have been clear about this point. But he conducted himself like a lover who observed a flaw in a woman he courted and turned to a trusted friend who before had interested him only slightly, his wife. He acted like the sorcerer's apprentice when the magic wand threatened to get out of hand. Breuer's behavior represents, to be sure, the most creditable testimony to his personal ethics, since he did not allow himself to be completely overcome by Anna O.; he thereby relinquished any influence on her neurosis and on neuroses in general, however.

The history of psychoanalysis clearly begins with an unchecked transference and countertransference relationship. In it Freud indeed recognized the transference, probably even saw it for the first time in this relationship, though he perhaps did not clearly recognize the countertransference; in any event he discreetly kept silent. But beyond this Freud was himself at the same time caught up in a transference relationship with Breuer that he himself likewise did not grasp.

THE FURTHER DEVELOPMENT OF TRANSFERENCE IN FREUD'S THEORY

From the initial article on psychoanalysis to the final years, statements by Freud on transference turn up again and again, admittedly not every time with new elaborations on the theme, but often with verbatim repetitions (which we can omit here). In the "Fragment of an Analysis of a Case of Hysteria" in 1905 Freud for the first time returned to the subject in detail:

> What are transferences? They are new editions or facsimiles of the impulses and phantasies which are aroused and made conscious during the progress of the analysis; but they have this peculiarity, which is characteristic for their species, that they replace some earlier person by the person of the physician. To put it another way: a whole series of psychological experiences are revived, not as belonging to the past, but as applying to the person of the physician at the present moment. Some of these transferences have

a content which differs from that of their model in no respect whatever except for the substitution. These then—to keep to the same metaphor—are merely new impressions or reprints. Others are more ingeniously constructed; their content has been subjected to a moderating influence—to *sublimation*, as I call it—and they may even become conscious, by cleverly taking advantage of some real peculiarity in the physician's person or circumstances and attaching themselves to that. These, then, will no longer be new impressions, but revised editions.

If the theory of analytic technique is gone into, it becomes evident that transference is an inevitable necessity. Practical experience, at all events, shows conclusively that there is no means of avoiding it, and that this latest creation of the disease must be combated like all the earlier ones. This happens, however, to be by far the hardest part of the whole task. It is easy to learn how to interpret dreams, to extract from the patient's associations his unconscious thoughts and memories, and to practise similar explanatory arts: for these the patient himself will always provide the text. Transference is the one thing the presence of which has to be detected almost without assistance and with only the slightest clues to go upon, while at the same time the risk of making arbitrary inferences has to be avoided. Nevertheless, transference cannot be evaded, since use is made of it in setting up all the obstacles that make the material inaccessible to treatment, and since it is only after the transference has been resolved that a patient arrives at a sense of conviction of the validity of the connections which have been constructed during the analysis.

Some people may feel inclined to look upon it as a serious objection to a method which is in any case troublesome enough that it itself should multiply the labours of the physician by creating a new species of pathological mental products. They may even be tempted to infer from the existence of transferences that the patient will be injured by analytic treatment. Both these suppositions would be mistaken. The physician's labours are not multiplied by transference; it need make no difference to him whether he has to overcome any particular impulse of the patient's in connection with himself or with some one else. Nor does the treatment force upon the patient, in the shape of transference, any new task which he would not otherwise have performed. It is true that neuroses may be cured in institutions from which psycho-analytic treatment is excluded, that hysteria may be said to be cured not by the method but by the physician, and that there is usually a sort of blind dependence and a permanent bond between a patient and the physician who has removed his symptoms by hypnotic suggestion;

but the scientific explanation of all these facts is to be found in the existence of 'transferences' such as are regularly directed by patients on to their physicians. Psycho-analytic treatment does not *create* transferences, it merely brings them to light, like so many other hidden psychical factors. The only difference is this—that spontaneously a patient will only call up affectionate and friendly transferences to help towards his recovery; if they cannot be called up, he feels the physician is 'antipathetic' to him, and breaks away from him as fast as possible and without having been influenced by him. In psycho-analysis, on the other hand, since the play of motives is different, all the patient's tendencies, including hostile ones, are aroused; they are then turned to account for the purposes of the analysis by being made conscious, and in this way the transference is constantly being destroyed. Transference, which seems ordained to be the greatest obstacle to psycho-analysis, becomes its most powerful ally, if its presence can be detected each time and explained to the patient.[19]

These passing observations in a work devoted to an entirely different subject indicate several refinements and elaborations that fit in as constituent elements in the structure of psychoanalytic theory. Clearly, in the transference the person of the therapist replaces one or more persons the patient knew earlier, whereby precisely during the analysis the feelings toward these persons are aroused and brought to consciousness. This notion has been kept unchanged and has been linked inextricably with the concept of transference. In this point already Freud exhibits clearly different notions vis-à-vis the earlier notions of "rapport."

Freud also introduces new distinctions in the type of the transferences, however. He speaks of "reprints" and "revised editions," in which images and fantasies linked to earlier persons are thus—simply in an altered form—transferred onto the physician. This alteration, here designated "sublimation," is not characterized in greater detail in this passage, and can be conceived of in a psychoanalytic sense only as the result of an intrapsychic process.

Already in the *Studies on Hysteria*, Freud established that transference should be something necessary for the therapy. But that transference represents a "creation of the disease," a type of neurotic symptom that takes the place of otherwise newly arisen neurotic symptoms, is a further elaboration on the transference idea, to which Freud later refers again and again.

Freud makes it clear, though, that with the earlier methods of psychotherapy based on hypnosis, symptomatic cures could result, but that the price for these was an indissoluable attachment of the patient to the physician. But as we have seen, Janet had previously indicated a technique whereby this attachment could be loosened. The psychoanalytic technique too, from this point on, recognizes the importance of resolving the transference and attributes the ultimate cure of neurotic (hysteric) symptoms, among other problems, to this.

A further change vis-à-vis the "rapport" in hypnotherapy is that the psychoanalytic technique arouses and permits not only positive transferences but also hostile ones, which with the older methods of psychotherapy would have necessitated discontinuing the therapy or led to a discontinuance by the patient. But the handling of hostile transferences is possible only because they are being raised to consciousness in the analysis and thereby constantly experience resolution. We recognise, of course, that in the psychoanalysis it is not always possible to resolve the positive transferences (thus bringing to an end the bond between analyst and patient), nor is it always possible to control the transferences here characterized as hostile (negative transferences) adequately and with positive effect on the analysis.

In the last of his five lectures held at Clark University in September 1909—the written version of which, according to Jones,[20] was completed only in December 1909—Freud devotes a detailed section to transference:

> I have not yet told you, Ladies and Gentlemen, of the most important of the observations which confirm our hypothesis of the sexual instinctual forces operating in neuroses. In every psychoanalytic treatment of a neurotic patient the strange phenomenon that is known as "transference" makes its appearance. The patient, that is to say, directs towards the physician a degree of affectionate feeling (mingled, often enough, with hostility) which is based on no real relation between them and which—as is shown by every detail of its emergence—can only be traced back to old wishful phantasies of the patient's which have become unconscious. Thus the part of the patient's emotional life which he can no longer recall to memory is reexperienced by him in his relation to the physician; and it is only this re-experiencing in the "transference" that convinces him of the existence and of the power of these unconscious sexual impulses. His symptoms, to take an analogy from chemistry, are precipitates of earlier experiences in the sphere of love (in the widest sense of the word), and it is only in the raised temperature of his experience of the transference that they can be resolved and reduced to other psychical products. In this reaction the physician, if I may borrow an apt phrase from Ferenczi, plays the part of a

catalytic ferment, which temporarily attracts to itself the affects liberated in the process. A study of transference, too, can give you the key to an understanding of hypnotic suggestion, which we employed to begin with as a technical method for investigating the unconscious in our patients. At that time hypnosis was found to be a help therapeutically, but a hindrance to the scientific understanding of the facts; for it cleared away the psychical resistances in a certain area while building them up into an unscalable wall at its frontiers. You must not suppose, moreover, that the phenomenon of transference (of which, unfortunately, I can tell you all too little to-day) is *created* by psycho-analytic influence. Transference arises spontaneously in all human relationships just as it does between the patient and the physician. It is everywhere the true vehicle of therapeutic influence; and the less its presence is suspected, the more powerfully it operates. So psycho-analysis does not create it, but merely reveals it to consciousness and gains control of it in order to guide psychical processes towards the desired goal. I cannot, however, leave the topic of transference without stressing the fact that this phenomenon plays a decisive part in bringing conviction not only to the patient but also to the physician. I know it to be true of all my followers that they were only convinced of the correctness of my assertions on the pathogenesis of the neuroses by their experiences with transference; and I can very well understand that such certainty of judgement cannot be attained before one has carried out psycho-analyses and has oneself observed the workings of transference.[21]

Although Freud expressed the opinion to his publisher Franz Deuticke that the lectures contained nothing new, and although the passage cited is in many respects a summary of his previously expressed views, there are here nonetheless several intellectual developments worthy of note.[22] Freud emphasizes in this passage, more than in earlier presentations, that sexual impulses underlie the transferences. From the father, mother, and sibling imagoes previously juxtaposed with equal emphasis a restriction to Oedipal relationships of this type has come about, thus foreshadowing the expansion of the psychoanalytic theory the next year (1910) with the Oedipus complex. In this passage is yet another allusion by Freud to hypnosis (or better, to hypnosis psychotherapy), with which similarities and differences are stressed.

Besides the restriction to Oedipal relationships this passage contains a broadening of the concept of the transference—Freud maintains that transference arises "in all human relationships," that it thus is not confined to the relationship between patient and analyst, and that it thereby also regulates the relationships of human beings with one another, as well as that between physician and patient. This observation actually applies to only one aspect of the transference relationship, namely to the revival of earlier relationships with other people. The observation is not applicable to the special relationship between psychotherapist and patient which affects the intensity and persistence of the transference. These two aspects of the transference relationship are today still not always clearly distinguished from one another.

Freud's only publication explicitly devoted to the problems of transference ("The Dynamics of Transference," 1912) was written to offer psychoanalysts clearer guidelines for the analytic technique.[23] Besides the detailed definition of transference we cited at the beginning of this chapter, this text is a recapitulation of diverse considerations on transference presented elsewhere. Certainly here more intensively than elsewhere Freud explores the question of why the transference is always put to the service of resistance when a repressed complex is touched upon. Transference in this passage is repeatedly characterized as *"the most powerful resistance* to the treatment," "the strongest weapon of the resistance," and an "admirably suited . . . means of resistance."[24] Freud explains that "controlling the phenomena of transference presents the psycho-analyst with the greatest difficulties," but he maintains emphatically "that it is precisely they [these difficulties] that do us the inestimable service of making the patient's hidden and forgotten erotic impulses immediate and manifest. For when all is said and done, it is impossible to destory anyone *in absentia* or *in effegie.*"[25] That Freud here terms it a duty "to strike dead," to kill the "erotic impulses" arising out of the transference is a significant secondary aspect. Freud also makes observations on countertransference in this context, but these should be discussed later. In his essay, "On Beginning the Treatment" (1913), Freud returns once more to the technical aspect; he writes:

> So long as the patient's communications and ideas run on without any obstruction, the theme of transference should be left untouched. One must wait until the transference, which is the most delicate of all procedures, has become a resistance.[26]

Among the *Introductory Lectures on Psycho-Analysis* (1917) the twenty-seventh is expressly dedicated to transference.[27] These lectures on the one hand reflect the experience of Freud's thirty-year lectureship and on the other sum up in an extremely clear, lucid, and easily comprehensible form the psychoanalytic system developed to that point. They thus rightly belong among the most often read portions of Freud's work. With regard to transference they simply represent a recapitulation and not a further development. However, little attention has ordinarily been paid to Freud's clear presentation in this text of his experiences with transference phenomena:

> Transference can appear as a passionate demand for love or in more moderate forms; in place of a wish to be loved, a wish can emerge between a girl and an old man to be received as a favourite daughter; the libidinal desire can be toned down into a proposal for an inseparable, but ideally non-sensual, friendship. Some women succeed in sublimating the transference and in moulding it till it achieves a kind of viability.[28]

From these formulations it can be seen that Freud has come to know transference in many variations, and certainly also in its hidden form, transformed by resistance and investigation of the resistance of the analyst. It again becomes clear that for the analyst transference represents on the one hand the most powerful ally, but on the other the greatest problem.

Freud came back to the problem of transference one last time in "An Outline of Psycho-Analysis" (1938), published posthumously.[29] During the final 20 years of Freud's psychoanalytic activity, there seem to be no major innovations or amplifications on the subject. In this final elaboration Freud assigns transference a position within the topographic system of classification developed in 1920, linking it here to the superego:

> If the patient puts the analyst in the place of his father (or mother), he is also giving him the power which his super-ego exercises over his ego, since his parents were, as we know, the origin of his super-ego. The new super-ego now has an opportunity for a sort of *after-education* of the neurotic; it can correct mistakes for which his parents were responsible in educating him.[30]

Of course, Freud immediately imposes a warning: The analyst should not dominate the patient, transforming him according to his ideal, but should always pay attention to the particularities of the patient. One more technical suggestion is elucidated here with greater clarity than elsewhere: "We think it most undesirable if the patient *acts* outside the transference instead of remembering. The ideal for our purposes would be that he should behave as normally as possible outside the treatment

and express his abnormal reactions only in the transference."[31] A recognized maxim of psychoanalytic treatment to this day, this rule is admittedly violated almost as often as not on the part of the patient, since
acting is constantly placed in the service of the resistance.

NEGATIVE TRANSFERENCE

Although Freud gave it a specific term, nothing is absolutely definitive
about negative transference outside of its tendency to introduce feelings
of hostility into the therapeutic relationship. Its significance thus is first
and foremost pragmatic. Certainly where friendly, over-excited, or seemingly intimate feelings enter into the therapy, one will always endeavor
to illuminate them. But feelings of hostility constantly and immediately
bring with them the danger of a discontinuation of the therapy. That
we heard nothing of such events from the preanalytical period justifies
the assumption that the negatively tinged relationship escaped the earlier psychotherapists as a phenomenon, either because the patients soon
disappeared from sight, or because the therapist did not care to boast
of such reactions. In the Freud-Jung correspondence, one quite often
reads an "avoidance" of therapy, probably still the simplest and most
common form of negative transference. But it says a great deal for Freud's
honesty and integrity that he not only recognized and named this phenomenon, but also put it in the service of therapy. This specific accomplishment of psychoanalysis to this day has not been adopted by any
other form of psychotherapy. Of course, Freud was ultimately unable
to give negative transference the "detailed examination" he felt it "de-
served."[32] And after his death this wish long went unfulfilled.

C. J. JUNG'S THEORETICAL CONSIDERATIONS ON TRANSFERENCE

Before we further explore specific problems of transference relationships, we should examine Jung's theoretical considerations on transference. In Jung's published work are few indications of the personal
significance of transference for him and his relationship with Freud.
Only in one passage in "The Psychology of the Transference" does he
come to speak of his personal relationship with Freud in connection
with transference:

> The enormous importance that Freud attached to the transference
> phenomenon became clear to me at our first personal meeting in
> 1907. After a conversation lasting many hours there came a pause.

> Suddenly he asked me out of the blue, "And what do you think about the transference?" I replied with the deepest conviction that it was the alpha and omega of the analytical method, whereupon he said, "Then you have grasped the main thing."[33]

Although Jung here attributes in his words an extraordinary importance to transference with his use of the topos "alpha and omega," it nonetheless becomes evident that its importance for Freud is, at least subjectively, considerably greater. This is indicated not only by Freud's use of their first meeting for the clarification of this question, but also by his hesitation.

Jung's theory, in fact, recognizes all the essential determinations of the Freudian school on the phenomenon of transference and countertransference, and Jung, too, refers to the rapport of the magnetists: "In the old pre-analytical psychotherapy, going right back to the doctors of the Romantic Age, the transference was already defined as 'rapport'."[34]

Jung, because of the transference phenomenon, ultimately was the first to call for a scholarly study. Jung's conception differs significantly from Freud's, however, above all in that it goes even further.

Only in 1945, at the age of 70, did Jung devote a specific, detailed study to transference ("The Psychology of the Transference"), in which he explains by means of a series of alchemistic images those aspects of transference he considers particularly significant.[35] Here, too, Jung admittedly presupposes familiarity with the basic phenomena of transference. Already in the introduction he states: "It is probably no exaggeration to say that almost all cases requiring lengthy treatment gravitate round the phenomenon of transference, and that the success or failure of the treatment appears to be bound up with it in a very fundamental way."[36] But Jung immediately puts himself at a distance from Freud:

> Although I originally agreed with Freud that the importance of the transference could hardly be overestimated, increasing experience has forced me to realize that its importance is relative. The transference is like those medicines which are a panacea for one and pure poison for another. In one case its appearance denotes a change for the better, in another it is a hindrance and an aggravation, if not a change for the worse, and in a third it is relatively unimportant. Generally speaking, however, it is a critical phenomenon of varying shades of meaning.[37]

Jung's description of the "transference neurosis" at first sounds conventional:

. . . a bond that corresponds in every respect to the initial infantile relationship, with a tendency to recapitulate all the experiences of childhood on the doctor. In other words, the neurotic maladjustment of the patient is now *transferred* to him. Freud, who was the first to recognize and describe this phenomenon, coined the term "transference neurosis."[38]

In a footnote at this point Jung sets out the difference more clearly. Here he quotes Freud:

Provided only that the patient shows compliance enough to respect the necessary conditions of the analysis, we regularly succeed in giving all the symptoms of the illness a new transference meaning and in replacing his ordinary neurosis by a "transference-neurosis."[39]

And Jung continues:

Freud puts down a little too much to his own account here. A transference is not by any means always the work of the doctor. Often it is in full swing before he has even opened his mouth. Freud's conception of the transference as a "new edition of the old disorder," a "newly created and transformed neurosis," or a "new, artificial neurosis,"[40] is right in so far as the transference of a neurotic patient is equally neurotic, but this neurosis is neither new nor artificial nor created: it is the same old neurosis, and the only new thing about it is that the doctor is now drawn into the vortex, more as its victim than as its creator.[41]

Jung also sees the factors of the countertransference and the involvement of the therapist in the specific relationship in a particular light: "It is inevitable that the doctor should be influenced to a certain extent and even that his nervous health should suffer. He quite literally 'takes over' the sufferings of his patient and shares them with him. For this reason he runs a risk—and must run it in the nature of things."[42] In the midst of his theoretical preliminary observations on the phenomenon of the transference Jung makes a startling personal confession: "I personally am always glad when there is only a mild transference or when it is practically unnoticeable. Far less claim is then made upon one as a person, and one can be satisfied with other therapeutically effective factors."[43] Of course, there may be an aftereffect here from some profound experiences of Jung's first years in psychotherapy. But far more than Freud he stresses that through the web of transference and countertransference a completely new phenomenon arises:

> The patient, by bringing an activated unconscious content to bear upon the doctor, constellates the corresponding unconscious material to him, owing to the inductive effect which always emanates from projections in greater or lesser degree. Doctor and patient thus find themselves in a relationship founded on mutual unconsciousness. . . . The greatest difficulty here is that contents are often activated in the doctor which might normally remain latent.[44]

Or again in a different formulation:

> The transference, however, alters the psychological stature of the doctor, though this is at first imperceptible to him. He too becomes affected, and has as much difficulty in distinguishing between the patient and what has taken possession of him as has the patient himself. This leads both of them to a direct confrontation with the daemonic forces lurking in the darkness. The resultant paradoxical blend of positive and negative, of trust and fear, of hope and doubt, of attraction and repulsion, is characteristic of the initial relationship.[45]

For Jung transference is composed not only of erotic feelings, but also of drives for power and possession, as well as of fear. Outside the relationship in the conscious and unconscious realm, according to Jung, the animus or anima of the therapist and the patient establish a relationship as well, so that in each case a complex constellation results. Not only is the relationship of psychotherapist and patient (and the converse) marked by this, but relations between human beings are also characterized by the most diverse transference relationships, especially in a lasting marriage. In any event, a social phenomenon results which figures extensively in the determination of societal relationships and culture. Once again, in Jung's words:

> The transference phenomenon is without doubt one of the most important syndromes in the process of individuation; its wealth of meanings goes far beyond mere personal likes and dislikes. By virtue of its collective contents and symbols it transcends the individual personality and extends into the social sphere, reminding us of those higher human relationships which are so painfully absent in our present social order, or rather disorder.[46]

TRANSFERENCE LOVE

Freud dedicated the essay "Observations on Transference-Love" (1915) to a problem relatively insignificant theoretically but extraordinarily significant pragmatically.[47] Jones observes that "he expounded with the utmost clarity the principles that should guide the analyst."[48] The question here is love in the literal sense, since Freud says: "What I have in mind is the case in which a woman patient shows by unmistakable indications, or openly declares, that she has fallen in love, as any other mortal woman might, with the doctor who is analysing her."[49] This phenomenon is of general significance, although it is explained throughout the essay in terms of a single concrete example, the love of a young girl for a male analyst. Freud comes to the following conclusions:

> We have no right to dispute that the state of being in love which makes its appearance in the course of analytic treatment has the character of a "genuine" love. If it seems so lacking in normality, this is sufficiently explained by the fact that being in love in ordinary life, outside analysis, is also more similar to abnormal than to normal mental phenomena. Nevertheless, transference-love is characterized by certain features which ensure it a special position. In the first place, it is provoked by the analytic situation; secondly, it is greatly intensified by the resistance, which dominates the situation; and thirdly, it is lacking to a high degree in a regard for reality, is less sensible, less concerned about consequences and more blind in its valuation of the loved person than we are prepared to admit in the case of normal love. We should not forget, however, that these departures from the norm constitute precisely what is essential about being in love.[50]

As we have seen, precisely in this direct connection, suggestive of sexuality, Freud differs from Jung, who wished to assign the phenomenon a more general significance bordering on the universal. In another passage Freud addresses directly the dangers for the analyst resulting from transference love:

> Again, when a woman sues for love, to reject and refuse is a distressing part for a man to play; and, in spite of neurosis and resistance, there is an incomparable fascination in a woman of high principles who confesses her passion. It is not a patient's crudely sensual desires which constitute the temptation. These are more likely to repel, and it will call for all the doctor's tolerance if he is to regard them as a natural phenomenon. It is rather, perhaps, a

woman's subtler and aim-inhibited wishes which bring with them the danger of making a man forget his technique and his medical task for the sake of a fine experience.[51]

These formulations, couched in terms of suggestions on technique, have a pragmatic and substantial background. We have already seen that, as in earlier forms of psychotherapy and in the inception of psychoanalysis too, transference love played a significant role, to which Freud alludes in an observation:

> I have recently disregarded this matter of discretion at one point, and shown how this same transference situation [namely transference love] held back the development of psycho-analytic therapy during its first decade.[52]

Although not expressly stated in the passage to which Freud is alluding (where Breuer's name is mentioned), Breuer's relationship with Anna O. is obviously intended.[53]

Freud points out that transference love becomes all the more acceptable, the more sublimated its expression is. Because of its limited moral and practical significance, this form of transference love was scarcely opposed by Freud. It is certainly not to be wished out of the early history of psychoanalysis. Freud's relationships with numerous earlier patients show that for him the abstinence ended at this point, although in the strict sense this meant a rule violation.

COUNTERTRANSFERENCE

Countertransference has been treated in the literature of psychoanalysis far less than has transference. Michel Neyraut first gave countertransference a central position in his book, *The Transference* (1974).[54] According to Neyraut, countertransference is actually more important than transference, since the commitment of the therapist to the therapy precedes all therapy. Diverging from the traditional point of view, Neyraut admittedly calls this empathic, still completely unformed feeling countertransference. With him countertransference is thus something extremely positive.

Countertransference is very seldom directly discussed in Freud's published work, and in his letters available thus far it is almost never mentioned. In addition, Freud's observations on countertransference are focused on a brief period, the years 1910 and 1911. James Strachey has suggested that Freud did not wish to see too many of the analyst's difficulties revealed to the general public.[55] The lack of corresponding discussions in his letters, however, shows that still other reasons for this are to be found in Freud's personality itself. These are also reflected in the few passages that treat countertransference. According to them, Freud viewed countertransference predominantly as a dangerous, difficult, and negative phenomenon that to be sure was not to be avoided, but was to be held in check with every available means.

Freud's first observation is found in a letter of June 5, 1910, to Oskar Pfister, in which the word countertransference is not mentioned, but from the context must be intended:

> The transference is indeed a cross. The unyielding stubbornness of the illness, because of which we abandoned indirect suggestion and direct hypnotic suggestion, cannot be entirely eliminated by analysis, but can only be diminished, and its relics make their appearance in the transference. These are generally conspicuous enough, and the rules often let one down, but one must be guided by the patient's character and not entirely give up one's personal note. In general, I agree with Stekel that the patient should be kept in sexual abstinence, in unrequited love, which of course is not always possible. The more you let him find love the sooner you will get his complexes, but the smaller is the final success, as he gives up the fulfilments of the complexes only because he can exchange them for the results of the transference. A cure has perhaps been achieved, but the patient has not attained the necessary degree of independence and security against relapse.[56]

In a painstaking study on the structural state of transference and countertransference, Werner Kemper has worked out the position of the negative countertransference and the affective reaction in the analytical situation.[57] In the event that the analyst detects an uneasiness or animosity, for example, or anxiety or perplexity in himself upon a remark by the patient, he should not be ashamed, but instead raise the following three questions:

> (1) To what that has just now transpired in the patient have I spontaneously reacted so affectively?
> (2) Why did that turn of events produce in me precisely this (and no other) particular emotional reaction?
> (3) What could the patient unconsciously have "intended" that he succeeded in assailing my analytical equanimity, causing an "unanalytical" emotional reaction?[58]

These questions comprise the measures through which the analyst not only observes and restrains his own impulses, but should make them effective for the therapy as well. Kemper has also established, in analogy to a structural model of transference, a model of countertransference which sums up schematically most recent discussion on this subject:

I. Deliberate sequences promoting the analysis on the part of the analyst—(a) fundamental readiness to help, (b) temporary identification, (c) acceptance of the patient's transferring projections, (d) distantiation by periodical retraction of (b) and (c) with a view to analytical clarification.

II. Unconscious sequences on the part of the analyst impairing the analysis—(a) transference to the patient adequate to structure, (b) projective transference inadequate to structure (1) to the patient, (2) to the analytical situation in general or to special events within this situation, (c) the analyst's reactions of protest against frustration imposed on him.[59]

In spite of the frank and public treatment Kemper and other psychoanalysts (for example Paul Parin, Annie Reich, Paula Heimann, and Gerhard Scheunert[60]) give the subject of countertransference—primarily negative countertransference—detailed case studies are noticeably absent which could register the definitive, distorting, or even destructive influence of the psychoanalyst's emotional attitudes on the course of the analysis or on the patient.

Negative countertransference and the transference reaction of the analyst to the transference of the patient present a special and difficult problem. The situation is especially difficult because the analyst finds himself in a position of advantage vis-à-vis the patient, since he can himself either propose interpretations or at least rate interpretations correct or false. When confronting the patient, he has at his disposal powerful resources derivable from the analysis. He can for example interpret for the patient as resistance every utterance that has aggrieved or perplexed him, and can thus in principle assume the error to be the patient's. The patient's nonacceptance of such a general interpretation can, moreover, be interpreted as resistance. Ultimately, if every means fails and the analysis—because of the analyst—goes no further, the diagnosis "neurosis" can be placed in doubt; it can be said that there is probably a question of a psychopathy, or at least of a particularly rigid structure, or perhaps an endogenous depression; with each assumption of this sort the analyst can feel himself exonerated.

TRANSFERENCE NEUROSES

The term "transference neuroses" is used by Freud in a twofold sense:

(1) In a nosographic sense. Transference neurosis then means simply a group of neuroses within the psychoneuroses (see Figure 1),
which are placed in opposition to the narcissistic neuroses. Pragmatically, one of the group of neuroses Freud first investigated
(anxiety hysteria, conversion hysteria, and obsessive-compulsive
neurosis) remained the basis of the psychoanalytic system. In contrast to the narcissistic neuroses, the capacity for transference formation in these neuroses is pronounced. In other words, all those
neuroses for which in Freud's original view a psychoanalytic treatment offers sufficient hope of success, since transference develops
as their driving force, are called transference neuroses.
(2) The more important connotation of the term "transference neurosis" belongs to a specific (the most important) episode in a psychoanalytic treatment. The clinical neurosis transforms itself after
a time into the transference neurosis (see Figure 2). In the transference—and as far as possible only in it—the neurotic repeats his
infantile conflicts. Within this transference neurosis every symptom of the disease takes on a new significance (transference significance) whose clarification through the analytic process leads to
the exposure of the infantile neurosis and therewith to the resolution of the neurosis.

In Freud's own terms this is expressed as follows:

The main instrument, however, for curbing the patient's compulsion to repeat and for turning it into a motive for remembering
lies in the handling of the transference. We render the compulsion

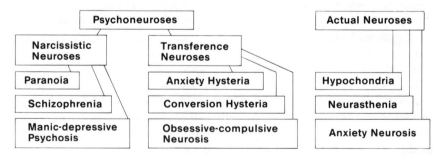

Figure 1. Nosologic system used by Freud.

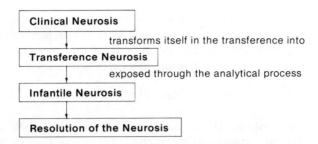

Figure 2.Development of a neurosis during its psychoanalytic treatment (according to Freud.)

harmless, and indeed useful, by giving it the right to assert itself in a definite field. We admit it into the transference as a playground in which it is allowed to expand in almost complete freedom and in which it is expected to display to us everything in the way of pathogenic instincts that is hidden in the patient's mind. Provided only that the patient shows compliance enough to respect the necessary conditions of the analysis, we regularly succeed in giving all the symptoms of the illness a new transference meaning replacing his ordinary neurosis by a "transference-neurosis" of which he can be cured by the therapeutic work. The transference thus creates an intermediate region between illness and real life through which the transition from the one to the other is made. The new condition has taken over all the features of the illness; but it represents an artificial illness which is at every point accessible to our intervention. It is a piece of real experience, but one which has been made possible by especially favourable conditions, and it is of a provisional nature. From the repetitive reactions which are exhibited in the transference we are led along the familiar paths to the awakening of the memories, which appear without difficulty, as it were, after the resistance has been overcome.[61]

The transference neurosis needs no proper cure. Its resolution takes place in any event little by little as the transference and its conditions are brought to consciousness.

Franz Alexander has pointed out that every neurotic—and even more every psychotic—patient tends to establish himself in the transference, to orient himself toward the secure (if at the same time always partially disappointing) relationships with the therapist, and because of this to neglect all (insecure) extratherapeutic relationships.[62] He must therefore always be encouraged to develop new interpersonal relationships outside the therapy. The resolution of a vestige of the transference is not common in life; even after a very long separation, meeting people again whose fate was once bound up with one's own often leads to a revival of old transferences, positive and negative alike, and these transferences are intrinsically part of a human being's existence in society.

TRANSFERENCE WITH THE NARCISSISTIC NEUROSES

In his early writings (1897) Freud placed the narcissistic neuroses (dementia praecox, paranoia, melancholia) in opposition to the transference neuroses (see Figure 1). The designation never took hold, and the concept behind it has proved more an impediment to the psychotherapy of the endogenous psychoses of today. It is difficult to say what led Freud to a theory that so necessitates resignation in therapy. The efforts toward a psychoanalysis of schizophrenia above all were numerous in the early years of psychoanalysis, in particular with Jung, who during the first phase of his correspondence with Freud described vividly this sort of institutional experience at Burghölzli. Jung ultimately set down his experiences in his study, "The Psychology of Dementia Praecox" (1907).[63] Freud's reasoning is based above all on the intractability of the endogenous psychoses when psychoanalytic therapy is used. In short, the theory holds that with those psychoses the object-libido is drawn back to the ego, and that therewith no further object-cathexes exist. The symptoms of the psychosis are interpreted as an attempt—admittedly hopeless—at reviving the object-cathexis. Therapy is therefore not practicable, since no transference neurosis develops. Freud did not further amend this view. We find it still in the *Introductory Lectures on Psycho-Analysis*:

> The narcissistic neuroses can scarcely be attacked with the technique that has served us with the transference neuroses. You will soon learn why. What always happens with them is that, after proceeding for a short distance, we come up against a wall which brings us to a stop. Even with the transference neuroses, as you know, we met with barriers of resistance, but we were able to demolish them bit by bit. In the narcissistic neuroses the resistance is unconquerable; at the most, we are able to cast an inquisitive glance over the top of the wall and spy out what is going on on the other side of it. Our technical methods must accordingly be replaced by others; and we do not know yet whether we shall succeed in finding a substitute.[64]

Only in his final sentence did Freud allow for some further developments. Transferences indeed are developed, although in a different way than with neuroses. The technique, however, did not have to be changed to overcome the resistance after all, but instead had to be transformed in a quite different way—which will not be explored further here—to offer an access for the assistance desired (cf. Frieda Fromm-Reichmann, Victor H. Rosen, Gaetano Benedetti).[65] For this reason almost all psychoanalysts today consider Freud's original determinations on the impossibility of transference formation with narcissistic neuroses to have been superseded by subsequent experiences. One of the few exceptions is Michel Neyraut, who continues to embrace Freud's position.

TRANSFERENCE IN POST-FREUDIAN PSYCHOANALYSIS

In the present study of transference we have mostly followed Freud himself. This in no way means that in the epoch of psychoanalysis after Freud no significance was ascribed to the phenomenon of transference. Quite the contrary. The literature on transference is extraordinarily extensive. So much common ground is in this literature, however, that for our purposes most of it can be omitted.

In the entire post-Freudian literature Freud's basic assumptions on the transference have not been examined or even called into question, in contrast to many of Freud's other propositions; this fact belongs to this common ground. One steadfast assumption is the notion that transference always represents the revival of past relational situations, and that it is a special feature of psychoanalytic therapy. These basic assumptions have for most psychoanalysts lost the character of theoretical constructs (which they are) and have been raised to the level of objective facts that in this regard need no further substantiation.

This transition from theory to fact is doubtlessly also linked to the psychoanalytic therapy experiences of the individual analyst that lead to confirmations of the theory of transference. Similarly, the post-Freudian discussion of transference has developed by and large out of problems of technique, bringing with it refinements in the concept of transference oriented toward the specific treatment situation. In one such refined sense, primarily through the work of Heinz Kohut, the topic of transference with narcissistic personality disorders has gained new relevance.[66]

Kohut's efforts are directed not toward schizophrenia and psychotic depressions, not even toward the so-called borderline conditions, but rather toward those personality disorders in which the self-cathexis stands at the heart of the process of defense, and which were long believed untreatable because of this. The work of analysis is constantly engaged in a not easily understood way in dealing with subtle transference manifestations. With Kohut the *mirror transference* and the *idealizing transference* take on key significance in the treatment of the narcissistic personality disorders.

During childhood there existed with the *mirror transference* a need for approval and acknowledgment by the person of reference (who should in this respect be a mirror). That person (for example, the mother) reacted to this need insufficiently or incorrectly, however. If the resulting mirror transference is formed in the therapy, the patient feels secure as long as the therapist acknowledges him. In Kohut's words, the question is one of a mobilization of the "grandiose self."[67] If the analyst's interpretation is felt to be incorrect, or simply inadequate, disruptions immediately occur, and the patient loses the feeling of wholeness which had been maintained with the aid of the transference.

Quite similarly, in the *idealizing transference* a fusion with a person of idealized strength and composure is revived. Here the question is in Kohut's words one of a mobilization of the parent imago in the therapy. With both types of transference, the analyst for his part forms transferences and countertransferences attuned to them. In both cases, the *narcissistic transference* serves to strengthen the self. Its analysis is therefore the primary subject of the psychoanalysis of the narcissistic personality disorders.

In a very similar fashion, special terms are coined by Otto Kernberg for the facets of the transference relationship which come to light in the treatment of borderline disorders.[68] There is an *oscillating transference*, for example, in which an alternating projection of fragments of the self takes place. With Kernberg too the analysis of the individual facets of the transference—likewise perceived as a revival of earlier relationships—is the essential therapeutic problem. In any event, the therapist must not only be aware of the most manifold variations of the transference, but also count on just as many countertransference reactions of his own.

TRANSFERENCE IN THE LACANIAN SCHOOL

Like most basic concepts of psychoanalysis, the technical concept of the transference has been subjected by Lacan to a thorough analysis, accompanied by his own insights. Lacan not only has devoted an individual work to the transference phenomenon ("Intervention sur le transfert"), but also has discussed it often in his seminars[69]:

The transference is a phenomenon in which subject and psycho-analyst are both included. To divide it in terms of transference and countertransference—however bold, however confident what is said on this theme may be—is never more than a way of avoiding the essence of the matter.[70]

Lacan goes to the essence of the psychoanalytic concept of transference as understood traditionally:

> . . . repetition of earlier situations, unconscious repetitions, acti-vation of a reintegration of history—history in a sense contrary to that of which I have spoken, since it is a question of an imaginary reintegration, in which, unknown to the subject, the past situation is only lived in the present insofar as the historical dimension is misrecognized by him—I have not said is *unconscious*, you will note.[71]

According to Lacan, the commonplace notion that transference rep-resents the repetition of a situation [from early childhood] is insuffi-cient.[72] And the most pervasive explanation, which makes transference the sum or succession of all the patient's positive or negative feelings toward the analyst, is questionable.[73] The subject of the entire post-Freudian literature on the transference concept matters little, namely the endless further dissection of these reactions, fixing the discussion com-pletely on the aspects thereby exposed.[74] A fundamental discussion of the problems of transference and their theoretical assumptions has been impeded by precisely this thinking. It could not even be said "that the different partial treatments existing simultaneously side by side com-plemented each other."[75]

Lacan's contribution works out the fundamentals of the transference:

> In its essence the effective transference in question is quite simply the act of speech. Each time one person speaks to another in a manner authentic and full, there is in the proper sense transference, symbolic transference—something happens that changes the na-ture of the two beings *en présence*.[76]

The transference concept cannot be resolved into constituent elements, Lacan writes at another point, but it is understood simultaneously in different realms: in the symbolic, the imaginary, and the real. Lacan's theory so pervades each of these individual formulations that to com-ment on them thoroughly would mean presenting the complete theory.

In brief, it maintains that in the communication between analyst and analysand the unconscious of both communicates in such a way that both come out of the analysis changed. This takes place in the symbolic realm. More precisely, the symbols of the unconscious, structured like a language, relate to one another. The psychoanalytic concepts Lacan has examined are related not so much to the hierarchical model of the id-ego-superego as to the three realms mentioned above, which are representative of his theory. The earlier psychoanalytic view, which saw transference (and countertransference) primarily as an obstacle to be overcome in the psychoanalytic treatment, is to be located on the imaginary level, according to Lacan.

Lacan brings the diversely branching post-Freudian discussion on transference back to Freud, and beyond this with Freud himself back to its fundamentals; this is important for the student. Lacan, moreover, illuminates the process of the transference in the light of his own theory of the unconscious.

TRANSFERENCE PSYCHOSIS

The term "transference psychosis" is seldom employed, although the clinical observation behind it is probably not infrequent. Crudely put, the question is one of psychoses in the clinical sense which breaks forth during a psychoanalytic treatment. Margaret Little, from whom come the first references and probably the term as well, stressed that transference psychoses arise with patients who cannot process transference interpretations.[77] In particular, the psychoanalytic situation loses its exemplary character, with the result that the image of the father, or the mother, or the like, is not simply *transferred* onto the analyst, but is real for the patient. The difference between real object and transference object, of which the patient otherwise always remains conscious in spite of all action and verbalization, vanishes. Thus typical schizophrenic patterns of thought and conduct are easily discerned.

Helmut Luft published the first two case studies soon after Little.[78] In these cases, the interruption of the therapy (through the absence of the therapist) brought out the psychosis. Obviously, here is only one possible situation leading to a psychosis. The detailed examination of a case by Walther T. Winkler gives us an in-depth look.[79] Winkler holds the view that the psychosis first establishes itself in the course of the psychoanalytic therapy, and he rejects the notion (one he had considered) that the psychosis could have existed earlier.

Winkler's patient had originally entered treatment because she felt disturbances in her concentration and her memory; she also felt a lack of human contact. In these complaints can be recognized fundamental schizophrenic disturbances which were joined only later by usual clinical schizophrenic symptoms. Under Winkler's psychoanalytic treatment an intensive transference then quickly developed, which offered the patient the prospect of replacing the lost human contact by means of the therapist. The dynamics of the transference relationship were then — understandably — perceived as a threat, so that Winkler could write that the "delusion formation" then manifesting itself had obviously arisen out of the transference conflict that was straining the patient quite heavily. The delusion takes the place of the transference and is by its nature not open to interpretation. The designation "transference psychosis" is in this respect justified, since the delusion proceeds in the therapy directly from the transference, and this remains thematic in the delusion as well.

Although the psychoanalytic therapy came to a standstill here, the catastrophe began only after treatment with neuroleptic drugs and the ensuing disappearance of the delusion. The patient reacted to this with a depression and committed suicide by hanging. These events reveal clearly the powerful psychical forces unleashed in the transference psychosis.

HANDLING OF TECHNIQUE IN THE PSYCHOANALYSIS

Considering the significance of transference phenomena in the psychoanalysis, very few aids for handling them can be enlisted from the literature by the young analyst. First and foremost he should approximate the ideal of the analyst, which would make specific suggestions on technique unnecessary indeed. According to Freud, placing the patient on the couch already belongs to the technique of transference:

> I hold to the plan of getting the patient to lie on a sofa while I sit behind him out of his sight. This arrangement has a historical basis; it is the remnant of the hypnotic method out of which psychoanalysis was evolved. But it deserves to be maintained for many reasons. The first is a personal motive, but one which others may share with me. I cannot put up with being stared at by other people for eight hours a day (or more). Since, while I am listening to the patient, I, too, give myself over to the current of my unconscious thoughts, I do not wish my expressions of face to give the patient

material for interpretations or to influence him in what he tells me. The patient usually regards being made to adopt this position as a hardship and rebels against it, especially if the instinct for looking (scopophilia) plays an important part in his neurosis. I insist on this procedure, however, for its purpose and result are to prevent the transference from mingling with the patient's associations imperceptibly, to isolate the transference and to allow it to come forward in due course sharply defined as a resistance.[80]

The clear regulation of the fee also belongs to the technique—even if today analysts no longer handle this as strictly as Freud did. Since the fact of being insured plays a significant role, the payment of the physician is therewith further removed from the person of the patient and the thought of a sacrifice absolutely precluded. The physician should begin with his interpretations only when the transference has resulted in a sufficiently strong bond, and he should take care that infatuation or hostility not become too intense. In other respects, the obvious rule maintains that transferences are to be worked through and should be resolved, in that the patient becomes conscious of resistances and repressions.

The termination of the transference, not identical with the termination of the treatment, is a special subject seldom treated. Freud emphasized, as we have seen, that with other forms of psychotherapy there exists a lifelong dependency. The conditions are not fundamentally different in psychoanalysis.

As Glover rightly stresses, the cases in which a classic analysis is terminated in the regular way are exceptional.[81] There are numerous reasons for this: physical illness, change of residence by either the patient or the analyst, and many other external reasons, in which it is difficult to separate the actual adversities of life from the resistances and counterresistances. The therapist has good reasons to declare the treatment concluded after the first successes, as this allows his capacities to be seen in a particularly favorable light. An interruption by the patient during an initial intense resistance seems more dangerous, though, since this attitude is often maintained for life. The same is true if the analyst after a time breaks off a treatment that he sees to offer little hope of success without being sufficiently clear about his own resistances.

With a discontinuation of the therapy at the wrong time, a lasting positive transference is at least as frequent as this form of lasting negative transference. It is questionable whether that sort of transference can be terminated anyway, since neither the patient nor the analyst can find sufficient reason to do so, and perhaps do not even consider it desirable. Michael Balint appropriately characterizes the situation when he says that at the end of the last session the patient normally leaves with tears in his eyes and that the analyst is also distressed.[82] Patients with whom the analyst has—even cautiously—pressed for a termination of the analysis often enough begin a new analysis after a time, usually with a new analyst, onto whom they can then transfer the (positive) transference. As is well known, no clear criterion exists for the termination of a psychoanalysis. Marion Milner is of the opinion that such a criterion does not exist in any event and that the patients themselves simply discontinue the analysis sooner or later.[83] In other cases, though, this does not occur, and many analysts have their patients return for a couple of hours from time to time even after the termination of the treatment; in doing so they still are able to invoke Freud, who calls for this procedure at least in the interest of the analyst.

We must confirm that the termination of a positive transference often does not take place, and that generally no one regrets this, although analytical therapy requires that the transference be exposed and thereby disposed of theoretically. It seems the case, however, that part of the invested libido is never withdrawn.

NOTES

[1]Carl Gustav Jung, "Wandlungen und Symbole der Libido," *Jahrbuch der Psychoanalyse*, 3 (1911-1912), 164; also in *Two Essays on Analytical Psychology*, vol. 7 of his *Collected Works*, ed. Herbert Read, Michael Fordham, and Gerhard Adler, trans. R. F. C. Hull (New York, 1953).

[2]Sigmund Freud, "The Dynamics of Transference," in *SE*, vol. 12, pp. 99-100.

[3]Henri F. Ellenberger, *The Discovery of the Unconscious: The History and Evolution of Dynamic Psychiatry* (New York: Basic Books, 1970).

[4]See *Mesmerism: A Translation of the Original Medical and Scientific Writings of F. A. Mesmer*, trans. and ed., George J. Bloch (Los Altos, CA: William Kaufman, 1980).

[5]Eugen Bleuler, *Dementia praecox oder Gruppe der Schizophrenien* (Leipzig, 1911).

[6]Claude Burdin and Frédéric Dubois, *Histoire académique du magnétisme animal* (Paris, 1841).

[7]Gotthilf Heinrich von Schubert, *Ansichten von der Nachtseite der Naturwissenschaft* (Leipzig, 1808); cf. Ellenberger, p. 153.

[8]Anon., *Mesmerism: Its History, Phenomena, and Practice, with Reports of Cases Developed in Scotland* (Edinburgh, 1843), pp. 101-106; cf. Ellenberger, p. 153.

[9]Pierre Janet, "L'influence somnambulique et le besoin de direction," *III. Internationaler Congress für Psychologie in München, 1896* (Munich, 1897), pp. 143-147.

[10]"Moral insanity": Term coined by J. C. Prichard in 1835 for " . . . madness consisting in a morbid perversion of the natural feelings, affections, inclinations, temper, habits, moral dispositions, and natural impulses, without any remarkable disorder or defect of the intellect or knowing and reasoning faculties, and particularly without any insane illusion or hallucination"; James Cowles Prichard, *A Treatise on Insanity*

and Other Disorders Affecting the Mind (London, 1835), p. 16. The term, in its English form or Germanized as "moralischer Schwachsinn," was intensely discussed in the nineteenth century in and out of medical circles, and was thus familiar to Freud's fiancée.

[11]Sigmund Freud, *Letters of Sigmund Freud: 1873-1939*, ed. Ernst L. Freud, trans. Tania and James Stern (London: Hogarth, 1970), pp. 55-56.

[12]Léon Chertok, "The Discovery of the Transference: Towards an Epistemological Interpretation," *International Journal of Psycho-Analysis*, 49 (1968), 560-576; "Freud in Paris (1885/86)," *Psyche*, 27 (1973), 431-448; letter to the editor, *American Journal of Psychiatry*, 132 (1975), 757-758.

[13]*SE* vol. 2, 266.

[14]*SE* vol. 2, 302 ff.

[15]*SE* vol. 14, 11-12.

[16]*SE* vol. 19, 280.

[17]Sigmund Freud, *Brautbriefe: Briefe an Martha Bernays aus den Jahren 1882-1886*, ed. Ernst L. Freud (Frankfurt am Main, 1968).

[18]Ernest Jones, *The Formative Years and the Years of Discovery: 1856-1900*, vol. 1 of *The Life and Work of Sigmund Freud* (New York: Basic Books, 1953), pp. 224-225; hereafter cited as Jones vol. 1.

[19]*SE* vol. 7, 116-117.

[20]Jones, *Years of Maturity: 1901-1919*, vol. 2 of *The Life and Work of Sigmund Freud* (New York: Basic Books, 1955), p. 211; hereafter cited as Jones vol. 2.

[21]*SE* vol. 11, 50-52.

[22]Jones vol. 2, 211.

[23]*SE* vol. 12, 99-108.

[24]*SE* vol. 12, 101-104 passim.

[25]*SE* vol. 12, 108.

[26]*SE* vol. 12, 139.

[27]*SE* vol. 16, 431-447.

[28]*SE* vol. 16, 442.

[29]*SE* vol. 23, 141-207.

[30]*SE* vol. 23, 175.

[31]*SE* vol. 23, 177.

[32]*SE* vol. 12, 106.

[33]Carl Gustav Jung, "The Psychology of the Transference," in *The Practice of Psychotherapy: Essays on the Psychology of the Transference and Other Subjects*, vol. 16 of his *Collected Works*, ed. Herbert Read, Michael Fordham, and Gerhard Adler, trans. R. F. C. Hull (New York, 1954), p. 172; hereafter cited as Jung vol. 16.

[34]Jung vol. 16, 177.

[35]Jung vol. 16, 163-323.

[36]Jung vol. 16, 164.

[37]Jung vol. 16, 164.

[38]Jung vol. 16, 170-171.

[39]*SE* vol. 12, 154.

[40]*SE* vol. 16, 444.

[41]Jung vol. 16, 171.

[42]Jung vol. 16, 171-172.

[43]Jung vol. 16, 172-173.

[44]Jung vol. 16, 176.

[45]Jung vol. 16, 182.

[46]Jung vol. 16, 323.

[47]*SE* vol. 12, 159-171.

[48]Jones vol. 2, 237.

[49]*SE* vol. 12, 159.
[50]*SE* vol. 12, 168-169.
[51]*SE* vol. 12, 170.
[52]*SE* vol. 12, 159.
[53]*SE* vol. 14, 11-12.
[54]Michel Neyraut, *Die Übertragung: Eine psychoanalytische Studie*, trans. Eva Moldenhauer (Frankfurt am Main, 1976); *Le transfert: Étude psychanalytique* (Paris, 1974).
[55]James Strachey, ed. and trans., *SE* vol. 14, 87, n. 1.
[56]Sigmund Freud and Oskar Pfister, *Psychoanalysis and Faith: The Letters of Sigmund Freud and Oskar Pfister*, ed. Heinrich Meng and Ernst L. Freud, trans. Eric Mosbacher (New York, 1963), p. 39.
[57]Werner Kemper, "Die Gegenübertragung," *Psyche*, 7 (1954), 593-626.
[58]Kemper, p. 621.
[59]Kemper, p. 625.
[60]Paul Parin, "Gegenübertragung bei verschiedenen Abwehrformen," *Jahrbuch der Psychoanalyse*, 1 (1960), 212; Annie Reich, "On Counter-Transference," *International Journal of Psycho-Analysis*, 32 (1951), 25-31, and "Bemerkungen zum Problem der Gegenübertragung," *Jahrbuch der Psychoanalyse*, 1 (1960), 183-195; Paula Heimann, "On Counter-Transference," *International Journal of Psycho-Analysis*, 31 (1950), 81-84; Gerhard Scheunert, "Zum Problem der Gegenübertragung," *Psyche*, 13 (1960), 574-593.
[61]*SE* vol. 12, 154-155.
[62]Franz Alexander, "The Significance of Emotional Attitudes in the Psychoanalytical Situation," *American Journal of Orthopsychiatry*, 3 (1933), 35-48.
[63]Carl G. Jung, "The Psychology of Dementia Praecox," in *The Psychogenesis of Mental Disease*, vol. 3 of his *Collected Works*, ed. Herbert Read, Michael Fordham, and Gerhard Adler, trans. R. F. C. Hull (New York, 1953), pp. 1-151.
[64]*SE* vol. 16, 423.
[65]Frieda Fromm-Reichmann, "Transference Problems in Schizophrenics," *Psychoanalytic Quarterly*, 8 (1939), 412-426, and in her *Psychoanalysis and Psychotherapy: Selected Papers of Frieda Fromm-Reichmann* (Chicago, 1959), pp. 117-128; Victor H. Rosen, *Style, Character and Language*, ed. Samuel Atkin and Milton E. Jucovy (New York, 1977); Gaetano Benedetti, *Klinische Psychopathologie* (Bern, 1964).
[66]Heinz Kohut, "Forms and Transformations of Narcissism," *Journal of the American Psychoanalytic Association*, 14 (1960), no. 2, 243-272; "The Psychoanalytic Treatment of Narcissistic Personality Disorders: Outline of a Systematic Approach," *Psychoanalytic Study of the Child 1968*, vol. 23, 86-113; see also the following note.
[67]Kohut, *The Analysis of the Self: A Systematic Approach to the Psychoanalytic Treatment of Narcissistic Personality Disorders* (New York: International Universities Press, 1971), p. 26.
[68]Otto F. Kernberg, "The Treatment of Patients with Borderline Personality Organization," *International Journal of Psycho-Analysis*, 49 (1968), 600-619.
[69]Jacques Lacan, *Ecrits* (Paris, 1966).
[70]Jacques Lacan, *The Four Fundamental Concepts of Psycho-Analysis*, ed. Jacques-Alain Miller, trans. Alan Sheridan (New York: Norton, 1978), p. 231.
[71]Jacques Lacan, *Les écrits techniques de Freud 1953-1954*, vol. 1 of *Le séminaire de Jacques Lacan*, ed. Jacques-Alain Miller (Paris, 1975), p. 127.
[72]Jacques Lacan, *Freuds technische Schriften*, ed. Jacques-Alain Miller, trans. Werner Hamacher (Freiburg, 1978), p. 86.
[73]Jacques Lacan, *Schriften I*, ed. Norbert Haas, trans. Norbert Haas, Klaus Laermann, Rodolphe Gasché, and Peter Stehlin (Frankfurt am Main, 1975), p. 191.
[74]Lacan, *Schriften I*, p. 191.
[75]Lacan, *Schriften I*, p. 192.

[76]Lacan, *Les écrits techniques de Freud 1953-1954*, p. 127.

[77]Margaret Little, "Über wahnhafte Übertragung (Übertragungspsychose)," *Psyche*, 12 (1958-1959), 258.

[78]Helmut Luft, "Übertragungspsychosen," *Nervenarzt*, 32 (1961), 199-210.

[79]Walther Thomas Winkler, *Übertragung und Psychose* (Bern, 1971).

[80]*SE* vol. 12, 133-134.

[81]Edward Glover, *The Technique of Psycho-Analysis* (New York: International Universities Press, 1955).

[82]Michael Balint, "On the Termination of Analysis," *International Journal of Psycho-Analysis*, 31 (1950), 196-199.

[83]Marion Milner, "A Note on the Ending of an Analysis," *International Journal of Psycho-Analysis*, 31 (1950), 191-193.

Chapter 7

Psychopathology

Michael H. Sacks

An immediate problem in the study of psychopathology is the distinction between the abnormal or pathological and normal. Consider the difference among persons and their attitude toward plane travel. The person with the plane phobia, an irrational and overwhelming fear of flying, confesses with embarrassment: "It is crazy, but I can't control it, so I stay away from planes." The second person says, "I don't like to travel in planes; I prefer to travel in trains. I like the slower pace and the chance to look at the scenery." On further questioning we learn that he often refuses business engagements important to his career because accepting them would require taking a plane. A third person who flies regularly hesitantly admits to feeling nervous at take-off and the need to have one or two drinks for relaxation. He sits in an aisle seat because he has learned that he is more comfortable if he does not have to look out the window. A fourth person feels no anxiety on planes despite a recent report of a major plane disaster.

Where does psychopathology begin in this series? Is it in the admitted phobic only? Does not the man with the "train preference" seem to have a disguised or latent phobia and the third to have a mild phobia which he controls with his alcohol and aisle seat? Finally, is the anxiety-free flier perhaps not a little bit too cool in his apparent detachment from the fear of flying? Clearly there is a continuum ranging from the inappropriate absence of any fear through a mild irrational fear that is controlled to a fear disguised as a preference to the full-blown phobia itself. Most psychopathology exists on such a continuum and it requires a judgment to specify where normality ends and psychopathology begins.

Another problem is that psychopathology need not be pathological in the usual sense of the word if we mean a disruption in the usual activities of everyday life. For example, a severe phobia of snakes rarely causes a city dweller any undue difficulties. Also, there is a psychopathology of everyday life that is often a source of amusement. A professor forgets his briefcase on the way to a lecture and returns to his apartment for it. Later at the lecture he opens his briefcase only to find it empty and realizes that the lecture is on his desk at home. In this instance, the professor's forgetting interferes with his lecture despite his best efforts not to forget. Freud was the first to draw attention to such incidents in his book "The Psychopathology of Everyday Life."[1] In it he catalogued many behaviors similar to forgetting which he called "symptomatic acts." They occur to all of us. Misspelling words that we know how to spell, mispronunciations, forgetting names, and slips of the tongue are some examples. Freud was led to call this "psychopathology" because in interesting ways the psychological mechanisms that cause such slips are strikingly similar to those that produce such distressing symptoms as a severe plane phobia.

Does this completely blur the distinction between normality and psychopathology? Thomas Szasz among others has been a severe critic of the concept of psychopathology. He argues that pathology refers to disease that can be demonstrated by an examination of the diseased organ. With most mental pathology we cannot demonstrate any disease in the brain. What is commonly called mental pathology is simply variations in behavior. To call these variations pathological is to introduce a false similarity between variation in behavior and the impaired function of a diseased organ.[2]

A social psychologist, D. L. Rosenhan, attempted to prove that psychiatrists could not distinguish normal from abnormal.[3] He sent normal people to emergency rooms of several psychiatric hospitals where they told psychiatrists that they were hearing a voice that said, "Thud hollow, empty"; they otherwise behaved in a completely normal way. They were all admitted to a psychiatric hospital with a psychiatric diagnosis of schizophrenia. It is not important to know what the diagnosis of schizophrenia means, but one characteristic is hallucinations, a perception such as hearing or seeing in the absence of any external stimulus causing it. Once these "pseudopatients" were in the hospital, they behaved normally. Rosenhan noted that the psychiatric staff did not recognize them as normal and discharged them later as patients in remission. He concluded that psychiatrists did not know how to tell psychopathology from normality.

Once a person is labeled as "crazy," Rosenhan further observed, he tends to be seen in a different way. So that, for example, one popular theory of schizophrenia in psychiatry is that one may become schizophrenic if born into a family with a weak, passive father and a strong, dominant, intrusive mother. The histories of the pseudopatients were rewritten to fit that theory during their hospitalization, even though their family history might have differed somewhat from that. Goffman had observed years earlier in *Asylums* that once a person is given the label of insane, he is viewed with certain expectations and his behavior tends to be interpreted as insane, even though it might not be.[4] Many pseudopatients took notes on the psychiatric wards, for example. This behavior was described by the nurses in their daily reports as "writing behavior," as if that were something abnormal. Rosenhan raises the question of whether psychopathology is a characteristic of individuals or whether it is instead a judgment made by observers which depends on their mental set or expectations. Normal behavior in the abnormal world of an emergency room or a psychiatric ward is perceived as abnormal.

Certainly psychopathology has its aspect of labeling. As Rosenhan shows, the situation plays a part in it, but this is not the entire picture. Genuine hallucinations are not part of normal everyday life. Rosenhan did not show that psychiatrists were unable to distinguish psychopathology. What he did show was that if a person lies, he can successfully deceive a person who is measuring psychopathology. In the same way, if you drink a vial of blood and go to the emergency room with a complaint that you had blood in your stool, you would easily fool the physician into thinking you might have an ulcer. It is very easy to fool someone into thinking that you are ill. One problem in all medicine is: How do you distinguish the person who has true pathology from the person who is pretending or lying? This is a particularly vexing problem in psychiatry, since for most psychopathology no validating instruments or tests tell us clearly if a patient has a disease. In medicine there are electrocardiograms and specific blood tests to confirm that a person has had a heart attack. There are no such tests for schizophrenia.

A second point is that Rosenhan's "normal patients" didn't behave normally. They lied to get into the hospital and once there they did not behave normally. If you place a normal person in a psychiatric hospital, he is going to demand to be released. None of his pseudopatients did that.[5]

Having established that psychopathology exists, let us distinguish two kinds: descriptive psychopathology and analytic psychopathology. Descriptive psychopathology attempts to describe as carefully as possible the signs and symptoms found in a patient. By "symptoms" is meant those subjective distressing concerns that patients complain of to doctors. For example, "I'm having anxiety," "I'm feeling very depressed," or "I have these voices that bother me," are symptoms. "Sign" refers to the objective observations of the physician. The patient's not smiling as he says he's depressed would be a sign. In descriptive psychopathology a collection of signs and symptoms which seem to occur together frequently is called a "diagnosis." A large part of descriptive psychopathology is the arranging of signs and symptoms into diagnostic systems.

Analytic psychopathology does this but also attempts to understand what the symptoms and signs mean. It looks for meaning. Why should an intelligent and normal-appearing individual develop a phobia? Different analytic theories exist but we shall focus today on the one developed by Freud. As an analytic psychopathologist Freud's primary interest was not in simply describing pathologic mental phenomena, but in attempting to unravel the underlying mechanism that caused them. For example, he was curious to understand why his patient, Anna O., developed a psychological or nonneurological paralysis of her arm, or why she had the strange and interesting symptom of being unable to talk in her native language while maintaining her capacity to speak in English. Such psychogenic physical symptoms as the paralysis of the arm combined with an amnesia also not of an organic or physical origin often occur together and are called hysteria. The value in understanding the mechanism producing the symptom is that it might suggest a treatment for it.

In the case of Anna O.,[6] Freud's colleague Breuer attempted to treat her hysteria by talking to her. In doing so he discovered the "talking cure"; as the patient talked and recalled the incidents that occurred at the time the symptoms had developed, there was often a release of emotion or a catharsis, with the disappearance of the symptom. We call this an "abreactive" treatment. It's still a very popular notion of what happens in psychiatric treatment. You go to a psychologist or psychiatrist, tell him what is happening to you, and with the release of emotion you feel better. This is the basic notion of psychopathology in Breuer and Freud's "Preliminary Communication."[7] It is a "toxic theory" of psychopathology. Basically, the theory maintains that if a strong emotion is experienced and for whatever reason is not completely discharged, it becomes encapsulated within the mind and is pushed into the unconscious. By unconscious we refer to that area of the mind outside of awareness. Despite being unconscious, the emotion exerts an influence, by causing the appearance of symptoms. It is an elegant and simple theory.

The theory of an upsetting or traumatic event producing an intense emotion which is not released but becomes encapsulated in the unconscious, where it produces symptoms that can be successfully treated by catharsis, is a practiced theory still. Primal Scream therapy, which was popular several years ago, is basically similar.[8] By recalling early childhood events in which parents were hurtful and releasing the pent-up, frustrated fury against them, symptoms are cured. Another place where this theory is still used is in the treatment of the traumatic neuroses. We have all seen a war movie in which a shell-shocked soldier is given an injection of truth serum and asked to relive the traumatic moment when his illness began. As the terrible memory, usually of his buddy's death, is recalled, the soldier gives an anguished cry of being glad that it was the buddy and not himself who was killed and then falls into a deep sleep and wakes cured. Breuer and Freud did exactly this by hypnosis.

The problem with the toxic theory of psychopathology is that it does not explain why initial emotion was so toxic in the first place. This problem was solved by developing a second theory—the conflict theory—of psychopathology. In the conflict theory, there is an impulse or a motive, and an opposing counterimpulse or countermotive. How might we explain the war neurosis with this theory? The impulse was "Better that my buddy be dead than I." The counterimpulse is the unspoken feeling "It is a terrible thing to wish someone else's death." This is a very common conflict among survivors—survivors of concentration camps and natural disasters as well as survivors of war. The individual is now experiencing two contradictory and simultaneous impulses; the result is anxiety.

By anxiety we mean a diffuse dread, which is evidence of our psyche or mental apparatus working under too severe a strain. It is analogous to the pain we feel when one of our physical systems, for example the muscular system, is operating under too severe a strain. Freud postulated that when the anxiety or mental anguish is too severe, the mind protects itself by repressing the anxiety and the conflict. Repression is one of a number of defenses the mind has against anxiety. In repression the conflict is pushed into the unconscious so that it is no longer in immediate awareness. This resolves the individual's anxiety at being torn between the simultaneous and contradictory impulse and counter-impulse. In a similar way, when a muscular pain becomes too severe, the limb becomes automatically fixed in the position that minimizes the pain. Now, once the conflict is in the unconscious, it returns to con-sciousness in the form of a symptom—the return of the repressed.

We can rewrite this theory by dividing the mind into id, ego, and superego. Such basic human impulses as sex, aggression, and depend-ency are in the *id*. Opposing these preemptive impulses desiring im-mediate gratification is the reality-oriented *ego*; the internal standards and ideals adopted from our parents and society are called the *superego*. The division of the mind into ego, id, and superego is called the *structural theory* of the mind.[9]

How do you get access to the unconscious? Early on Breuer and Freud used hypnosis. Freud stopped using hypnosis, however, because he was not a very good hypnotist and was convinced it was not necessary. By letting patients *free associate*, he could gain access to the unconscious. Free association is a process in which patients say whatever comes into their mind, without first censoring it. As he began to use this technique, Freud noted that many neurotic patients frequently recalled traumatic sexual events. He repeatedly heard that they had been seduced as a child by a parent or a relative. This led him to hypothesize that the cause of the adult neurosis was an actual traumatic sexual event in childhood, which in adulthood was reactivated. As he continued his work and his own self-analysis, he realized that an actual seduction had not occurred, only the fantasy of one. He also realized that sexual impulses were a very normal part of infantile development.

In the theory of infantile sexuality Freud proposed an early oral phase at which the infant focuses sexual energy or libido around the mouth. Later at two or three it begins to focus around the anus, and from four to six it focuses around the genitals, the phallic period; it is finally directed toward an object of the opposite sex in the Oedipal period.[10] During this development sexuality, or libido, moves from one area into another. The Oedipal period comes to a close at age six or seven with a massive repression of sexuality. During puberty, the repression is lifted and adult heterosexual activity begins. Freud maintained, however, if there is a trauma during childhood or the sexual urge is too strong, an interference of normal libidinal development or progress results. This interference causes a fixation point, that is, a point of vulnerability in the child's development. The analogy Freud used was that of an army advancing. If part of the troops are left at a particular point, the fixation point, the forward movement of the army is impaired. Once such a fixation point is established, the child is unable to master fully the subsequent periods of development, especially the Oedipal period. At this point the child may develop the symptoms of a childhood neurosis. This is usually transient. Later in adulthood a particularly difficult conflict will cause a reawakening of the childhood neurosis, now transformed into an adult neurosis.

Although most analytic psychopathologists accept that adult psychopathology can be understood only with reference to the childhood antecedents, controversy exists over whether the childhood antecedent must necessarily be, as Freud insisted, an unresolved childhood sexual conflict. Jung and Adler separated from Freud over this issue. Both argued that there were sources for childhood conflict other than sexuality. Adler, for example, emphasized the child's struggle with his inferiority to older siblings and parents because of his immaturity.[11] Such contemporary psychoanalysts as Margaret Mahler[12] have drawn attention to the role of childhood conflicts over establishing separation and individuation from parents.

Here is an example from a patient in psychoanalysis over a period of five years. He came for treatment as a graduate student; he felt intensely frustrated because whenever he reached the point of writing his Ph.D. thesis, he would delay it by taking more courses or doing further research. Finally, he began to realize that something was preventing him from achieving the doctorate. This inability to permit oneself to attain a success is called a "success phobia." Along the way this patient also revealed that he suffered from premature ejaculation. Central in this young man's character was his pride in himself at being an intensely normal and caring person. His ideal was of an early Christian saint who would not injure even an insect. Over time it emerged that this man was struggling with the impulse of aggression. He denied feeling angry when situations seemed to justify an angry response. The counterimpulse against the aggression was an intense fear of counteraggression or retaliation. For this man, completing his Ph.D. thesis was equal to an aggressive act, for which he feared retaliation, so that the closer he got to the Ph.D., the more he became fearful of this retaliation. He solved the conflict by developing not a symptom, but an inhibition. He just couldn't bring the act to completion.

Further exploration revealed that obtaining the Ph.D. was perceived as winning a prize and was related to a prize he wished to win as a child, the attention and devotion of his mother. The way to winning your mother is to eliminate the father competitively. As the father is seen as a rival, the fear of his retaliation becomes a powerful element. Thus, writing the Ph.D. was unconsciously perceived by the patient as the winning of his mother and the removal of his father. The inhibition was a resolution of the conflict between the wish to defeat his father and win his mother for himself and the fear of his father's retaliation. This is a classic representation of an Oedipal conflict.

As a child he had a phobia, a childhood neurosis: It was a phobia of bridges which occurred around the age of five. What became clear was that the fear of falling off the bridge related to a fear of falling into the water where he would be injured. Through the use of dreams and free association the patient was able to appreciate the unconscious symbolism of his childhood phobia and how it related to his Oedipal conflict. The fear of falling into the water was the fear of falling into the vagina, which was perceived as dangerous because, once in the vagina, he would meet up with his father. And his father, in this unconscious fantasy, would say, "What are you doing here? This place belongs to me," and at that point, the patient would be castrated. Hence, the adult symptom of the premature ejaculation was in part motivated by having to get out of the dangerous vagina as quickly as possible. Here we see the childhood neurosis of a bridge phobia reoccurring in the adult as a success phobia and premature ejaculation.

Thus far we have discussed conflict and how conflict can produce symptoms and inhibitions. It also produces character. Wilhelm Reich appreciated that every aspect of a person's appearance—his personality, the way he walks, talks, and dresses—is an expression of a conflict.[13] In the above patient the conflicts with aggression produced not only a success phobia and premature ejaculation symptoms but also his character. For example, he rarely protested openly against insults to him and tended to be submissive instead. He rarely competed in sports despite being athletic. He had a quiet, unassertive, and gentle character.

Since everyone has character traits, when do we call character traits pathological? To define pathology in character is not as easy as it is in neuroses. The neurotic person says, "Doctor, I'm in trouble, I hurt." He talks about the intense distress of his symptoms. But a character disorder has no symptoms. People with character pathology usually do not have insight into the fact that something is wrong with them, and they don't feel distress. The people who feel the distress are those who live with them, because often the pathological traits offend others. One such character is the obsessive character, who is classically described as stubborn, stingy, and orderly. Such individuals often insist that everything be done in a precisely planned way according to their wishes. This, together with a tendency toward parsimony and possessiveness, completes the picture. The central conflict in this character disorder is around rage and derives from the anal phase.[14]

When the child is about two, the infantile sexuality is focused around the anus. The child at this point has no repugnance of feces; in fact, he may be quite comfortable playing with them. Children who soil in their diapers begin to cry only when the feces gets cool and uncomfortable. Once toilet training begins, the mother attempts to discipline the child to be orderly about defecation. A struggle ensues—the battle of the potty. The child derives a pleasure from stooling when and where the impulse moves him, but this causes trouble with the parents who are in the process of socializing him. If the struggle is not successfully surmounted at this stage, there will be a fixation at the anal stage. This person is going to be concerned with a conflict between his spontaneously and undisciplined attitude toward defecation and his wish to gain the approval of his parents: "I have to submit to what my parent is telling me, or else I will be abandoned, my parent won't love me, but damn it, I want to do it the way I want to do it."

What we see in this kind of character are struggles between submissions and defiance. But over what kind of issues? Cleanliness and time! People fixated at this stage tend as adults to either be very meticulous about their cleanliness, that is, they're on the submission side of the conflict, or they tend to make a point of being messy; they are on the defiant part of the conflict. Note however that in this situation the conflict results in no subjective distress. The individual often prides himself on his character trait of cleanliness or messiness. Often it only causes a problem for the person who's living with him.

The same is true of time. Time is involved because the parents expect the toileting to be completed at a particular time. People with fixation at the anal stage tend to be either meticulous about time (the submission) or careless about appointments (defiance). Also, there are often concerns about money, with either hoarding or excessive generosity. Hoarding represents the defiance aspect of the conflict while excessive generosity is the submission aspect—"I will give what is asked of me because otherwise I might lose my mother's love." Money becomes equated with feces in the conflict, since both are seen as valuable to the parents, who take an intense interest in them. In this way a conflict derived from the anal phase produces definite character traits that, because of inflexibility and disregard of the wishes of others, can be considered pathological.

These traits deriving from the anal period need not be pathological. Neatness and orderliness are desirable traits if not carried to excess.

Thus, a conflict at the anal stage can produce a neurosis, pathological character traits, or desirable character traits. But what if it occurs in the following way? The person is defiant about the stool and wants to smear it all over the place. Over time this impulse is "tamed" and the person becomes an artist who does his smearing on a canvas.

If a conflict can produce a neurosis, a character disorder, normal character, and a creative artist, then obviously nothing in the conflict itself is pathological. Why develop a neurosis rather than a character disorder or an expression of the conflict in creativity? And why develop a fixation to the anal period in one case and the Oedipal in another? In early analytic theory, there was a focus mostly on the sexual instincts and how they progressed from one phase to another. Depending on the strength of the impulse and the environmental conditions, many possible outcomes could occur. If the mother was too demanding during the anal period, that might lead to an anal fixation. Some families take toilet training as a matter of fact and there's no great struggle with it. In other families, there is great difficulty. Another factor is that there is something constitutional, something inborn in the child. This inborn quality could be a very strong anal instinct. Alternatively it could be the strength of the ego. Such ego capacities as talent and the ability to control one's instincts by sublimating them into creative behavior might be qualities that are inherent in the individual from birth.

This concludes our overview of psychopathology from a psychoanalytic perspective. What remains, however, is to define what we mean by psychopathology more clearly. Since conflict can produce neurosis, inhibitions, character, creativity, and the normal "symptomatic acts" of everyday pathology, it is not a helpful guide. Whatever the conflict that produced the absentminded professor's forgetting his lecture notes, it in itself will not define whether the forgetting is pathological. At this point, however, this question might better be phrased in terms of how much the symptom interferes with his life. Does it result in an inadequate lecture? If it does, it is behavior that is maladaptive—that is, apparently self-defeating. If it causes only a mild embarrassment, then we can more easily dismiss it as just an interesting mental phenomenon and really not an abnormal pathological behavior. In conclusion, I should suggest that a judgment in the degree to which a behavior seems to be maladaptive leads us to define it as pathological. The involved individual may be aware of it, as in my patient with the success phobia, or he may not be if it is a character problem simply. In either case, if it prevents him from gaining a reasonable amount of satisfaction from work, friends, family, and recreation, we might say it is pathological.

NOTES

[1]Sigmund Freud, (1904) "The Psychopathology of Everyday Life." *SE* vol. 6, 3-63.

[2]Thomas Szasz, *The Myth of Mental Illness* (New York: Hoeber, 1961).

[3]D. L. Rosenhan, "On Being Sane in Insane Places," *Science*, 179 (1973), 250-258.

[4]E. Goffman, *Asylums* (Chicago: Aldine, 1962).

[5]R. Spitzer, "On Pseudoscience in Science, Logic in Remission and Psychiatric Diagnosis: A Critique of Rosenhan's 'On Being Insane in Insane Places,' " *Journal of Abnormal Psychology*, 84 (1975), 442-452.

[6]J. Breuer and S. Freud, "Studies on Hysteria" *SE* vol. 2, 1-47.

[7]Breuer and Freud, *SE* vol. 2, 3-17.

[8]A. Janov, *The Primal Scream* (New York: Putnam, 1970).

[9]Sigmund Freud, (1973). "The Ego and the Id." *SE* vol. 19, 3-66; Charles Brenner, *A Elementary Textbook of Psychoanalysis* (Garden City, N.Y.: Anchor Books, 1974), pp. 30-125.

[10]Sigmund Freud, (1905) "Three Essays on the Theory of Sexuality." *SE* vol. 7, 125-243.

[11]Henri Ellenberger, *The Discovery of the Unconscious* (New York: Basic Books, 1970), pp. 571-656.

[12]Margaret Mahler, and M. Furer, *On Human Symbiosis and the Viscissitudes of Individuation*, vol. 1 *Infantile Psychosis* (New York: International Universities Press, 1966).

[13]Wilhelm Reich, *Character Analysis* (New York: Noonday, 1949).

[14]Sigmund Freud, "Character and Anal Erotism" (1905), *SE* vol 9, 168-175.

Chapter 8

Narcissism

Otto F. Kernberg

The clarification of the concept of "narcissism" is complicated by two parallel and complementary levels of conceptualization of this term. Within a first level of discussion, that of psychoanalytic theory or "metapsychology" (that is, a consideration of structural, dynamic, economic, adaptive, and genetic principles of mental functioning), narcissism is defined as the libidinal investment of the self. The self, within that theoretical formulation, is a substructure of the system ego, a substructure that reflects the integration of all the component self-images or self-representations that develop throughout all the experiences of interactions with other human beings ("objects" in metapsychological language). In contrast, the investment of libido in such objects and in their psychic representations ("object representations") constitutes "object libido." Object libido is in a dynamic relationship with "narcissistic libido" invested in the self.

The second level of the concept of narcissism is the clinical one, which has to do with the clinical syndromes that characterize patients with abnormal self-esteem regulation. Our self-esteem or self-regard usually fluctuates according to the gratifying or frustrating experiences we have in our relationships with others, and according to our evaluation of the distance between our goals and aspirations, and our achievements and success. Beyond these commonsense observations, clinical experiences indicate that there are complex relations between self-esteem, on the one hand, and predominant affects or moods, the extent to which various self-representations are integrated or dissociated, and the vicissitudes of internalized object relations (the reciprocal relations between self- and object representations), on the other. How are the clinical and metapsychological conceptualizations of narcissism related? Why the two levels of discourse? The first, more difficult conceptualization provides us with models of unconscious psychic functioning that explain the clinical phenomena we observe.

For example, metapsychological analysis postulates that self-esteem regulation is dependent, among other factors, on the pressures that the superego exerts on the ego: the stricter the superego (the more excessive the infantile morality of unconscious demands for perfection and prohibitions), the more self-esteem may be lowered. At bottom, such a lowering of self-esteem would reflect a predominance of self-directed aggression (stemming from the superego) over the libidinal investment of the self.

Or, as another example, a lowering of self-esteem may be caused by the lack of gratification of instinctual needs, of both a libidinal and aggressive nature (reflected in dependent, sexual, and aggressive strivings). In other words, unconscious ego defenses that repress the awareness and expression of instinctual needs would impoverish the ego (self) of gratifying experiences and thus "deplete" libidinal ego (self) investments and diminish self-esteem.

As still another illustration of the relation between the metapsychological and the clinical: The internalization of libidinally invested objects in the form of libidinally invested object representations may greatly reinforce the libidinal investment of the self—the presence, in our mind, of the images of those we love and by whom we feel loved strengthens our self-love. As a French song by George Brassens has it: "There are friends in the forest of my heart." In contrast, when excessive conflicts around aggression weaken our libidinal investments of others and, secondarily, their corresponding object representations, the libidinal investment of the self and self-love also suffer.

In clinical psychiatry, we find three types of abnormal or pathological self-esteem regulation, reflecting at the same time three levels of severity of pathological narcissism. The first type is represented by the frequent cases of personality disorders or character pathology wherein the regulation of self-esteem seems to be overly dependent on expression of or defenses against childish gratifications that are normally abandoned in adulthood. For example, a woman suffering from a hysterical character neurosis may feel secure in her self-esteem only when admiration for her beauty is coupled with admiration for her "sexual innocence." She is abnormally retaining an infantile equation of goodness and sexual innocence. Here we find patients with neurotic but essentially deep and stable relationships with other people, with a solid, well-integrated concept of their self, and whose characterological difficulties have, as one function among others, that of preserving self-esteem in accordance with childhood aspirations and prohibitions. This is a very frequent and relatively mild disturbance that need not concern us further here.

A second, more severe, but relatively infrequent, type of pathological narcissism is typically represented by some cases of homosexuality in which the homosexual partner is loved as a representation of the self, while the patient himself unconsciously reenacts the attitude of a parent from whom he expected love in the past. In other words, the patient identifies with a certain libidinal object of his past while projecting his libidinally invested self onto another person. Self-esteem regulation here is more pathological, and it was the study of male homosexuals with these characteristics that stimulated Freud[1] to develop his original model of narcissistic object love. In these cases, there is still a capacity for deep and stable relations with others, and, if the required object relations of these patients are fulfilled, their self-esteem regulation may still be under satisfactory control.

A third, frequent, and very severe type of pathological narcissism is represented by the narcissistic personality or narcissistic personality disorder, one of the most challenging syndromes met with in clinical psychiatry. Patients with narcissistic personality are extremely self-centered and self-referential, and whatever is going on around them they apply to themselves. If a discussion is going on, for instance, the degree to which they contribute to it is far more important to them than the subject being discussed. Their grandiosity is so marked that it led one psychoanalyst to describe them as having a "Nobel Prize Complex."[2] Although narcissistic personalities feel immensely superior to everybody else, they are not self-sufficient; to the contrary, they are terribly dependent upon admiration from others, and unless other people constantly feed them with admiration and praise, their self-esteem collapses. They are then overwhelmed with feelings of inferiority, for theirs is a world of extremes—they are either the best or the worst.

Narcissistic personalities carry these warped views over into their relationships with other people. They have no empathy for others; other people exist only to serve their needs. There are some people they admire because they have something that these patients themselves would like to acquire, but their relations with such admired people are often parasitic and sometimes exploitative. There are other people these patients devalue or depreciate, from whom they expect nothing and who, emotionally speaking, do not exist for them. Finally, there are people these patients experience as potential enemies, who they perceive as harshly critical and derogatory and/or potentially exploitative, enemies who they must fight or escape from.

Pathological narcissists have enormous problems with envy. Melanie Klein[3] was the first to call attention to the intimate connection between envy and gratitude. Patients with narcissistic personality experience both conscious envy, which consumes them, and unconscious envy, against which they defend themselves by various means, and which I shall describe shortly. Unlike normal people, however, they do not experience gratitude. Normal people accept the idea that other people are valuable and worthy of their esteem. Not so the pathologically narcissistic. They are drawn to people who have something they want to acquire for themselves. Once they acquire it, they discard other persons, who have lost the only value they had. Hence, narcissists' relations with others are parasitic and sometimes exploitative.

Consider, for example, love relations. These patients' love, whether it be of a man for a woman or of a woman for a man, contains large quantities of envy, as well as a need for admiration and devotion. A narcissistic man's need is to conquer the woman. He may do this by simply having a series of sexual adventures—one-night stands—or by seeing to it that the woman becomes completely dedicated to him over a period of time. In either case, as soon as she becomes "his," she becomes devalued and spoiled for him.

A woman with a narcissistic personality has exactly the same relation toward men: She may see men's admiration of her as a tribute that reinforces her self-esteem, and she may graciously love men as long as they admire her. Once she has absorbed the admiration, she loses all interest and moves on to the next man. Or she may maintain a more stable relation, for example, with husband and/or a lover, as long as it is clear that she does not "belong" to anybody but that he belongs to her. Psychoanalytic exploration regularly reveals that the devaluation that takes place is in the service of eliminating the envy the other person has aroused.

How does psychoanalysis explain the narcissistic personality? Freud's only paper on the subject was written in 1914, before he had advanced either his structural or dual-instinct theories. He included the words

"An introduction" in the title of his narcissism paper, clearly indicating that his ideas on the matter were still not firmly set. Freud conceived of libido as being invested, at first, solely in the self, what he called autoerotism. Over time, libido was directed onto other people (psychoanalysts call these "objects" in order to distinguish them from "subjects"). Freud's ideas about narcissism evolved gradually, so that what now seems like a compact "package" has at points a lack of internal consistency and completion.

Freud assumed that the newborn infant was unaware of a world outside himself, that libido was invested in an undifferentiated ego-id. He called this early stage of development "primary narcissism." As the infant gradually became aware of a world outside himself, he invested libido in "objects." But when the infant experienced unpleasure (pain or frustration), he withdrew this object libido and directed it back onto the ego, a phenomenon Freud called "secondary narcissism." Thus, the early psychoanalytic literature treats libido as if there were a system of communicating vessels in the psyche: the more libido invested in the ego (today we say "self"), the more narcissistic the individual; the more libido invested in other people, the more the individual is capable of object love. Narcissism, then, and object love were complementary, or even contradictory, to each other, and presumably, pathological narcissism could be explained by an abnormal predominance of libidinal investment of the self, to the detriment of libidinal investment in other people ("external objects").

More recently, however, metapsychological thinking has shifted toward the assumption that libidinal investment of self and objects originate simultaneously, and that the differences between normal and pathological libidinal investments in the self and objects depend not on a quantitative distribution of libido, but on the structural characteristics of the self- and object representations. In this view, normal narcissism and normal object investments go hand in hand, while pathological investments of the self and of objects and object representations go together.[4]

Of the new ways of looking at the problem of narcissism, two major currents[5] seem to have taken hold in this country, Heinz Kohut's[5] and my own. Both views originally developed from Freud's thinking, but Kohut, departing from classical psychoanalytic theory, evolved what has come to be known as "the psychology of the self."

The events Kohut considers crucial to producing narcissistic pathology occur very early in life, before the child enters the Oedipal phase of development. The concepts of superego and of conflict are conspicuously absent from his theory. Aggression is not primary, although "healthy self-assertiveness" is. Aggression, in the form of narcissistic rage[6] is the result of frustration of normal narcissistic needs.

Normal narcissistic needs consist of the need to be admired and the need to admire. The mother's love and admiration for her baby permit the baby to develop normal grandiosity. (Kohut coined the term "grandiose self," which I have adopted. I have added "pathological" to it, because I consider pathological the grandiosity he regards as normal.) The baby feels omnipotent and grandiose; the mother's love for the baby confirms his grandiosity. The gleam of approval in her eye mirrors the baby's feeling of grandiosity. And a little later on, the mother's ability to gratify the baby's needs permits the baby to idealize her.

Kohut introduced the term "bipolar self,"[7] which he considered a psychological configuration having its own initiative and supraordinate to Freud's[8] psychic structures of id, ego, and superego. One pole of this bipolar self derives from the infantile exhibitionistic grandiosity; the other pole derives from the infantile idealizing needs. The grandiose self is not pathological, Kohut says, but has, in the narcissistic personality, remained at an infantile stage because its development has been thwarted. The parent has not provided a sufficient gratification of infantile grandiose and idealizing needs.

Kohut sees narcissism as having its own line of development, separate from, though not independent of, object relations. He has little to say about object libido—he does not seem particularly interested in it. He coined the term "selfobject" to describe what he conceptualized as the infant's early relation to others. The infant sees the other as distinct from himself only in the sense of being aware that the other is serving his needs. The infant does not conceive of the other as being an autonomous entity—as a person in his/her own right.

Kohut's treatment of patients with narcissistic personality disorder is based on his theory that these patients are suffering from unmet infantile needs for mirroring and idealizing. Failure on the part of the parents to meet these needs resulted in the patient's having a self of great fragility. Under excessive stress, this fragile self fragments or splits apart. The patient feels depleted, depressed, anxious, hypochondriacal, or even paranoid.

In treatment, the analyst's interpretations remove defenses so that the patient will become aware of his infantile (archaic) wishes for approval. Awareness of the infantile wishes results in the formation of new structures which can transform these wishes into more mature forms; instead of requiring instant gratification, the patient gradually learns to postpone gratification, for example. While these changes are occurring in the patient, he uses the analyst as a support, as a substitute for the deficient parent of his infancy and childhood—as what Kohut calls a "selfobject." Psychic structures are then gradually built up in the ego by a process Kohut calls "transmuting internalization." Kohut stresses that this process of transmuting internalization occurs by means of working through in the transferences.

These transferences are of two types—a mirroring transference and an idealizing transference. The analyst permits the development of these transferences so that the patient feels he is totally approved of by a therapist he feels is perfect. Although Kohut originally recommended this type of treatment for people suffering from pathology in the narcissistic segment, he later stressed the universality of the need for mirroring and idealization throughout the entire life span. He has consistently left untouched the subject of object relations.

My own views on pathological narcissism are based very much on the work of two leading psychoanalytic theoreticians, Edith Jacobson[9] and Margaret Mahler,[10] and have been spelled out over the past several years.[11] To Jacobson I owe my concept of how the ego and superego structures come into being, and the functions of self- and object representations as constituent substructures of ego and superego. Mahler's developmental theory of separation-individuation, which uses Jacobson's ideas, correlates remarkably well with the hypothesis I arrived at from the clinical study of the borderline personality organization. Although important differences exist between the borderline personality and the narcissistic personality, both reflect a derailment in ego development that occurs during the same developmental phase of childhood.

In describing how the ego develops, I follow Jacobson in using the term "mental representation." (A mental representation is simply a psychoanalytic way of conceptualizing how experiences are psychically registered.) In contrast to Kohut, I consider object relations integral to development; my own approach to the subject of narcissism is through what I have called an ego psychological object relations theory.

Although recent infant research[12] is suggesting that babies are capable of extremely fine discrimination in the first few weeks of life, from about the second to the fifth month of life the baby begins to develop primitive representations of the self and of the object, but does not yet differentiate one from the other. This period corresponds to Mahler's symbiotic phase of development. These condensed representations of self and objects are of two kinds, depending on the experience leading to their formation. If the experience is pleasurable, a positive self-object representation is established; if the experience is unpleasurable, a negative self-object representation is established.

This is a condition which, abnormally retained, one also finds in psychosis. During intensive psychotherapy with a schizophrenic, either the patient is enraged, and the therapist is perceived as a bundle of rage which cannot be differentiated from the patient's, or the patient is ecstatic and happy, and the therapist is seen as a bundle of happiness which merges with the patient. In either case, the patient cannot differentiate himself from the therapist: There are some psychotic patients who cannot tell whose thoughts they are thinking.

Mahler's next stage of development is that of separation-individuation, which starts in the fifth to eighth month of life, and continues to the thirty-sixth month. Now the infant can begin to differentiate between the self and the object, and begin to build up self-representations and object representations, but cannot yet integrate the two. In the latter part of this stage—the subphase of rapprochement—the "good" and "bad" self-representations are still separate, and the same is true for the object representations. Children at this stage of development know the difference between themselves and others, but they do not have the capacity to integrate contradictory aspects of either themselves or others; they tend to see themselves as totally good or totally bad, and to see others the same way. This incapacity is typical of the so-called borderline patient and of the person with pathological narcissism, whose pathology is in many ways similar to that of the borderline patient.

The next level of development, according to Mahler, is that of emotional object constancy, a term used to describe the capacity for being able to maintain a "good" representation of others even when the others are frustrating or "bad." In other words, "good" and "bad" aspects of objects are now firmly linked or integrated. This phase of development is characterized by the establishment of both self- and object representations that can incorporate libido and aggression — love and hate — simultaneously. In other words, the child can now accept the idea that one person can be both lovable and hateful; he can accept and tolerate ambivalence.

The developmental theory just described is not consistent with Freud's theory of the progression from autoerotism via narcissism to object love. On the contrary, libidinal and aggressive investment of self and objects proceeds simultaneously, and there is a continuous interaction between the two types of investment.

The psychic development of the narcissistic personality does not proceed smoothly to the phase of object constancy. Some time between the ages of three and five, the narcissistic personality, instead of integrating positive and negative representations of self and of objects—"on the road to object constancy"[13]—puts together all the positive representations of both self and objects, as well as idealized representations of self and objects. This constitutes an extremely unrealistic and idealized idea of himself, and a pathological, grandiose self is the result. Fostering the development of a pathological grandiose self are parents who are cold, rejecting, yet admiring. The narcissistic personality devaluates the real objects, having incorporated those aspects of the real objects he wants for himself. All the negative aspects of himself and others he dissociates from himself, represses, or projects onto others. He is thus left with a very grandiose, if thoroughly unrealistic, idea of himself. The mechanisms I have described allow the patient to express his aggression through devaluating others. All the rage these patients are attempting to deny as existing within themselves is projected onto others. The others are then seen as enemies, to be either avoided or engaged in controversy.

The ideal self- and object representations that would normally become part of the superego are incorporated into the pathological grandiose self. This leads to a superego containing only the aggressively determined components (the early prohibitive and threatening aspects of the parental images distorted under the impact of the projection onto them of the child's own aggressive impulses). This excessively aggressive superego also tends to be dissociated and projected, which leads to further development of "persecutory" external objects and to the major loss of the normal functions of the superego in regulating self-esteem, such as monitoring and approval.

The devaluation of others, the emptying out of the internal world of object representations, is a major contributing cause of those patients' lack of normal self-esteem and also determines their remarkable lack of capacity for empathy with others. Their sense of internal void can only be compensated for by endless admiration from others, and by efforts to control others to avoid the envy that would otherwise be caused by the autonomous functioning, enjoyment of life, and creativity others enjoy.

Throughout the years, the individual with narcissistic personality disorder becomes significantly impoverished. He finds it difficult to come to terms with aging, with the loss of physical attractiveness, health, and power aging entails. His grandiose self cannot accept the passage of time. The lack of accumulation of an internal wealth of relations with others increases his sense of loneliness. The envy of others and of other people's creativity interferes with his enjoyment of culture and art. He dreads the future and begins to envy his own past because of the losses that it brings to mind. He tends to live in an eternal present that is ahistorical and alienating. Frequent results of these developments are deepening depressions in middle age and beyond, as well as secondary neurotic symptoms such as somatic complaints, sexual difficulties, drug abuse, and alcoholism.

In my view, in the treatment of the narcissistic personality one must analyze the pathological grandiose self into all of its components, rather than gratify the patient's need to be admired or his need to idealize the analyst. I interpret these idealizations as protective measures against the activation of the dissociated or repressed bad self- and object representations. These idealizations and the patient's grandiosity are, in other words, one type of defense against the primitive conflicts having to do with the stage of development, the stage of separation-individuation in which intense preoedipal aggression and preoedipal libidinal impulses are involved. When I clarify with the patient his idealizations of others—particularly the therapist—and the patient's grandiosity, there is indeed a falling apart of the grandiose self—a "fragmentation" of a kind. But behind that fragmentation emerge the primitive object relations, both libidinally and aggressively tinged, that characterize the separation-individuation stage of development. I analyze these until the patient is able to integrate the good and bad aspects of the self-representations, and the good and bad aspects of object representations. I try to help the patient, not by fostering a better adaptation of the pathological grandiose self, but by its resolution through interpretive techniques, which permits the recovery and normal development of self- and object representations, now freed from the obstructive effect of the pathological grandiose self. In consequence, normal object-relations, as well as normal self-love, become reinstated and both develop further. The theory and the corresponding technique of my approach of treatment have, I believe, an effect in terms of simultaneously improving the narcissistic and the object-related segment of the personality.

The study of the narcissistic personality has permitted the clarification of general issues of narcissism, both normal and pathological, and has permitted the development of psychoanalytic theory in new and exciting areas relevant to infant and child development, as well as to the diagnosis and treatment of character pathology.

NOTES

[1] Sigmund Freud (1914). "On Narcissism," *SE* vol. 14, 66-102.

[2] H. Tartakoff, "The Normal Personality in our Culture and the Nobel Prize Complex." In R. M. Loewenstein et al. (eds.), *Psychoanalysis: A General Psychology.* (New York: International Universities Press, 1966), pp. 222-252.

[3] M. Klein, *Envy and Gratitude.* (New York: Basic Books, 1957).

[4] H. G. Van der Waals, "Problems on Narcissism." *Bulletin of the Menninger Clinic* 29, 1965, 293-311.

[5] H. Kohut, *The Analysis of the Self.* (New York: International Universities Press, 1971); "Thoughts on Narcissism and Narcissistic Rage." *The Psychoanalytic Study of the Child,* 27, 1972, 360-400; *The Restoration of the Self.* (New York: International Universities Press, 1977).

[6] Kohut, 1972.

[7] Kohut, 1977.

[8] Sigmund Freud (1923). "The Ego and the Id," *SE* vol. 19, 3-66.

[9] E. Jacobson, *The Self and the Object World.* (New York: International Universities Press, 1964).

[10] M. Mahler, *On Human Symbiosis and the Vicissitudes of Individuation.* (New York: International Universities Press, 1968), *Selected Papers.* (New York: Jason Aronson, 1979); M. Mahler, F. Pine, and A. Bergman, *The Psychological Birth of the Human Infant.* (New York: Basic Books, 1975).

[11] O. Kernberg, *Borderline Conditions and Pathological Narcissism.* (New York: Jason Aronson, 1975); *Object Relations Theory and Clinical Psychoanalysis.* (New York: Jason Aronson, 1976); *Internal World and External Reality.* (New York: Jason Aronson, 1980).

[12] M. L. Hoffman, "Toward a Theory of Empathic Arousal and Development." In M. Lewis and L. Rosenblum (eds.), *The Development of Affect.* (New York: Plenum Press, 1978), pp. 227-256; C. Izard, "On the Ontogenesis of Emotions and Emotion-Cognition Relationships in Infancy." In M. Lewis and L. Rosenblum (eds.), *The Development of Affect.* (New York: Plenum Press, 1978) pp. 389-413; C. Izard and S. Buechler, "Emotion Expressions and Personality Integration in Infancy." In C. Izard (ed.), *Emotions in Personality and Psychopathology.* (New York: Plenum Press, 1979), pp. 447-472.

[13] Mahler, 1979.

PART II

The Context of Psychoanalysis

Chapter 9

The Scientific Status
of Psychoanalysis

Barbara Von Eckardt

INTRODUCTION

Freudian psychoanalysis represents a fascinating and ingenious attempt to answer a host of deep and perplexing questions about human nature. But what exactly is the status of Freud's contribution to psychoanalysis? How ought we to regard it?

Any assessment of Freud's contribution requires some set of criteria for evaluation. But this in turn requires that we decide on the *sort* of achievement psychoanalysis is. Is it, for example, literature or science? Or some combination of the two? Obviously, how we choose to categorize psychoanalysis will make a big difference in what standards are relevant for assessment. For example, a scientific theory is regarded as good only if it is empirically well supported, or highly predictive, or heuristically valuable in generating research questions. But none of these "good-making" characteristics are relevant to a work of literature.

Thus, when we ask about the scientific status of psychoanalysis, we can be asking one of two questions. The first concerns the categorization of psychoanalysis as a contribution. Ought psychoanalysis be assessed as a *scientific* contribution? The second concerns the assessment itself, given that we have chosen an appropriate set of standards. For example, assuming psychoanalysis to be scientific, is it *good* science? To what extent does it meet the standards of an important, or acceptable, scientific contribution? In this chapter, we will be concerned with only the first question, namely: Is psychoanalysis scientific at all?

Our discussion will be limited in two ways. First, we shall focus primarily on articulating and assessing various negative challenges to the scientific status of psychoanalysis which have been made or hinted at in the philosophical literature of the past 20 years. For the most part, these negative challenges have taken the following form:

> Premise A: To be scientific, something must have a certain property N.
> Premise B: Psychoanalysis does not have property N. Therefore, psychoanalysis is not scientific.

It has been argued, in other words, that for something to be scientific, it must meet a certain necessary condition. And it has further been claimed that psychoanalysis fails to meet this condition. Focus on such challenges potentially limits our treatment of the question of the scientific status of psychoanalysis because, should we decide that these challenges have not been successful, then the answer to our question will remain inconclusive. For we will have shown only that the case against psychoanalysis has not been made—not that it *could* not be made on other grounds.

Second, we shall consider only two out of the three possible component subquestions which make up our larger question. The term "psychoanalysis" can be taken to refer to any of three things:

> (1) a body of claims, that is, a set of theories and hypotheses concerning human nature, the workings of the mind, the nature of mental illness, etc.;
> (2) a methodology for investigating the mind and for establishing the psychoanalytic theories; or
> (3) a therapeutic technique based on the psychoanalytic theories and hypotheses.

All three of these have been impugned as being unscientific at some time or another by somebody. What is important to note is that it may well take *independent* arguments to establish that psychoanalysis is unscientific in any of these three senses. Suppose, for example, that one could establish that the theory was unscientific. It would not necessarily follow from this that the methodology or the therapeutic technique was unscientific. The reason is that the necessary condition *relevant* to points 1, 2, and 3, respectively, may be different. Thus, we really have three questions, not one: Is psychoanalytic theory scientific? Is the psychoanalytic methodology scientific? And, is the psychoanalytic therapeutic technique scientific? In what follows, we shall be concerned only with the scientific status of psychoanalytic theory and of the psychoanalytic methodology.

One final preliminary remark: It is appropriate to raise the question of the scientific status of psychoanalysis, or to challenge this status, only if there is, at least, some *prima facie* presumption in favor of its being scientific. In contrast, one would not raise the question of the scientific status of, say, Shakespeare's *Romeo and Juliet*. With respect to this point, it may be important to distinguish between psychoanalysis as it was originally conceived by Freud and psychoanalysis in its present form. Among psychoanalytic practitioners today, there appears to be no consensus on the question of whether psychoanalysis is scientific. Some believe that it is; others prefer to think about it in other ways—in terms of hermeneutics, for example. But there is no doubt Freud himself intended psychoanalysis to be scientific. He was trained as a scientist and throughout his writings one finds allusions to the scientific character of the theories he is developing.[1] Thus, whatever the views of current practitioners, Freud's own attitude supplies enough reason to take the issue of the scientific status of psychoanalysis seriously.

THE SCIENTIFIC STATUS OF PSYCHOANALYTIC THEORY

The Challenge

Among philosophers, the scientific status of psychoanalytic theory first became a topic of discussion in the early 1950s, when several prominent philosophers of science—among them Karl Popper and Ernest Nagel—wrote rather strong criticisms of psychoanalytic theory, arguing that it was not scientific. Karl Popper's views first appeared in a paper entitled "Science, Conjectures and Refutations." He wrote:

> I found that those of my friends who were admirers of Marx, Freud, and Adler, were impressed by a number of points common to these theories, and especially by their apparent *explanatory power*. These

theories appeared to be able to explain practically everything that happened within the fields to which they referred. The study of any of them seemed to have the effect of an intellectual conversion or revelation, opening your eyes to a new truth hidden from those not yet initiated. Once your eyes were thus opened you saw confirming instances everywhere: the world was full of *verifications* of the theory. Whatever happened always confirmed it. . . . The most characteristic element in this situation seemed to me the incessant stream of confirmations, of observations which "verified" the theories in question; and this point was constantly emphasized by their adherents. . . . The Freudian analysts emphasized that their theories were constantly verified by their "clinical observations."[2]

Somewhat later, Popper continues:

I could not think of any human behavior which could not be interpreted in terms of either theory. It was precisely this fact—that they always fitted, that they were always confirmed—which in the eyes of their admirers constituted the strongest argument in favor of these theories. It began to dawn on me that this apparent strength was in fact their weakness.[3]

In contrast, the confirmation of Einstein's theory of gravitation, according to Popper, resulted from a prediction which, on the basis of currently available scientific beliefs and without knowledge of the theory, no one would have expected to come true. This was the prediction that light from a distant star would be bent near the sun. The success of this prediction constituted strong support for the theory precisely because it was so "risky."

On considering this contrast between psychoanalytic theory and Einstein's theory of gravitation, Popper in the winter of 1919-1920 came to the following conclusions:

(1) It is easy to obtain confirmations, or verifications, for nearly every theory—if we look for confirmation.
(2) Confirmations should count only if they are the result of *risky predictions*, that is to say, if, unenlightened by the theory in question, we should have expected an event which was incompatible with the theory—an event which would have refuted the theory.
(3) Every "good" scientific theory is a prohibition: it forbids certain things to happen. The more a theory forbids, the better it is.
(4) A theory which is not refutable by a conceivable event is non-

scientific. Irrefutability is not a virtue of a theory (as people often think) but a vice.

(5) Every genuine *test* of a theory is an attempt to falsify it, or to refute it.

(6) Confirming evidence should not count except when it is the result of a genuine test of the theory; and this means that it can be presented as a serious but unsuccessful attempt to falsify the theory.[4]

Ernest Nagel's critique of psychoanalytic theory was very similar. He wrote:

My first difficulty with Freudian theory nevertheless is generated by the fact that while it is unobjectionable for a theory to be couched in terms of theoretical notions, the theory does not seem to me to satisfy two requirements which any theory must satisfy if it is to be capable of empirical validation. . . .

[F]irst, . . . it must be possible to deduce determinate consequences from the assumptions of the theory, so that one can decide on the basis of logical considerations, and prior to the examination of any empirical data, whether or not an alleged consequence of the theory is indeed implied by the latter. . . .

[S]econd, . . . even though the theoretical notions are not explicitly defined by way of overt empirical procedures and observable traits of things, *some* theoretical notions must be tied down to fairly definite and unambiguously specified observable materials, by way of rules of procedure variously called "correspondence rules," "coordinating definitions," and "operational definitions."

An immediate corollary to these requirements is that since a consistent theory cannot imply two incompatible consequences, a credible theory must not only be *confirmed* by observational evidence, but it must also be capable of being *negated* by such evidence. In short, a theory must not be formulated in such a manner that it can always be construed and manipulated so as to explain whatever the actual facts are, no matter whether controlled observation shows one state of affairs to obtain or its opposite.

In respect to both of these requirements, however, Freudian theory in general, and the metapsychology in particular, seem to me to suffer from serious shortcomings.[5]

The Notion of Falsifiability

In this section, I shall attempt a precise formulation of the condition of falsifiability so that we shall be in a better position to assess the scientific status of Freudian theory. We shall use Popper's version as our starting point. It will turn out, however, that his notion of falsifiability suffers from a serious difficulty for which a solution is far from obvious. At that point, we will explore the problem of finding an adequate alternative.

Based on the above quote and other passages from Popper's work,[6] we can reconstruct Popper's version of falsifiability. Let "T" represent a system or set of statements which constitutes a theory; let "P" represent a singular statement which expresses a prediction, and let "IC" represent a singular statement describing some set of initial conditions relevant to the theory. Then

> Popper's Version of Falisifiability
> T is falsifiable just in case there exists a P and there exists an IC such that
> (a) The conjunction of T and IC entails P
> (b) IC does not entail P alone
> (c) The conjunction of T and IC is consistent
> (d) IC is "acceptable"
> (e) P can be rejected on the basis of observation
> (f) P is a "risky" prediction.

Condition (d) states that IC must be "acceptable." This means that either there must be independent scientific evidence to support IC, or IC is highly plausible relative to one's background beliefs.

Condition (e) requires that P can be rejected on the basis of observation. What Popper says is that P must be a "basic statement." A basic statement is one whose logical form is something like "there is a so-and-so in the region k" or "such-and-such an event is occurring in the region k," where the things or events in question are ordinary macroscopic entities. Although he refers to such statements as "observable," he rejects the view that observation is somehow epistemically pure or unsullied by our knowledge of theory. Further, he rejects the view that perceptual experiences can in themselves justify such statements. Rather, his view is that the acceptance or rejection of a basic statement requires a *decision* on our part, and this decision may very well involve interpretation of the facts observed, even interpretation in the light of theories.[7] Thus, the primacy of basic statements rests not in some inherent epistemic privilege but simply in the fact that intersubjective agreement about them is relatively easy to secure.

Condition (f) states that P must be a "risky" prediction. Basically, a risky prediction, for Popper, is one which would be assigned a low probability, or which we would not expect, on the basis of our available background beliefs at the time the falsifiability of T is being assessed. Note that both conditions (d) and (f) suggest the need for relativization to a time of assessment and a community of believers. The issue of relativization will be discussed shortly when we attempt to reformulate Popper's version of falsifiability in the face of difficulties.

Now is it true that for a theory to be scientific it must be falsifiable in this sense? A consideration of the relationship between theory and data by philosophers of science in recent years[8] suggests that this version of falsifiability is much too strong. It is too strong in the sense that it will rule out as scientific theories we consider paradigmatically scientific (such as physics). The reason is simple: For most, if not all, paradigmatically scientific theories, the theory alone cannot entail a prediction of the required "observational" kind.

The original view of the logical positivists was that theory and observation were mediated by so-called correspondence rules, consisting either of explicit or partial definitions of the theoretical vocabulary in terms of an observational vocabulary. In recent years, however, it has been argued that the so-called "received view" of correspondence rules vastly oversimplifies the relationship between a theoretical hypothesis undergoing test and the observable evidence adduced in its support. Careful examination of scientific case studies has revealed that theory and data are often mediated by a complex array of auxiliary propositions: hypotheses from related theories, theories of measurement and of the data, assumptions about the experimental situation, and assumptions about the ways in which the putative theoretical states causally influence the observable states-of-affairs.[9]

That theories are connected with observable results only via a mediating link of auxiliary hypotheses has important implications for the justification of theories. Although it has long been recognized that no single experiment can ever conclusively verify a theory or hypothesis, it has frequently been maintained that a single experiment can falsify a theory. Such an experiment was known as a "crucial experiment." But, as the nineteenth-century philosopher, historian of science, and physicist, Pierre Duhem, pointed out, if theories confront data only in conjunction with other theories or hypotheses, then if a theory's prediction is not borne out, the most one can conclude is that *either* the theory *or* one of the auxiliary hypotheses is wrong.[10]

Popper's original version of falsifiability clearly needs revision. At first blush, such revision appears an easy task. Why not simply require the existence of a set of auxiliary hypotheses A in conjunction with the theory T and the statement of initial conditions IC in order to entail the prediction P? In other words, why not adopt the following formulation?

Crude Modified Version of Falsifiability
T is falsifiable just in case there exists a P, an IC, and an A such that
(a) The conjunction of T and IC and A entails P
(b) The conjunction of IC and A does not entail P
(c) The conjunction of T and IC and A is consistent
(d) IC is "acceptable"
(e) P can be rejected on the basis of observation
(f) P is a "risky" prediction.

The reason is simple. The above version of falsifiability can no longer serve the function which Popper intended falsifiability to serve, namely, to provide a principle of demarcation between science and nonscience. Without further constraints on what can count as an appropriate set of auxiliary hypotheses, *any* theory will be falsifiable.[11] No matter how abstract or unempirical a theory may be, it will always be possible (it is even easy) to make up a logically appropriate set of auxiliary hypotheses. Suppose, for example, that the theory in question is that a cloud of perfect spirituality is hovering over Yale. Then, there are hundreds, possibly thousands, of auxiliary hypotheses that will satisfy the Crude Modified Version of Falsifiability. Here's one: If a cloud of perfect spirituality is hovering over Yale, then every ice cream cone bought on September 20, 1980, in New Haven will be strawberry-flavored. Clearly, something has gone wrong. And, equally clearly, what is required is the introduction of additional constraints on what can count as an appropriate auxiliary hypothesis. But what constraints?

At this point, we seem to have two basic options, neither of which is totally satisfactory. The first is to make the notion of falsifiability what the philosophers call "factive": to require of both IC and A that they be *true*. If we are really interested in whether or not a theory can be determined to be *false*, then the logic of modus tollens[12] requires precisely such a move. However, there is a cost—the usefulness of falsifiability as a principle of demarcation is seriously diminished. The difficulty is not that the Factive Version fails to draw any boundary at all, as with the Crude Modified Version, or that it obviously draws it in the wrong place. The difficulty is, rather, that it fails to provide a readily applicable set of conditions capable of *settling* a controversial case. What it can do, however, is set the stage for a more focused debate, for example, a debate on whether a set of appropriate true auxiliary hypotheses exists. But this limited usefulness falls far short of Popper's original intentions.

The second alternative is to make the notion that philosophers call "epistemic." This involves constraining the set of auxiliary hypotheses by requiring that they be *available and accepted by a research community*. I do not mean accepted in an idle way; I mean accepted in the sense that the researchers would actually be prepared to conduct research on the assumption that they are true. Such a modification, of course, relativizes the falsifiability of a theory to a research community at a time. And while it makes the notion of falsifiability more readily applicable to a controversial case, such as psychoanalytic theory, it has a number of problems of its own. The fundamental problem has to do with fixing the referent of "research community" in a satisfactory way. On the one hand, if we apply the term too liberally, we run the risk of making our notion of falsifiability too weak again. On the other, if we apply the term strictly, we run the risk of begging the question, for we may be considering a genuine research community to be the only one that is in the business of testing falsifiable theories. To make the problem more concrete: In deciding whether psychoanalytic theory is scientific, ought we to regard psychoanalysts as members of a research community or not? As we shall see, whether we do makes a difference to whether we take psychoanalytic theory to be falsifiable or not.

Once we see the need to modify Popper's original formulation of falsifiability to include reference to auxiliary hypotheses, there seems to be no clearly adequate alternative formulation. Nevertheless, despite this less than satisfactory situation, we will persist in our inquiry. For even though our standards of assessment are not in the best of shape, it will still be of interest to see how Freudian psychoanalytic theory will bear up when we attempt to apply them. For this purpose, we shall keep in mind both modified versions we have discussed. They are what I shall call the "Modified Factive Version of Falsifiability" and the "Modified Epistemic Version of Falsifiability."

The Modified Factive Version of Falsifiability
T is falsifiable just in case there exists a P, an IC, and an A such that
(a) The conjunction of T and IC and A entails P
(b) The conjunction of IC and A does not entail P

(c) The conjunction of T and IC and A is consistent
(d) IC is available, acceptable, and true
(e) P can be rejected on the basis of observation
(f) P is a "risky" prediction
(g) A is available, acceptable, and true.

The Modified Epistemic Version of Falsifiability
T is falsifiable at time t for a research community RC just in case
there exists a P, an IC, and an A such that
(a) The conjunction of T and IC and A entails P
(b) The conjunction of IC and A does not entail P
(c) The conjunction of T and IC and A is consistent
(d) IC is acceptable to RC
(e) P can be rejected on the basis of observation
(f) P is a "risky" prediction
(g) A is available and accepted by RC.

As we have seen, the Modified Epistemic Version of Falsifiability allows us to relativize the falsifiability of Freudian theory in two ways:
first, relative to a set of auxiliary assumptions, and second, relative to
a research community. Are there alternative sets of auxiliary assumptions and alternative research communities that might be relevant for
such an assessment? The answer is yes. There have been two very
different attempts to justify Freudian theory. The first, carried out by
Freud during his lifetime and pursued by orthodox Freudians even today, relies heavily on the so-called psychoanalytic method; the second
began in the 1940s when psychologists became interested in testing
Freudian theory experimentally. As we shall see, both attempts made
use of auxiliary assumptions peculiar to the research methodology being
employed. These facts suggest that, in considering the falsifiability of
Freudian theory, we ought to distinguish between its falsifiability relative
to the set of auxiliary assumptions *available to and accepted by Freud* and
its falsifiability relative to auxiliary assumptions *added later to the theory
for the purpose of testing it empirically*. Further, they suggest that we ought
to consider it relative to two research communities: the first consisting
of *Freud himself and the orthodox Freudians*, and the second consisting of
contemporary experimental psychologists.

Thus, two variables are relevant to our evaluation, each of which has
two relevant values. In other words, in applying the Epistemic Version
of Falsifiability, we are seeking answers to the following four questions:

(Q1) Is Freudian theory falsifiable for orthodox Freudians relative
to some set of original auxiliary assumptions?

(Q2) Is Freudian theory falsifiable for contemporary experimental psychologists relative to some set of original auxiliary assumptions?
(Q3) Is Freudian theory falsifiable for orthodox Freudians relative to some set of added auxiliary assumptions?
(Q4) Is Freudian theory falsifiable for contemporary experimental psychologists relative to some set of added auxiliary assumptions?

The four possible situations relevant to falsifiability are represented in a 2 x 2 matrix in Figure 1. For convenience, we shall call Freudian theory in conjunction with any original auxiliary assumptions the "Original Extended Theory"; in contrast, Freudian theory in conjunction with any auxiliary assumptions added since Freud's time for experimental purposes will be called the "New Extended Theory."

In applying the Factive Version of Falsifiability, reference to a research community drops out and we must take a stand on the *truth* of each set of auxiliary assumptions. In doing so, we can either align ourselves with one of the above research groups or take a novel stand.

| | RESEARCH COMMUNITY | |
	Orthodox	Experimental
AUXILIARY ASSUMPTIONS		
Original	(Q1)	(Q2)
Added	(Q3)	(Q4)

Figure 1. Factors Relevant to Epistemic Falsifiability

Epistemic Falsifiability of the Original Extended Theory

The Sexual Trauma Theory

In a recent paper, the contemporary philosopher of science, A. Grünbaum, gives four sets of examples to show that Freudian theory is falsifiable. Of these, only one set is relevant to the status of the Original Extended Theory.[13] Grünbaum describes these examples thus:

Ten years before Popper precociously formulated his demarcation criterion at the age of seventeen, Freud himself had recognized (1909)[14] the following refutation: The best available evidence concerning the actual life history of his "Rat Man" Paul Lorenz had *refuted* his prior hypothesis as to the specifics of the sexual aetiology

which he had postulated for adult obsessional neurosis. . . . Similarly
for Freud's abandonment . . . of his erstwhile 1896 view of the role
of passive infantile experiences (of seduction) in the traumatic aetiology of hysteria.[15]

The theory relevant to both examples is one of Freud's earliest theories
on the aetiology of the neuroses. Let us call it the "Sexual Trauma
Theory." According to this theory, the "specific cause" of each of the
neuroses (hysteria, obsessional neurosis, neurasthenia proper, and anxiety neurosis) is a "particular disturbance of the economics of the nervous
system" which has as its *source the subject's sexual life, whether . . . a
disorder of his contemporary sexual life or important events of his past life"*
(Freud's emphasis).[16] Furthermore, each kind of neurosis is associated
with a different kind of sexually traumatic specific cause. Neurasthenia
proper is associated with immoderate masturbation or spontaneous
emissions; anxiety neurosis with enforced abstinence or unconsum-
mated genital excitation; hysteria with a childhood sexual seduction;
and, obsessional neurosis with a pleasurable childhood sexual experience.

Now, is this theory falsifiable? I should think so. Suppose we were
interested in testing the hypothesis concerning the specific cause of
hysteria, namely, if a person suffers from a hysterical neurosis, he or
she will have experienced a childhood seduction. Testing such a hypothesis poses two basic probems: first, the problem of diagnosing someone as a hysteric, and second, the problem of finding evidence for an
event that occurred in the past. And although both of these are serious
problems, they are primarily *methodological.* As far as I can see, they do
not render the theory nonfalsifiable.

Freud himself rejected the hypothesis that hysteria stemmed from a
childhood seduction for several reasons. Three of these involve reasoning which roughly fits our falsifiability model. The first reason was that
the analyses he conducted on the basis of the seduction hypothesis were
not going well. Here he was clearly assuming that if the theory were
true, they would be going well. The second was that if the theory were
true and his beliefs about the frequency of hysteria correct, then the
frequency of "perverted acts against children" would have to have been
extremely high. This did not seem "credible." And, finally, he reasoned
that if the theory were true "the secret of infantile experiences" should
be revealed in the delirious states of psychotics; this did not happen.[17]

Thus, I agree with Grünbaum that these examples show one subtheory
of Freud's Original Extended Theory to be falsifiable. But because they

involve the Sexual Trauma Theory I believe them to be of limited interest. The reason is that this Freudian theory is not what most challengers of Freud have had in mind. (Nor is it the one the experimental psychologists have been interested in.) What challengers of Freud have had in mind has been the more mature, typically Freudian subtheories, in which the specific cause of neurosis is taken from the realm of observable phenomena (for example, actual seductions) and placed inside the head. What about that theory? Is it falsifiable?

The Libido/Wish Theory

To understand Freud's later thinking on the aetiology of the neuroses, we must start with a brief sketch of his views on psychosexual development and the nature of the libido.[18]

At the time Freud wrote his "Three Essays on Sexuality," which articulated his theory of psychosexual development, the conventional view regarding human psychosexual development was that the sexual instinct is absent in childhood, only setting in at puberty, and that it is manifested as attraction to the opposite sex for the aim of sexual union. One of Freud's major innovations was to alter this conventional view. To do so, he distinguished between a sexual *object*, the object toward which the sexual instinct is directed, and the sexual *aim*, the act toward which the instinct tends. And he argued against the conventional view that there were deviations with respect to both sexual objects and sexual aims.

He also argued that the development of human sexuality begins in infancy. Normal development follows a pattern, according to Freud, of various stages of sexuality: infantile sexuality, latency, puberty, and adult sexuality. Within the period of infantile sexuality, Freud distinguished a number of substages: the oral, the anal, the genital, and the Oedipal. Each of these stages and substages is characterized by both a certain kind of object choice and a certain kind of aim. For example, the first three substages of the infantile stage take the sexual object to be the self and the sexual aim to be pleasure by manipulation of stimuli to the various erogenous zones. In contrast, the Oedipal stage is characterized by the choice of an object other than the self, namely, the mother.

In addition to describing psychosexual development in terms of stages, Freud also gave a description in terms of the workings of an internal force called the *libido*. Libido, according to Freud, is the energy under the control of the sexual instinct. It is capable of both variation in quantity and variation of direction. In particular, it can be directed upon various objects, either in actuality (via action) or merely mentally (in fantasy), or it can be employed for various aims. It can also change its direction from one set of objects and aims to another—what Freud called "displacement." Four basic principles govern the workings of the libido:

(1) In normal development, libidinal energy is transferred from one set of objects and aims to another according to the maturational pattern of psychosexual stages.

(2) Due to a variety of causes, some energy can become permanently attached to a certain set of objects or aims. This is called *fixation*.

(3) The energy also can return to an object or aim characteristic of an earlier developmental stage. This is called *regression*. Regression occurs when normal development is prevented.

(4) In particular, when regression occurs, the libido returns to prior points of fixation.

Freud illustrated these four basic principles with an analogy of a migrating people. Imagine a group of people moving across a country. At various way stations in their travels, they leave smaller groups to settle. This is the analog of fixation. But then they come to the border of the country and are prevented from going any further. So instead of remaining there, they return to their fellow men at the various way stations. This is the analog of regression. We can readily understand why a group of people in this sort of situation would return to their friends and fellow men at the way stations. Why the libidinal energy regresses to points of fixation is not so clear, but it is an important tenet of Freud's theory.

The formation of a neurosis, according to Freud, requires the existence of a certain precondition in the past, as well as certain conditions in the present. The precondition is the fixation of the libido at some stage of sexual development. Such fixation occurs to many people for a variety of reasons and is not uncommon. What produces the formation of a neurosis, however, is that, in addition to this fixation, certain present conditions are satisfied in adult life. First, the libido must be externally frustrated from seeking satisfaction for some reason or other. This may be because of some kind of traumatic event.[19] When this happens, regression occurs to an earlier fixation point such that the libido tries to become directed upon an infantile type of object. This, however, leads to a conflict with the adult ego, which has internalized various standards of conduct and hence rejects an infantile form of satisfaction. The libido is thus forced to elude the censorship of the ego somehow in order to express its wish. It does this by employing any of a variety of processes which the unconscious makes available for the purpose of disguise, for example, condensation, displacement, or projection. Thus, the outcome is the formation of a symptom which is both caused by and expresses the libidinal wish in symbolic form. As Freud writes: "Two things combine to constitute the meaning of a symptom, its whence and its whither or why, that is, the impressions and experiences from which it sprang, and the purpose which it serves."[20]

To understand how Freud's Libido/Wish Theory of the etiology of the neuroses is falsifiable relative to his own auxiliary assumptions, one must understand the method he developed to "test" this theory. The method, of course, was the so-called psychoanalytic method of interpretation. Freud was quite explicit about the importance of its role in the justification of his theory. For example, at one point he wrote:

> The question may, however, be raised of where convincing evidence is to be found in favour of the alleged aetiological importance of sexual factors in the psychoneuroses, in view of the fact that the onset of these illnesses may be observed in response to the most commonplace emotions or even to somatic precipitating causes. . . . To such a question I would reply that the psycho-analytic examination of neurotics is the source from which this disputed conviction of mine is derived. If we make use of that irreplaceable method of research, we discover that *the patient's symptoms constitute his sexual activity* (whether wholly or in part), which arises from the sources of the normal or perverse component instincts of sexuality. . . . Anyone who knows how to interpret the language of hysteria will recognize that the neurosis is concerned only with the patient's repressed sexuality.[21]

Now why did Freud consider his psychoanalytic method so "irreplaceable"? As the quote makes clear, for Freud the *evidence for the etiological role of sexual factors in neurosis* was that neurotic symptoms had a certain meaning or significance, and it was only the psychoanalytic method which could reveal this meaning. In other words, in Freud's view, symptom formation was *caused* by the repression of unacceptable material in virtue of the fact that symptoms constituted an *expression* of such material. What the repression of unacceptable material caused was not symptoms *per se* but symptoms with a certain meaning. Thus, if the meaning of his patients' symptoms could be discovered, the precise nature of that meaning would constitute evidence for the precise nature of the repressed material which had caused the symptom. Specifically, if it turned out that all the symptoms of Freud's patients were, in fact, expressions of sexual wishes, then this would constitute evidence in favor of his sexual etiology hypothesis.

Let us now see how the Epistemic Version of Falsifiability can be satisfied. We shall take T to consist of the following three propositions:

> T 1   The specific cause of psychoneurosis is the occurrence of an unacceptable sexual wish in childhood which is subsequently repressed.
> T 2   Unless they are somehow brought to consciousness, such repressed wishes persist in the unconscious indefinitely.
> T 3   Such repressed wishes express themselves not only in symptoms but also in dreams, slips of the tongue, jokes.

Now, given the assumption that a certain patient, Miss X, is suffering from psychoneurosis (= IC), T allows us to infer that Miss X will have dreams with a certain (latent) content, namely, the unacceptable sexual wish of her childhood. If we then add the following auxiliary hypothesis pertaining to the method of interpretation, T satisfies the epistemic condition of falsifiability:

> A*: If an expert practitioner employs the method of interpretation with respect to a dream D, then, under normal conditions, D has a certain (latent) content M if and only if the expert practitioner assigns M to D.

The prediction is then:

> P: An expert practitioner of the method of interpretation will assign M = an infantile sexual wish to the dreams of Miss X.

This is certainly a risky prediction; independently of believing Freud's theory, one would not have expected someone's dream to be interpreted that way. Furthermore, it is easy to see what would falsify the prediction: It would be falsified just in case an expert practitioner of the method of interpretation assigned any other content beside "M = an infantile sexual wish" to the patient's dreams.

Critics of Freud may very well balk at granting falsifiability to Freudian theory on the basis of this account. The reason, of course, is that the auxiliary hypothesis A* which we have claimed was accepted by Freud is probably not acceptable to them. And with good reason. For A* presupposes both that latent content is an objective property of dreams and that the method of interpretation is an objective method for ascertaining the nature of that latent content. *Both of these are highly questionable assumptions.* They were assumptions accepted by Freud, however, and hence, if we opt to characterize falsifiability epistemically, we must conclude that, relative to the research community of orthodox Freudians, the Original Extended Theory (even in its mature form) is falsifiable. On the other hand, since contemporary experimental psychologists would reject the method of interpretation as a way of obtaining reliable data for testing Freudian theory, we must also conclude that, relative to the research community of experimental psychologists, the Original Extended Theory is not falsifiable. These results are summarized in Figure 2.

	RESEARCH COMMUNITY	
	Orthodox	Experimental
AUXILIARY ASSUMPTIONS		
Original	Falsifiable	Not Falsifiable
Added	—	

Figure 2. Falsifiability of the Original Extended Theory

Epistemic Falsifiability of the New Extended Theory

There exists today a whole cottage industry for the testing of Freudian theory.[22] As we noted previously, what is involved in such tests is the formulation of new auxiliary hypotheses sufficient to permit some sort of experimental prediction. And relative to these added auxiliary hypotheses, which are, of course, accepted by the experimental psychologists doing the testing, many aspects of Freudian theory are, again, perfectly falsifiable. As an example, we shall describe a study done to test Freud's hypothesis concerning the nature of paranoia.

Because neurosis always involves regression to an earlier developmental stage, it became necessary for Freud to elaborate on his story of psychosexual development as he tried to account for the details of diverse forms of neurosis. In the case of paranoia, a number of revisions were required. First, he posited a stage of narcissism between the earlier infantile, autoerotic stages and the first stage of object selection. Second, he divided the prelatency stage of object selection into two substages: a stage of homosexual impulse and a stage of heterosexual impulse. He described these new stages as follows:

There comes a time in the development of the individual at which he unifies his sexual instincts (which have hitherto been engaged in auto-erotic activities) in order to obtain a love-object; and he begins by taking himself, his own body, as his love-object, and only subsequently proceeds from this to the choice of some person other than himself as his object. This half-way phase between auto-erotism and object-love may perhaps be indispensable to the normal course of life; but it appears that many people linger unusually long in this condition, and that many of its features are carried over by them into the later stages of their development. The point of central interest in the self which is thus chosen as a love-object may already be the genitals. The line of development then leads on to the choice of an outer object with similar genitals—that is, to homosexual object-choice—and thence to homosexuality.[23]

The detailed path of symptom formation for paranoia was then described by Freud, thus: The precondition is a fixation somewhere between the stages of autoeroticism, narcissism, and infantile homosexuality. Given an external frustration, regression occurs to this fixation point, resulting in the emergence of an unconscious, infantile, homosexual wish. Naturally, such a wish is unacceptable to the ego. Hence, to be expressed it must be disguised in one of the ways available to the unconscious. In this case, the wish is disguised by a combination of projection and reversal. "I love him" becomes "I hate him" which, in turn, becomes "He hates me." Thus, the persecution complex typical of a paranoid is formed.

The research I shall describe was done by H. S. Zamansky.[24] The hypothesis which Zamansky attempted to test was this: The paranoid delusion represents a defensive attempt to control and repress unacceptable homosexual wishes by the mechanism of projection. Let us call this the "Psychoanalytic Theory of Paranoid Delusion." To test this hypothesis, Zamansky reasoned as follows: If Freud's theory concerning paranoia is correct, then

if an individual with strong homosexual urges is placed in a situation in which there is an equal opportunity for attraction to either a member of his own sex or of the opposite sex, he should manifest by his behavior (if the task is appropriately disguised) a greater attraction to the member of his own sex, and a lesser attraction to the opposite sex, than would the heterosexually oriented person.[25]

In contrast, if such an individual is placed in a setting where his sexual preferences are being overtly evaluated, then he should defensively express a greater preference for women than for men.

Zamansky's strategy, then, was to devise two experimental tasks for his subjects, one that somehow got at their unconscious preferences and one that probed their conscious preferences. If these tasks in fact did what they were supposed to, then the Psychoanalytic Theory of Paranoid Delusion would predict that paranoid subjects would show a preference for males on the task probing their unconscious preferences but would show a preference for females on the task probing conscious preferences. The details of Zamansky's experiment looked like this:

Stimuli
Pairs of pictures were presented to subjects. These pictures consisted of various combinations of male and female figures, and scenes with and without homosexually threatening themes.

Tasks
Unconscious preference task: Subjects were exposed to pairs of pictures and asked to decide which picture had the greater overall surface area. While they were looking at the pictures, the experimenter monitored how much time was spent looking at each picture.

Conscious preference task: Subjects were exposed to the same pairs of pictures and asked which picture they preferred. The experimenter recorded these responses.

Subjects
The subjects included 20 male paranoids and 20 male nonparanoid schizophrenics.

The logic of this attempt to test part of Freud's theory should be clear. The theory T that we are trying to test is the Psychoanalytic Theory of Paranoid Delusion, that is, the claim that paranoids suffer from repressed homosexual wishes. To use T to generate a prediction, we must make various auxiliary assumptions. We need a description of the experimental setup as provided above; in addition, we must connect the theory with possible results of the experimental tasks. Zamansky made the following assumptions:

(1) Men with paranoid delusions, when compared with men without these delusions, will spend more time on male than female

pictures in the unconscious preference task.

(2) Men with paranoid delusions, when compared with men without these delusions, will express a greater preference for women than for men as this expression becomes more explicit or conscious.

Note that these assumptions are not part of Freud's theory *per se* but are required to make a prediction using Zamansky's task. The predictions are, of course, that the paranoid subjects chosen for Zamansky's experiment will act in accordance with the above assumptions. Note that these predictions satisfy Popper's requirement that a prediction be risky. Independent of the theory in question, there is no reason to expect paranoid and nonparanoid subjects to act differently on something like Zamansky's tasks.

As it turned out, Zamansky's predictions were borne out.[26] Hence, the Psychoanalytic Theory of Paranoid Delusion received a certain amount of confirmation. What is of greater interest to us, however, is that the theory *could* have been falsified relative to Zamansky's experimental assumptions.

Thus, we now have the answer to one more of our epistemic falsifiability questons. Freudian theory *is* falsifiable relative to auxiliary assumptions added for the purpose of experimental test and relative to the community of experimental psychologists who are carrying out such tests.

Two more questions remain regarding the falsifiability issue. First, is the New Extended Theory falsifiable relative to the orthodox Freudian community? And, second, what about falsifiability in its factive form?

There is some evidence for believing that Freud, at least, would not have accepted the new auxiliary assumptions required for the purposes of experimental test, and, hence, would have considered his theory *nonfalsifiable* relative to such assumptions. The evidence is this. In the early 1930s, an American psychologist named Rosenzweig wrote to Freud informing him that he had experimental evidence in support of some aspect of Freud's theories. Freud wrote in reply:

My dear Sir,

I have examined your experimental studies for the verification of the psychoanalytic assertions with interest. I cannot put much value on these confirmations because the wealth of reliable observations on which these assertions rest make them independent of experimental verification. Still, it can do no harm.[27]

Thus Freud seems to have regarded clinical observation as completely sufficient for justifying his theories; experimental evidence was simply superfluous, on his view.

Epistemic and Factive Falsifiability: Conclusions

We can now sum up our results relevant to the Epistemic Version of Falsifiability:

(1) The Original Extended Theory is falsifiable relative to the orthodox Freudian community but is not falsifiable relative to the experimental psychological community.
(2) The New Extended Theory, in contrast, is not falsifiable relative to the orthodox Freudian community but is falsifiable relative to the experimental psychological community.

These results are represented in Figure 3.

	RESEARCH COMMUNITY	
	Orthodox	Experimental
AUXILIARY ASSUMPTIONS		
Original	Falsifiable	Not Falsifiable
Added	Not Falsifiable	Falsifiable

Figure 3. The Epistemic Falsifiability of Freudian Theory

As we have seen, what underlie this pattern of results are differences of opinion regarding the sort of auxiliary assumptions that are appropriate for the "testing" of Freudian theory. For the orthodox Freudians, the appropriate auxiliary assumptions connect tenets of the theory with the use of the method of interpretation; for the experimental psychologists, in contrast, they connect tenets of the theory with particular experimental test situations and tasks. Thus the divergent falsifiability judgments of the two communities basically come down to a difference in methodological commitments.

Now, what about falsifiability in the factive sense? Recall that according to the Factive Version of Falsifiability, the set A of auxiliary hypotheses must be not only acceptable to whoever is making the judgment, but also *true*. Empirical propositions can never be proved true, of course, so the best we can do in assessing the factive falsifiability of a theory is to make a judgment of truth based on the best available evidence and the best possible arguments.

In my view, there are serious methodological difficulties connected with the method of interpretation; hence, I believe that the auxiliary assumption A* which we have taken to be part of the Original Extended Theory is false. (This point will be argued below.) Furthermore, I reject Freud's view that experimental test procedures are irrelevant for the justification of psychoanalytic theory. If psychoanalytic theory makes empirical claims and if psychoanalytic researchers seek acceptance of the theory *on scientific grounds,* then the theory must be submitted to the sort of test procedures sanctioned by the scientific community at large—that is, experimental or quasiexperimental tests. Thus, there are no *a priori* grounds for rejecting what we have called "added" assumptions. With respect to the truth of any particular set of auxiliary assumptions, such as, for example, those used in Zamansky's experiment, judgment must be made on a case-by-case basis. Ultimately, if the theory is empirically vindicated and we can devise alternative measures for the presence or absence of such particular theoretical states as paranoia, then perhaps such auxiliary assumptions as Zamansky's can themselves be subjected to experimental test. But initially we may have to be content with mere plausibility considerations or with simply regarding an auxiliary assumption as true, unless there is evidence to the contrary.

In sum, in my view, the factive falsifiability of Freudian theory is the same as its epistemic falsifiability with respect to the experimental psychological community. The Original Extended Theory is not falsifiable, whereas the New Extended Theory is. This judgment rests primarily on the claim that the original Freudian research methodology is not scientifically acceptable. Thus, to justify my view, I must now turn to a consideration of the scientific status of Freud's research methodology.

THE SCIENTIFIC STATUS OF FREUD'S RESEARCH METHODOLOGY

The scientific status of Freudian psychoanalysis has been challenged with respect not only to its theories, but also to its methodology.[28] However, despite the repeated presentation by critics of certain features of Freud's methodology as problematic, the challenge to Freud's method has never been as clearly formulated as the challenge to his theory. The difficulty is, of course, that if such a challenge is to assume the same logical structure as Popper's and Nagel's challenge with respect to psychoanalytic theory, then something must be said about what makes a research methodology scientific. And this is a notoriously difficult and controversial topic.[29] Nevertheless, to get a clearer picture of the scientific status of the Freudian methodology, I shall attempt to tackle this difficult question. I shall try not only to identify those aspects of Freud's methodology which are troublesome, but also to indicate *why* they are troublesome in the light of standard scientific practice.

The Requirement of a Good Scientific Test

One thing that distinguishes science from other efforts to answer questions about our world is that scientists have developed rather stringent rules for the *acceptability* of an answer. Since in general answers are sought which are true or at least approximately true, the point of these methodological canons is to maximize the probability of an accepted answer being a true one.

Two of the most important properties of a hypothesis or theory relevant to its acceptability are:

(1) the explanatory power of the theory, that is, the extent to which it can explain relevant data (not only how much data it can explain but how well compared to rival theories); and
(2) the predictive success of the theory on good scientific tests.

That a theory or hypothesis can explain some set of relevant data is a minimal condition of its acceptability. But more than this is required because, given any set of data, there is always more than one possible explanation. The role of the second property, thus, is to distinguish among these possible explanations. Popper's notion of a risky prediction permits us to distinguish between explanations which follow from our background beliefs and those which follow from the theory under consideration. But this is not enough, for there may be more than one *new* way of explaining the data. Thus, a good scientific test distinguishes, in principle, between the theory in question and rival theories (both old and new) to as great an extent as possible.

According to Ronald N. Giere, a good scientific test requires the following:

A good test of a theoretical hypothesis, H, requires an experiment or set of observations that involve the hypothesis, H, initial conditions, IC, auxiliary assumptions, AA, and a prediction, P, such that the following two statements are *true*.
Condition 1. If [H and IC and AA], then P.
Condition 2. If [Not even approximately H and IC and AA], then very probably Not P.[30]

Condition 1 simply states that P is a prediction that can be made on the basis of theoretical hypothesis H, given certain additional assumptions. Condition 2 is similar to Popper's requirement of a risky prediction. Note, however, the difference. A prediction is risky if the probability of P is low given our background beliefs. Condition 2 is stronger: It states that the probability of P must be low whenever H is not even approximately true. That is, no theory or hypothesis significantly different from H ought to assign P a high probability, where IC and AA are true. Obviously, this stronger requirement is not one which can, in practice, be justified easily. But, nevertheless, it serves an important methodological function, for it encourages scientists to try to distinguish the hypothesis undergoing test not only from currently held beliefs, but also from other possible rivals. In other words, it encourages them to be creative in thinking up alternative ways of explaining the available data to see whether any alternatives might make predictions similar to H.

Freud's reliance on clinical observation

A number of aspects of Freud's methodology are troublesome when compared to this scientific ideal. First, Freud restricted himself to clinical observation as the basis for confirming his theories. This emphasis on clinical observation was, undoubtedly, initially the result of his interest in using his theories as a basis for therapy, but the restriction was more than just a practical one. As we have seen, Freud made it a matter of principle.

The difficulty with this restriction to clinical data is not that it makes prediction impossible, as some have thought, but that, for the most part, it makes prediction on the basis of a good scientific test impossible. The reason is this. A good scientific test, as we have seen, is one which *discriminates* between the theory under consideration and rival theories. It is a test which, if successful, significantly cuts down the class of hypotheses compatible with the data. To be in a position to make the kind of prediction required by a good scientific test with confidence almost always demands extremely subtle manipulation and control of the many variables which are relevant to the domain under study. That is what experimental control is all about. Rival theories often make similar predictions over a wide range of circumstances. To distinguish between them one must be able to isolate that one circumstance which will make a difference. But this is precisely what is impossible if one bars the use of experimental manipulation in principle. A reliance on data acquired by observation rather than experimental control is a reliance on data determined by circumstances as they *happen to occur* rather than as they are required by the demands of a good scientific test.[31]

Freud's reliance on explanatory power

In fact, for the most part, Freud did not even avail himself of the predictive possibilities that exist within the clinical setting. He seems to have believed that a theory could be justified solely on the basis of its explanatory power. If we take a close look at how Freud came to adopt his various theories, we see that he typically proceeded in the following way. First, he starts with various background assumptions—either inherited from other thinkers or determined by those of his own theories to which he is already committed. These, in conjunction with various observations, give rise to certain questions. Next, he attempts to formulate an answer to these questions and this answer constitutes his tentative hypothesis. He then attempts to justify his hypothesis by seeking further observations explainable by the hypothesis. If he finds such additional observations, he takes the hypothesis to be confirmed. However, if he comes upon evidence which does not fit his hypothesis, then the original hypothesis is frequently revised. The revised version is then tentatively accepted until such time as further recalcitrant data are found. Note that at no time in this process is the tentatively accepted hypothesis—either original or revised—subjected to rigorous predictive tests. As long as it can explain all relevant data at hand, Freud regards it as acceptable.[32]

A good illustration of Freud's research methodology can be found in the early development of Freud's ideas on the origins of neurosis. Freud's first theory of neurosis was developed jointly with Josef Breuer, a Viennese physician, on the basis of Breuer's experiences with a patient known as "Anna O." Anna was a woman of 21 who came to Breuer suffering from a host of "physical and psychological disturbances," including rigid paralysis and loss of sensation on her right side, impaired vision, a nervous cough, an aversion to eating, and impaired speaking abilities. In working with this patient, Breuer discovered that if, under hypnosis, Anna was able to express certain fantasies and memories connected with the original formation of her symptoms, then these symptoms would disappear. In addition to this discovery, two further observations played a critical role in suggesting to Freud and Breuer the explanation for Anna's symptomatology and behavior under hypnosis. First, they noted that all the memories, expression of which led to symptom reduction, stemmed from the time she was nursing her sick father, a time when she had to constantly suppress her feelings and emotions. This led to the view that it was precisely these unexpressed feelings and emotions which were at the root of her difficulties. As Freud put it:

> One was driven to assume that the illness occurred because the affects generated in the pathogenic situations had their normal outlet blocked, and that the essence of the illness lay in the fact that these "strangulated" affects were then put to an abnormal use. In part they remained as a permanent burden upon the patient's mental life and a source of constant excitation for it; and in part they underwent a transformation into unusual somatic innervations and inhibitions, which manifested themselves as the physical symptoms of the case. For this latter process we coined the term "hysterical conversion."[33]

The second observation was that the patient exhibited two states of consciousness, her normal state and a state of so-called *absence*. In the normal state, Anna had no memories of her pathogenic experiences, nor was she aware of the connections between these experiences and her symptoms. In contrast, during her periods of absence—and also during hypnosis—memories of these past, emotionally-charged experiences seemed to surface. The explanation of this fact, according to Freud, would have been "a most awkward business," were it not for the study of hypnotism.

> The study of hypnotic phenomena has accustomed us to what was at first a bewildering realization that in one and the same individual there can be several mental groupings, which can remain more or less independent of one another, which can "know nothing" of one another and which can alternate with one another in their hold upon consciousness.[34]

Freud goes on to say that a particularly striking case of this splitting of consciousness is the phenomenon of posthypnotic suggestion when a command given under hypnosis is subsequently carried out involuntarily, in the normal state. In fact, it was precisely this phenomenon of posthypnotic suggestion which Freud and Breuer used as a partial model for the etiology of hysterical conversion. What, then, made the difference in the case of Anna O.? Using posthypnotic suggestion as a model, Breuer suggested that the additional requirement was experiencing the pathogenic trauma in a hypnoidal state. On this view, according to Freud, "excitations occurring during these hypnoid states can easily become pathogenic because such states do not provide opportunities for the normal discharge of the process of excitation."[35] Hence, the formation of the symptom.

This, then, was the original theory. In attempting to apply this early theory to other patients, Freud discovered two facts that made him unhappy with the original picture. The first was that hypnosis was not really necessary for patients to bring their suppressed memories to consciousness. Instead of hypnosis Freud found he could use a technique of simply insisting to patients in their normal state that they could remember. Second, however, he found that using this new technique, his patients' attempts to recall forgotten memories were frequently accompanied by a great deal of mental struggle and what he came to call *resistance*. He first described this discovery in the case study of Elisabeth von R.:

> Throughout the analysis I made use of the technique of bringing out pictures and ideas by means of pressing on the patient's head, a method, that is, which would be unworkable without the patient's full co-operation and willing attention. Sometimes, indeed, her behaviour fulfilled my highest expectations, and during such periods it was surprising with what promptitude the different scenes relating to a given theme emerged in a strictly chronological order. . . . At other times there seemed to be impediments of whose nature I had no suspicion then. When I pressed her head she would maintain that nothing occurred to her. I would repeat my pressure and tell her to wait, but still nothing appeared. The first few times when this recalcitrance exhibited itself I allowed myself to be led into breaking off the work; it was an unfavourable day; we would try another time. Two observations, however, decided me to alter my attitude. I noticed, in the first place, that the method failed in this way only when I found Elisabeth in a cheerful state and free from pain, never when she was feeling badly. In the second place, that she often made such assertions as that she saw nothing, after she had allowed a long interval to pass during which her tense and preoccupied expression of face nevertheless betrayed the fact that a mental process was taking place in her. I resolved, therefore, to adopt the hypothesis that the procedure never failed: that on every occasion under the pressure of my hand some idea occurred to Elisabeth or some picture came before her eyes, but that she was not always prepared to communicate it to me, and tried to suppress once more what had been conjured up. I could think of two motives for this concealment. Either she was applying criticism to the idea, which she had no right to do, on the ground

of its not being important enough or of its being an irrelevant reply to the question she had been asked; or she hesitated to produce it because—she found it too disagreeable to tell. I therefore proceeded as though I was completely convinced of the trustworthiness of my technique. I no longer accepted her declaration that nothing had occurred to her, but assured her that something *must* have occurred to her. . . . By thus insisting, I brought it about that from that time forward my pressure on her head never failed in its effect. I could not but conclude that I had formed a correct opinion of the state of affairs. . . . In the course of this difficult work I began to attach a deeper significance to the resistance offered by the patient in the reproduction of her memories and to make a careful collection of the occasions on which it was particularly marked.[36]

To account for these two new facts (that is, that hypnosis was not necessary for recall of suppressed memories and that patients were subject to resistance), Freud modified the original Freud-Breuer theory by positing the existence of a force which he called *repression*. This force was designed to play a significant role in both the etiology of the patient's illness and in his or her response to therapy. Several years later, Freud explained his new theory of the etiology of neurosis thus:

All these [pathogenic situations which we had come to know] had involved the emergence of a wishful impulse which was in sharp contrast to the subject's other wishes and which proved incompatible with the ethical and aesthetic standards of his personality. There had been a short conflict, and the end of this internal struggle was that the idea which had appeared before consciousness as the vehicle of this irreconcilable wish fell a victim to repression, was pushed out of consciousness with all its attached memories, and was forgotten. Thus the incompatibility of the wish in question with the patient's ego was the motive for the repression; the subject's ethical and other standards were the repressing forces. An acceptance of the incompatible wishful impulse or a prolongation of the conflict would have produced a high degree of unpleasure; thus unpleasure was avoided by means of repression, which was thus revealed as one of the devices serving to protect the mental personality.[37]

In addition to explaining the onset of the neurotic process, the existence of the repressive force could be used to explain the phenomenon of resistance. Freud had only to assume that the same force which caused the forgetting in the first place was still operating in the present in the therapeutic context, preventing easy access to the forgotten material.

In fact, Freud was so impressed with the explanatory value of his repression hypothesis vis-à-vis the phenomenon of resistance that he reported the following in his "Five Lectures on Psycho-analysis": "I gave the name of 'repression' to this hypothetical process, and *I considered that it was proved by the undeniable existence of resistance*" (my emphasis).

Now, why did he consider it proved? The only possible answer is that he regarded it proved because of its *explanatory value*. And this was so because he regarded a high degree of explanatory power to be sufficient for the justification of a scientific theory. But, as we have seen, according to the standard scientific methodology this is not enough. A theory is not sufficiently justified unless it has been submitted to a variety of good scientific tests. And here Freud's methodology systematically falls short.

The Requirement of Objectivity

There is an additional requirement for assessing a theory or hypothesis in a scientific way—whether in terms of its explanatory power or in terms of its success on good scientific tests—and that concerns the nature of the data against which the assessment is made. The traditional way of putting this requirement is to say that data must be *objective*. But what do we mean by this?

Naively, to say data are objective is to say that they reflect the way things really are (in the object) rather than something in the person (subject) gathering the data. On the logical positivists' view of science, such objectivity was insured because the data of science were to be derived by observation, and observation, under suitable conditions, was regarded as immediate and untainted access to the observable properties of objects. Observable properties were simply there, in the real world; anyone who observed them properly, no matter what their conceptual commitments or beliefs might be, would be able to ascertain their existence and nature.

In recent years, this view has been severely criticized. Drawing largely on work in the psychology of perception, such critics as Norwood R. Hanson and Thomas Kuhn have suggested that observation always involves interpretation and such interpretation is relative to a person's conceptual apparatus, beliefs, expectations.[39] Observation is—as the slogan goes—"theory-laden." If we accept this revised view of observation, and there is ample psychological evidence to support it, then someone committed to the requirement that the data of science be objective seems faced with a dilemma. As Israel Scheffler remarks:

> Observation needs to be construed as independent of conceptual-
> ization if conceptualization is not to be simply arbitrary; yet, it
> cannot plausibly be thought to be independent of conceptualiza-
> tion. On the contrary, it is shot through with interpretation, ex-
> pectation, and wish. So, on the one hand, observation must be
> independent, and, on the other hand, it cannot be. To suppose it
> is independent commits us to an implausibly pure observational
> given, and makes a mystery of observational control over thought.
> To suppose, on the other hand, that it is not independent commits
> us rather to the view that apparent observational control is always
> circular and hence incapable of restricting the arbitrariness of con-
> ceptual differences. In any event, the standard notion of obser-
> vation as providing objective control over conception needs to be
> abandoned.[39]

Many contemporary philosophers of science, having accepted the
view that observation is theory-laden, have in fact opted for the second
horn of Scheffler's dilemma, regarding the acceptance and rejection of
scientific theories as more a matter of psychology, sociology, and politics,
than of rationality. As Scheffler has pointed out, however, this nonra-
tional picture of science is not entailed by acceptance of the view that
observation is theory-laden, for the dilemma described above is a false
one. It is possible for observation to be both theory-laden and theory-
neutral in all the ways that matter: theory-laden in a way that satisfies
the demands of empirical findings in the psychology of perception, yet
theory-neutral in the sense that what one observes is not influenced by
the *particular* theory undergoing assessment. That the scientific theories
and hypotheses to which we are committed *can* and often do influence
our perception of the world does not entail that they *must* do so. The
ideal of objective data is possible at least to this extent: that data relevant
to a given theory T can be collected by someone whether or not he or
she believes in T or even, in fact, whether or not he or she has knowledge
of T. Giere puts the point this way: The prediction of a good scientific
test "must be a statement that can reliably be determined to be true or
false using methods that do not themselves presuppose that the hypothesis in question is true."[40]

Scientists have become increasingly aware of the ways in which an
experimenter's bias toward his pet hypothesis can affect the outcome
of an experiment. With animal subjects, bias often operates in the re-
cording of observations; with human subjects, it can be unintentionally

conveyed in the communication of experimental instructions. The result of this increasing knowledge about the potential pitfalls of experimenter bias has not been despair over the inevitable irrationality and arbitrariness of scientific theorizing. Rather, it has been the adoption of new and more stringent controls to minimize or eliminate such bias. For example, the use of so-called double blind experimental procedure has become standard for experimentation with human subjects where important policy consequences hang on the outcome of experiments, for example, in drug and other medical research.[41]

In sum, we shall take the requirement of objectivity to be this: Data used for the empirical assessment of a scientific theory T must be objective, at least in the minimal sense that such data are determined independent of any commitment to T. The phrase "to determine a datum" here means "to determine the truth of a statement (we can call it a 'possible datum statement') describing a possible state-of-affairs which, if it were *actual*, would be regarded as an empirical datum."

Freud's use of interpreted data

We have seen that the data Freud relied on most heavily for the justification of his mature etiological hypotheses were data concerning the meaning or significance of his patient's dreams, slips of the tongue, jokes, and symptoms. All were regarded by Freud as expressions of the unconscious and all thus could be used to make inferences concerning the character of a person's repressed unconscious states. The procedure Freud developed for getting at these unconscious states consisted in eliciting from the patient descriptions of thoughts, feelings, and memories, reports of dreams, unconscious verbal slips, plus associations to each of these, and then subjecting this "clinical material" to a process of interpretation. The results of this process were *interpretations* which then constituted the evidential basis for his theoretical claims.

We have argued that a necessary condition of a research methodology being scientific is that the data it uses as the basis for accepting or rejecting a candidate hypothesis must be objective. The question now before us is this: Does the psychoanalytic method satisfy this requirement of objectivity? I shall argue that it does not—at least in its original Freudian form. It does not because the process which Freud used to arrive at interpretations which he took to be correct was theoretically-biased in an unacceptable way.

To make our case, we should first examine how Freud himself describes the method of interpretation at various points in his career.

Initially, Freud appears to have regarded the process of interpretation as a rule-governed procedure, whose correct utilization insured that the practitioner would sooner or later arrive at a correct interpretation. In 1904, he described the method thus:

> Freud has developed . . . an art of interpretation which takes on the task of, as it were, extracting the pure metal of the repressed thoughts from the ore of the unintentional ideas. This work of interpretation is applied not only to the patient's ideas but also to his dreams, which open up the most direct approach to a knowledge of the unconscious, to his unintentional as well as to his purposeless actions (symptomatic acts) and to the blunders he makes in everyday life (slips of the tongue, bungled actions, and so on). The details of this technique of interpretation or translation have not yet been published by Freud. According to indications he has given, they comprise *a number of rules, reached empirically, of how the unconscious material may be reconstructed from the associations,* directions on how to know what it means when the patient's ideas cease to flow and experiences of the most important typical resistances that arise in the course of such treatments.[42]

By 1923 his picture is quite different. The process of interpretation is now no longer seen as a rule-governed procedure. Rather, Freud conceives of it as a process of insightful problem-solving. Assigning an interpretation to a dream is like finding the solution to an extremely complicated jigsaw puzzle. The solution is not obtained by following rules, but by trial and error coupled with creative insight. Despite his altered conception, however, this view has something important in common with the rule-governed procedure. In both cases, the method of interpretation is regarded as a *discovery procedure,* such that if the procedure is carried out correctly, discovery of the actual meaning of the phenomenon being interpreted will result. What insures the correct outcome on Freud's first picture of the procedure are the rules themselves: what insures the correct outcome on the insightful problem-solving view are a number of *constraints* which must be satisfied for something to count as a solution to the problem. When an analyst considers whether or not a given interpretation is correct, according to Freud:

> What makes him certain in the end is precisely the complication of the problem before him, which is like the solution of a jig-saw puzzle. A coloured picture, pasted upon a thin sheet of wood and fitting exactly into a wooden frame, is cut into a large number of

pieces of the most irregular and crooked shapes. If one succeeds in arranging the confused heap of fragments, each of which bears upon it an unintelligible piece of drawing, so that the picture acquires a meaning, so that *there is no gap anywhere in the design and so that the whole fits into the frame—if all these conditions are fulfilled, then one knows that one has solved the puzzle and that there is no alternative solution.*[43]

Freud is clearly assuming that "gestalt" constraints analogous to those for a jigsaw puzzle apply in an interpretation, and that if these constraints are satisfied, a given interpretation will be correct.

He is not always this confident about the reliability of his procedure, however. As early as the 1917 lectures, he acknowledges that the physician may infer something "wrongly." But he does not seem to regard the problem as a serious one, for "anything that has been inferred wrongly by the physician will disappear in the course of the analysis; it must be withdrawn and replaced by something more correct."[44] What he means, of course, is that any mistaken interpretations will be corrected in the course of a *successful* analysis, that is, one in which the patient succeeds in overcoming inner resistances and achieving positive inner change.

This point is discussed at length 20 years later. Distinguishing between "interpretation," which applies to "some single element of material, such as an association or a parapraxis," and "construction," when one "lays before the subject of the analysis a piece of his early history that he has forgotten,"[45] Freud now compares construction to an archaeologist's excavation of some dwelling place that has been destroyed and buried. The new metaphor allows him to recognize that constructions, like archaeological hypotheses, are subject to "difficulties and sources of error." That is, no *discovery procedure* can guarantee the correctness of the proposed construction or hypothesis. This recognition gives rise to the following question: "What guarantee [do] we have while we are working on these constructions that we are not making mistakes and risking the success of the treatment by putting forward some construction that is incorrect."[46] His answer, in short, is that "only the further course of the analysis enables us to decide whether our constructions are correct or unserviceable,"[47] in particular, what further associations the proposed construction gives rise to in the patient, whether the analysis is therapeutically successful, and whether the patient comes to accept the truth of the construction.

This last picture of the method of interpretation does not so much undercut the insightful problem-solving view as force a revision in it. Individual interpretations (that is, interpretations of elements of the manifest content of a dream, single slips of the tongue, single symptoms, etc.) are arrived at by insight. To be correct, however, such interpretations must satisfy two sets of constraints: internal and external. The internal constraints are the gestalt constraints mentioned previously. Roughly, individual interpretations are correct only if they fit together into a meaningful whole—a "construction" in Freud's mature terminology—which makes sense of all the clinical material. But this is not sufficient, for Freud now admits that such an internally coherent construction might be false. Thus, as a further guarantee of its correctness, it must satisfy an external constraint: It must be a construction which, roughly speaking, plays a central role in a successful analysis.

If we assume this amalgamated picture to reflect fairly closely both Freud's mature view and his practice, we can now understand why Freud devotes so little time to *defending* the sample interpretations he gives us in his writings, especially in the context of the case studies. Explicit defense is not required, for what justifies a given interpretation in his view is given implicitly. The case studies present individual interpretations as part of a *whole construction*; furthermore, they are, presumably, case studies of *successful* (at least, in Freud's mind) analyses. In other words, that any given interpretation satisfies both internal and external constraints is implicit in the context in which these interpretations are given to the reader.

We are now in a position to evaluate Freud's method of interpretation as good scientific method. Precisely, what is it about Freud's use of the method of interpretation which raises questions about its scientific status?

We have argued that a research methodology is scientific only if the data it uses for the empirical assessment of candidate hypotheses and theories are arrived at independently of any commitment to the hypotheses and theories in question. Freud claimed his theories to be empirically well supported primarily on the basis of interpretative claims arrived at by the method of interpretation. These interpretative claims constituted his "data." The issue, then, is whether these interpretative claims were arrived at independently of the theory they were designed to support. The answer is clearly "no," but there are both simple-minded and more complex accounts which lead to this answer.

First, the simple-minded account. If we look carefully at the interpretations Freud offers us in his various case studies, it becomes readily apparent that his theoretical commitments strongly influence the kind of interpretations he comes up with. This happens in two ways. First, he often either actively solicits key associations (the material upon which interpretations are based) from his patients or actually supplies them himself.[48] Second, in arriving at interpretations that satisfy the gestalt constraints, the fundamental guiding principle which Freud seems to employ is "closeness of fit" with his theory. That is, what makes the separate interpretative pieces fit together is no more than that they all fit the theory.[49]

However, that his theory plays a significant role in the *generation* of interpretative claims is not alone sufficient to undercut the objectivity of Freud's interpretative data. For if the method of interpretation is construed along the lines of a hypothesis formation and test model, it is perfectly legitimate to *generate* interpretations (now, interpretative *hypotheses*) in the light of one's favorite theory so long as they will be subject to test procedures capable of ruling out the incorrect interpretations on independent grounds.[50] Thus, insofar as Freud supplements his internal constraints to guarantee the correctness of his interpretations with some theory-independent check, the existence of the above kinds of theoretical bias does not entail that data arrived at by the method of interpretation fails the requirement of objectivity. The problem arises only given the "theory-ladenness" of the Freudian interpretations coupled with a second fact, namely *that the external constraint which Freud relies on to insure the correctness of his interpretations is inadequate to do the job.* This, then, is the complex account of why Freud's method of interpretation fails the requirement of objectivity.

Grünbaum has recently discussed in considerable detail the pitfalls associated with using claims of therapeutic success as empirical support for Freudian theory.[51] In particular, he argues that Freud's reliance on the success of an analysis to vindicate the correctness of an interpretation offered in the context of that analysis is based on an inference with the following logical structure:

Tally Argument
(1) The analysis of Miss X was successful.
(2) A successful analysis is possible only if the patient solves his or her conflicts and overcomes his or her resistances; but this, in turn, is possible only if the interpretations offered the patient "tally" with what is real in him (i.e., are correct) (Necessary Condition Thesis)[52]
(3) Therefore, the interpretations which played a central role in Miss X's analysis must be correct.

It is by making implicit use of inferences with the above structure that Freud determines which of the interpretations he has generated he will regard as correct. Since the argument *form* is valid, the legitimacy of his validation procedure hangs on the status of the Necessary Condition Thesis.

Showing that the therapeutic success of psychoanalysis exceeds the spontaneous remission rate is not sufficient to justify the Necessary Condition Thesis, as Grünbaum has pointed out. It must further be shown that the relative success is due to features of the analytic situation *characteristic* of the psychoanalytic method, such as the use of the method of interpretation. But this is precisely what has not been shown. In fact, outcome studies suggest (a) that the success of psychoanalytic therapy may be due to *incidental* features of the situation, such as the establishment of a trust relationship between two people,[53] and (b) that nonanalytic therapeutic techniques can be equally effective. Since the Necessary Condition Thesis claims that the utilization of a correct interpretation is a necessary condition of therapeutic success, insofar as (a) or (b) are true, the Necessary Condition Thesis will be false.

There seems to be no reason for accepting the second premise of the Tally Argument, and hence the soundness of the argument itself, except a prior commitment to Freudian theory. But to the extent that such a commitment constitutes the basis for using the Tally Argument for determining the correctness of an interpretation, the resulting interpretative "data" will not be objective.

SUMMARY AND CONCLUSIONS

"Psychoanalysis" refers to a set of theories and hypotheses, a research methodology, and a therapeutic technique. Since what makes a theory scientific may be distinct from what makes a research methodology scientific, and what makes a research methodology scientific may be distinct from what makes a therapeutic technique scientific, any detailed exploration of the question of the scientific status of psychoanalysis must deal separately with each of its aspects. In this paper, we consider only the question of the scientific status of Freudian theory and the question of the scientific status of Freud's research methodology.

Philosophers of science generally agree that a necessary condition of a theory's being scientific is that it be falsifiable. Psychoanalytic theory has been charged with being unscientific on the grounds of being unfalsifiable. To evaluate this challenge, we should look more closely at what is meant by "falsifiability." It turns out that all obvious formulations of the notion of falsifiability are inadequate. The Popperian version presupposes that a theory T conjoined with a statement of initial conditions IC can itself entail an observable prediction P. Since most paradigmatically scientific theories do not satisfy this assumption, the Popperian version is too strong. However, the simple addition of auxiliary assumptions to the formulation results in a notion of falsifiability which is far too weak. An adequate version requires the addition of constraints on what sort of auxiliary assumptions may be added. Such constraints can be of two kinds. Either we can require that the auxiliary assumptions must be *accepted* by a research community or we can require that they must be *true*. The first requirement results in the relativization of falsifiability to a research community (the "Modified Epistemic Version"); the second requires a judgment as to the truth of the auxiliary assumptions in question (the "Modified Factive Version").

We consider first the falsifiability of Freudian theory on the Epistemic Version. Two kinds of auxiliary assumptions and two research communities are relevant to the assessment: assumptions used by Freud himself vs. assumptions added for the purpose of experimental test, and the orthodox research community vs. the experimental psychological community. We call Freudian theory plus the original assumptions the "Original Extended Theory" and Freudian theory plus the added assumptions the "New Extended Theory." A consideration of the acceptability of each of these kinds of assumptions to the two research communities yields the following conclusions:

> (1) The Original Extended Theory is falsifiable relative to the orthodox Freudian community but is not falsifiable relative to the experimental psychological community.
> (2) The New Extended Theory, in contrast, is not falsifiable relative to the orthodox Freudian community but is falsifiable relative to the experimental psychological community.

With respect to the Factive Version of Falsifiability, I argue that we ought to reject Freud's original auxiliary assumptions concerning the validity of the method of interpretation, but that there is no *a priori* reason to rule out experimental auxiliary assumptions as true. Thus on the Factive Version, the Original Extended Theory is not falsifiable whereas the New Extended Theory is.

An assessment of the Freudian research methodology requires that we say something about what makes a research methodology scientific. Two requirements are discussed: the so-called requirement of a good scientific test and the so-called requirement of objectivity. I argue that the way Freud typically went about justifying his theoretical claims fails both of these requirements. His research methodology fails the requirement of a good scientific test because of his reliance on the clinical setting for gathering data and because of his reliance on explanatory power as a sufficient mark of truth. It fails the requirement of objectivity because the sort of data he relied on most heavily, interpretative data, was typically arrived at by assuming the truth of the very theories it was intended to support.

An interesting result of our investigation is that the answers to our three component questions turn out to bear on one another in several ways. To decide whether the Original Extended Theory is factively falsifiable requires an assessment of Freud's research methodology. Furthermore, to decide whether the research methodology is scientific requires an assessment of the scientific status of the therapeutic technique in the form of an evaluation of the so-called Necessary Condition Thesis.

Is psychoanalysis scientific? We can summarize our findings in this way: Freudian theory is perfectly scientific in the sense of being a *candidate* for scientific testing, so long as we do not restrict ourselves to Freud's methodological assumptions. However, since Freud's own research methodology was seriously deficient from a scientific point of view, the *orthodox* grounds for regarding the theory as empirically well founded are not acceptable. Neither Freudian interpretations which appear to support the theory nor the success of analysis as a therapeutic technique provide scientifically acceptable evidence for the truth of the theory. Thus, although the theory can be considered scientific in the minimal sense, whether it will prove to be *good* science remains to be seen.

NOTES

[1]See, for example, Sigmund Freud, "The Claims of Psycho-analysis to Scientific Interest," first published in *Scientia* 14 (1913), 240-250; 369-384; also included in *SE* vol. 13, 165-193.

[2]Karl R. Popper, *Conjectures and Refutations: The Growth of Scientific Knowledge* (New York: Harper Torchbooks, 1968), pp. 34-35.

[3]Popper, p. 35.

[4]Popper, p. 36. When Popper speaks of "falsifying" a theory here, he means, of course, something like "determining it to be false (i.e., not true)."

[5]Ernest Nagel, "Methodological Issues in Psychoanalytic Theory," in *Psychoanalysis, Scientific Method, and Philosophy*, ed. Sidney Hook (New York: New York University Press, 1959), p. 39.

[6]See especially Karl Popper, *The Logic of Scientific Discovery* (New York: Harper & Row; Harper Torchbooks, 1965), pp. 84-92.

[7]See Popper, *Logic*, p. 107, n. 3.

[8]F. Suppe, *The Structure of Scientific Theories* (Urbana: University of Illinois Press, 1974), pp. 16-27, 102-110, gives a useful summary of the history of this discussion.

[9]See K. Schaffner, "Correspondence Rules," *Philosophy of Science*, 36:280-290; P. Suppes, "Models of Data" in *Logic, Methodology, and Philosophy of Science: Proceedings of the 1960 International Congress*, eds. E. Nagel, P. Suppes, and A. Tarski (Stanford: Stanford University Press, 1962), pp. 252-261; and P. Suppes, "What is a Scientific Theory?" in *Philosophy of Science Today*, ed. Sidney Morgenbesser (New York: Basic Books, 1967), pp. 55-67.

[10]Pierre Duhem, *The Aim and Structure of Physical Theory*, (Princeton: Princeton University Press, 1954), published originally in 1906, pp. 188-190. Popper's own stand on these matters is not entirely clear. In some places, he seems to concede the Duhemian point. See, for example, *Conjectures and Refutations*, p. 112. Yet, in other places, he continues to maintain the possibility of a crucial falsifying experiment. I suspect the problem is that he believes Duhemian revision always consists in the *addition* of ad hoc hypotheses to the theory being tested, rather than the modification of auxiliary hypotheses which are required from the outset.

[11]A similar point is made by Michael Martin in "Mr. Farrell and the Refutability of Psychoanalysis," *Inquiry*, 7 (1964), 81-82. There he argues that if "T is a refutable theory" means it is "possible to give theory T, in which the relation between the theoretical and observational language is extremely vague and ambiguous, a clear and unambiguous formulation," then such paradigm cases of irrefutable theories as that the Absolute is perfect and is developing in history or that an all-good, all-powerful God exists will be refutable. The reason is that one can always add correspondence rules designed to link them with observational consequences.

[12]Modus tollens is the logical principle which licenses the following sort of inference:

If α then β.

It is not the case that β.

Therefore, it is not the case that α.

where "α" and "β" are linguistic variables for which any sentence may be substituted. For us to conclude that α is false on the basis of such an argument, we must assume that the two premises of the argument are *true*.

[13]See Adolf Grünbaum, "Is Freudian Psychoanalytic Theory Pseudo-Scientific by Karl Popper's Criterion of Demarcation?" *American Philosophical Quarterly*, 16 (April, 1979), 131-141. Unfortunately, Grünbaum does not attempt to spell out what falsifiability comes to in any detail and thus fails to distinguish the question of the falsifiability of the theory relative to auxiliary hypotheses accepted by Freud and the question of its falsifiability relative to auxiliary hypotheses expressly formulated by research psychologists for the purpose of testing the theory.

[14]"Notes Upon a Case of Obsessional Neurosis," *SE* vol. 10, 155-318.

[15]Grünbaum, p. 137. Grünbaum credits C. Glymour ("Freud, Kepler and the Clinical Evidence" in *Freud*, ed. Richard Wollheim (New York: Anchor Books, 1974)), for noting the first example.

[16]Sigmund Freud, "Heredity and the Aetiology of the Neuroses" (1896) *SE* vol. 3, 149.

[17]Sigmund Freud, *Letters to Wilhelm Fleiss, Drafts and Notes: 1887-1902*, eds. Marie Bonaparte, Anna Freud, and Ernst Kris (New York: Basic Books, 1954), p. 216.

[18]The theory of neurosis to be sketched is taken from Freud's *General Introduction to Psychoanalysis* (New York: Simon & Schuster, Inc.: Pocket Books, 1975), pp. 255-386, a set of lectures originally presented from 1915-1917. The theory of psychosexual development is taken from "Three Essays on Sexuality" in *SE* vol. 7, 135-243.

[19]Freud defines a traumatic experience thus: "An experience which we call traumatic is

one which within a very short space of time subjects the mind to such a very high increase of stimulation that assimilation or elaboration of it can no longer be effected by normal means, so that lasting disturbances must result in the distribution of the available energy in the mind." See *General Introduction*, p. 286.

[20]*Ibid.*, p. 295.

[21]Sigmund Freud, "My Views on the Part Played by Sexuality in the Aetiology of the Neuroses," *SE* vol. 7, 278. See also Freud's "Three Essays on Sexuality," same volume, for a similar statement.

[22]For a review of recent work, see S. Fisher and R. P. Greenberg, *The Scientific Credibility of Freud's Theories and Therapy* (New York: Basic Books, 1977).

[23]Sigmund Freud, *Three Case Studies* (New York: Collier Books, Macmillan, 1963), p. 163.

[24]H. S. Zamansky, "An Investigation of the Psychoanalytic Theory of Paranoid Delusions," *Journal of Personality*, 26 (1958), 410-425.

[25]Zamansky, p. 411.

[26]The paranoid subjects tended, on the average, to look 1.49 seconds longer at pictures of men in the unconscious preference task when pairs of pictures were presented consisting of one female picture and one male picture. This was significant at beyond the .001 level. When paranoid subjects were asked to state which picture they preferred, they selected a significantly greater number of female pictures than they did when their preference was assessed by determining which picture they tended to look at longer. In contrast, the control group manifested the same degree of preference when asked explicitly and when monitored for fixation. Out of nine male-female picture pairs, paranoids preferred, on the average, 5.75 female pictures on the basis of verbal preference but only 2.80 on the basis of fixation preference. The control subjects preferred 5.80 on the basis of verbal preference and 5.60 on the basis of fixation preference. The difference for the experimental group was significant at the .001 level.

[27]Quoted from D. Shakow and D. Rapaport, *The Influence of Freud on American Psychology* (Cleveland: World Publishers, 1968), p. 129.

[28]Concern over Freudian methodology has been expressed by philosophers and experimental psychologists, as well as by analysts themselves. With respect to the philosophical literature, see, especially, the following: Ernest Nagel, "Methodological Issues in Psychoanalytic Theory," in *Psychoanalysis, Scientific Method, and Philosophy*, ed. Sidney Hook (New York: New York University Press, 1959), pp. 38-56; Michael Martin, "The Scientific Status of Psychoanalytic Clinical Evidence," *Inquiry*, 7 (1964), 13-36; Frank Cioffi, "Freud and the Idea of a Pseudo-Science," in *Explanation in the Behavioural Sciences*, eds. Robert Borger and Frank Cioffi (Cambridge: University Press, 1970), pp. 471-499; and, more recently, Adolf Grünbaum, "Epistemological Liabilities of the Clinical Appraisal of Psychoanalysis," *Psychoanalysis and Contemporary Thought*, 2 (1979), 451-526.

[29]There are even philosophers of science who take the extreme view that there is no such thing as scientific methodology—that, as it were, "anything goes." See Paul Feyerabend, *Against Method* (London: Verso, 1975).

[30]Ronald N. Giere, *Understanding Scientific Reasoning* (New York: Holt, Rinehart and Winston, 1979), p. 94. Although Giere's formulation will do for our purposes, it is not entirely satisfactory from a technical point of view. This is because it is unclear what notion of probability Giere has in mind in Condition 2. A technically satisfactory formulation would include elaboration on this point.

[31]A similar point is made by Grünbaum specifically with respect to the validation of causal claims in the clinical setting. See "Epistemological Liabilities of the Clinical Appraisal of Psychoanalytic Theory," p. 509.

[32]In a recent book on Freud, the psychoanalyst Erich Fromm vindicates Freud's scientific method by describing the *norm* in a way which comes close to our description of Freud's method. He writes:

What is the procedure today which constitutes the scientific method both in the natural sciences and in legitimate social science?

(1) The scientist does not start out from nothing; rather his thinking is determined by his previous knowledge and by the challenge of unexplored areas.

(2) Most minute and detailed exploration of phenomena is the condition of optimal objectivity. It is characteristic of the scientist that he has the greatest respect for the observable phenomena: many great discoveries have been made because a scientist paid attention to a small event which was seen but ignored by everybody else.

(3) On the basis of the known theories and the optimum of detailed knowledge, he formulates a hypothesis. The function of a hypothesis should be to bring some order to the observed phenomena and to arrange them tentatively in such a way that they seem to make some sense. It is also essential that the researcher is capable at every moment of observing new data which may contradict his hypothesis and lead to its revision and so *ad infinitum*.

(4) This scientific method requires of course that the scientist is at least relatively free from wishful and narcissistic thinking; that is to say, that he can observe the facts objectively without distorting them or giving them inadequate weight because he is so eager to prove that his hypothesis is right.

Erich Fromm, *Greatness and Limitations of Freud's Thought* (New York: Harper & Row, 1980), p. 12.

What Fromm leaves out, of course, is the importance of *testing* a theory or hypothesis once it has been formulated and tentatively accepted. Like Freud, Fromm seems to believe that a theory is acceptable so long as it "bring[s] some order to the observed phenomena" and there are no data which contradict it. But as I have tried to argue, this constitutes only a minimal condition of acceptability.

[33]Sigmund Freud, "Five Lectures on Psycho-analysis," in *SE* vol. 11, 18.

[34]*SE* vol. 11, 19.

[35]*SE* vol. 11, 19.

[36]Sigmund Freud, "Case Histories," *SE* vol. 2, 153-154.

[37]Sigmund Freud, "Five Lectures," *SE* vol. 11, 24.

[38]Thomas Kuhn, *The Structure of Scientific Revolutions* (Chicago: University of Chicago Press, 1962), and Norwood R. Hanson, *Patterns of Discovery* (Cambridge: University Press, 1958).

[39]Israel Scheffler, *Science and Subjectivity* (Indianapolis: Bobbs-Merrill, 1967), p. 23.

[40]Giere, p. 95.

[41]For a review of some relevant literature, see James R. Craig and Leroy P. Metze, *Methods of Psychological Research* (Philadelphia: Saunders, 1979).

[42]Sigmund Freud, "Freud's Psycho-analytic Procedure," *SE* vol. 7, 252. My emphasis.

[43]Sigmund Freud, "Remarks on the Theory and Practice of Dream Interpretation," *SE* vol. 19, 116. My emphasis.

[44]Sigmund Freud, "Introductory Lectures on Psycho-analysis (1916-1917)", *SE* vol. 16, 452.

[45]Sigmund Freud, "Constructions in Analysis," (1937), *SE* vol. 23, 261.

[46]*SE* vol. 23, 261.

[47]*SE* vol. 23, 265.

[48]For particularly blatant examples of this practice, see Freud's interpretation of Dora's first dream in "Fragment of an Analysis of a Case of Hysteria," *SE* vol. 7, 64-93.

[49]Frank Cioffi puts the point this way:

Examination of Freud's interpretations will show that he typically proceeds by beginning with whatever content his theoretical preconceptions compel him to maintain underlies the symptoms, and then, by working back and forth between it and the explanadum, constructing persuasive but spurious links between them. It is this which enables him to find allusions to the father's coital breathing in attacks of dyspnoea, fellatio in *tussis nervosa*, defloration in migraine, orgasm in an hysterical loss of consciousness, birth pangs in appendicitis, pregnancy wishes in hysterical vomiting, pregnancy fears in anorexia, an accouchement in a suicidal leap, castration fears in an obsessive preoccupation with hat tipping, masturbation in the practice of squeezing blackheads, the anal theory of birth in an hysterical constipation, parturition in a falling cart-horse, nocturnal emissions in bedwetting, unwed motherhood in a limp, guilt over the practice of seducing pubescent girls in the compulsion to sterilize banknotes before passing them on, etc. ("Freud and the Idea of the Pseudo-science," p. 497).

Detailed documentation for this point can be found in Joseph Wolpe and Stanley Rachman, "Psychoanalytic Evidence: A Critique Based on Freud's Case of Little Hans," in *Critical Essays on Psychoanalysis*, ed. Stanley Rachman (New York: Macmillan, 1963), pp. 198-220, and Sebastiano Timpanaro, "The Freudian Slip," *New Left Review*, 91 (May/June, 1975), 43-56.

[50]This is a perfectly legitimate procedure *once the theory has been established*. What is at issue is the legitimacy of arriving at an interpretation in the light of a theory which has not yet been empirically justified and for which the interpretation is to count as evidence.

[51]Grünbaum, "Epistemological Liabilities of the Clinical Appraisal of Psychoanalytic Theory."

[52]Grünbaum's formulation of the Necessary Condition Thesis is slightly different, namely, "Only psychoanalytic interpretations that 'tally with what is real' in the patient can mediate veridical insight, and such insight, in turn, is causally necessary for the successful alleviation of the patient's neurosis" (*ibid.*, p. 464). This thesis is attributed to Freud based on the following quote. Speaking about a patient in analysis, Freud writes: "After all, his conflicts will only be successfully solved and his resistances overcome if the anticipatory ideas he is given tally with what is real in him" ("Introductory Lectures," p. 452).

[53]For a discussion of this point, see A. K. Shapiro and L. A. Morris, "The Placebo Effect in Medicine, Psychoanalysis, and Psychological Therapies," in *Handbook of Psychotherapy and Behavior Change*, eds. A. E. Bergin and S. L. Garfield (New York: Wiley, 1978), pp. 369-410.

Chapter 10

Freud's *Three Essays on the Theory of Sexuality:* A Problem in Intellectual History

Sander L. Gilman

In the past few years there has been more and more interest in seeing Sigmund Freud's contribution to depth psychology in the light of the intellectual and historical milieu of fin-de-siècle Vienna. Frank J. Sulloway, in his *Freud: Biologist of the Mind* (New York: Basic Books, 1979), pointed out again Freud's debt to late nineteenth-century science. To understand Freud, however, it is necessary to abandon the compartmentalization of knowledge which the very title of Sulloway's volume suggests. He sees the "universe" of biological knowledge as somehow discrete from other manners of seeing man. What strikes us most in an examination of Freud's thinking in the light of the history of ideas is how his views continued and expanded upon problems and solutions found in a wide range of areas, from the physiology of Ernst Brücke and Hermann Helmholtz to the popular theater of Theodor Herzl, Arthur Schnitzler, and Hermann Bahr. Rather than attempting a superficial reading of Freud's thought in the light of certain problems in the history of ideas, which would be encyclopedic in scope, I have decided to concentrate on one exemplary problem from Freud's *Three Essays on the Theory of Sexuality* (1905). This volume, more than any other, gave Freud's name its slightly disreputable tinge through the presentation of his theory of infantile sexuality.

THE PUZZLE

We begin with a conundrum set by a master puzzle solver. Steven Marcus, in his lucid introduction to the American paperback edition of Freud's *Three Essays on the Theory of Sexuality* (1905), presents the riddle so:

> One can add as a piece of crowning confusion the following leap in the dark from the second essay. In his discussion of the polymorphous perverse sexuality of children Freud pauses for an illustration: "In this respect children behave in the same kind of way as an average uncultivated woman in whom the same polymorphous perverse disposition persists. Under ordinary conditions she may remain normal sexually, but if she is led on by a clever seducer she will find every sort of perversion to her taste, and will retain them as part of her own sexual activities. Prostitutes exploit the same polymorphous, that is, infantile, disposition for the purposes of their profession; and considering the immense number of women who are prostitutes or who must be supposed to have an aptitude for prostitution without becoming engaged in it, it becomes impossible not to recognize that this same disposition to perversions of every kind is a general and fundamental human characteristic." One doesn't know where to look for a handle to these remarks. It is even difficult to frame a context that might make discussion of them pertinent. Perhaps we can do no better than repeat the waggish observation that it is very difficult to know the meaning of a statement about Freud being right or wrong since he is always both.[1]

Resolving the puzzle of Freud's illustration with its analogy to childhood sexuality, polymorphous perversity and prostitution requires "framing the context" in which the stereotypes of female sexuality were generated in fin-de-siècle Vienna. An understanding of the various models of female sexuality which existed side by side at the turn of the century can supply the missing interrelationship among the diverse elements in Marcus' riddle. As he suggests, Freud's views are neither "right nor wrong," but rather reflect an amalgam of the inconsistencies and contradictions surrounding the idea of female sexuality in 1905. To pinpoint these inner tensions, an example documenting the overlapping of various stereotypes can be very revealing.[2] The borderland between the stereotypes of childhood sexuality, proletarian sexuality, and the prostitute exists in the image of the child prostitute. Here the child serves as the sexual object, with all the mystique surrounding sexuality, childhood, and approachability preserved. With this image we can begin our unraveling of Marcus' puzzle.

THE MEDICO-LEGAL BACKGROUND

The view that sexuality exists in early childhood permeates the medical literature of the late eighteenth and nineteenth centuries, at least in the extensive literature dealing with masturbation and its results.[3] Masturbation came to be viewed as the central medical problem since it was seen to be the cause of physical collapse and, as Voltaire observed, premature death.[4] The medical literature on female masturbation, such as D. M Rozier's monograph on the "secret habits of the woman," first published in 1825, stressed the permanent damage to the development of the psyche as well as to the organism.[5] Masturbation was viewed as a deviant sexual state leading to other pathologies, including sexual ones.

By the 1880s the primary role which masturbation had played as the major etiology of mental as well as physical illness had all but vanished from the medical literature. Richard Krafft-Ebing, in his *Psychopathia sexualis* (1888), viewed the entire problem of childhood masturbation as peripheral.[6] He was able to summarize the half-dozen cases taken from contemporary sources quite cursorily. While all dealt with varieties of masturbation, only two resulted in further sexual activity. One described an eight-year-old girl "who consorted with boys of the age of ten or twelve" after a history of masturbation, and the other a girl who from the age of seven "practised lewdness with boys." Hermann Rohleder refers to the latter case in his *Lectures on the Sexual Drive* (1901), condemning the activities of this "horror of a child" ("Ein solches Scheusal von Kind").[7] In a lecture held before the Viennese Psychiatric and Neurological Association in 1902, Alfred Fuchs described two cases of sexuality in children. The first was a case of masturbation in a 20-month-old boy, the second a case of mutual masturbation which led to further sexual activity in a two-year-old girl.[8] In all these cases the sexual activity of the child in the form of masturbation is viewed as pathological. Only in the case of the female children, however, is further sexual activity perceived as a pathological result of early childhood masturbation. Indeed, Krafft-Ebing's report of the eight-year-old girl who "consorted with boys of the age of ten or twelve" condemns the girl as "devoid of all child-like and moral feelings" without any comment on the sexuality of her youthful partners.

The labeling of sexual activity—whether masturbatory, heterosexual, or homosexual—as pathological when found in children reflects the stereotype of the "pure child" present in Romantic thought.[9] The early nineteenth century saw the child almost as noncorporeal, the polar opposite to the pathological sensuality of the masturbator. Jakob Christoph Santlus, in his *Psychology of the Human Drives* (1864), stressed the acquisition of sexuality in the normal course of maturity. Female sexuality was also thought to assume a mode of development different from male sexuality, for the normal female acquired sexual awareness only at the moment of menarche: "How many girls are not horrified when they begin to menstruate and with the menses the first sexual sensations are felt."[10] In the female all sexuality existing before puberty was perceived as pathological, while in the male only masturbatory sexuality was so understood.

While the medical literature of the time condemned or ignored early sexual activity in females, the public health texts of the nineteenth century could not treat this question quite as cavalierly, for in Vienna's daily life the existence of child prostitutes could not be ignored. While parallel references to the existence of at least 200 regular prostitutes under the age of 12 in Liverpool during 1857[11] cannot be cited for Vienna, certain extrapolations can be made from the statistics available concerning registered prostitutes in the last third of the nineteenth century. During the first decade of registration, from 1873 to 1883, the majority of registered prostitutes in Vienna were legally minors.[12] The minimum age for registration during this decade was 14, which meant that more than 50 percent of the approximately 1500 registered prostitutes were between the ages of 14 and 21. Indeed, in the first year of registration (1873), 14 15-year-old prostitutes were registered and in the following year there were an additional three 14-year-olds and four 15-year-olds. The youthfulness of registered prostitutes replicates the findings of the age of prostitutes in Edinburgh for a similar time in the nineteenth century.[13] One can extrapolate from the Viennese statistics, as one can from those from Edinburgh, that a trade in child prostitution existed in Vienna as it did in Great Britain and elsewhere in Europe during the nineteenth century.

By the first decade of the new century, the Viennese laws concerning the registration of prostitutes were tightened. In the regulations dated June 1, 1911, the minimum age for registration had risen to 18, with, however, a caveat: "Minors may be assigned to supervision . . . only when complete moral indifference, without any hope of betterment, had been unmistakeably ascertained."[14] The law covered all minors, even those below the legal age of registration, if their actions revealed a total and innate lack of the moral standards of the dominant society. This, of course, is the social category for the child prostitute. The higher age limit emphasizes the gap between the arbitrary legal definition of the child and the realities of daily life in Vienna.

The existence of child prostitution in Vienna during the mid-nineteenth century can be further extrapolated from Friedrich Hügel's programmatic public health study of 1865, which proposed the establishment of registration for prostitutes and the opening of licensed brothels. One of his central aims was the elimination of child prostitution. He wished to exclude all prostitutes under the age of 16 from his proposed houses of prostitution.[15] In reality, only prostitutes younger than 14 were excluded from registration, once this was introduced as a result of the 1873 Viennese World's Fair. Hügel's work also offers a 20-point catalogue of the sources of prostitution.[16] This list bears examination since it reflects the dominant male (Viennese) view of the nature of the prostitute and the causes for her deviant behavior. The list begins with the "bad education of girls in general, but especially those from the lowest classes." Girls are exposed to the "immoral discourses and acts" of their parents and the ubiquitous boarders *(Bettgeherleute)*, whose presence in most lower-class homes was an economic necessity. The home is thus the breeding ground for future prostitutes. The poverty of the home makes the luxurious life of the prostitute attractive. Also within the home the initial sexual experience occurs. The seduction of the child by her parents is common. "Fathers and daughters living together in concubinage; —fathers living off the ill-gotten gains of the daughters . . .". Poverty, unemployment, low payment for female workers are paralleled by Hügel to the biological and psychological weaknesses of the female. She is physically weaker, more given to "coquettery, love of pleasure, dislike of work, desire for luxury and ostentation, love of ornament, alcoholism, avarice, immorality, etc." These are seen as the innate qualities of the lower-class, poorly educated female.

Lord Acton, in the classic mid-Victorian study of prostitution (1857), had prefigured Hügel's categories, seeing the origin of prostitution as being "derived from the vice of women": "Natural desire. Natural sinfullness. The preferment of indolent ease to labour. Vicious inclination strengthened and ingrained by early neglect, or evil training, bad associates, and an indecent mode of life. Necessity, imbued by the inability to obtain a living by honest means consequent on a fall from virtue. Extreme poverty. To the black list may be added love of drink, love of dress, love of amusement."[17] While Acton, like Hügel, finds in the economic pattern of nineteenth-century society the catalyst that creates the prostitute, he also sees the potential for prostitution as inherent in the lower-class female.

The inherent tendency of lower-class females to enter into prostitution is reflected in the image of the female as the active seductress. Acton sees the woman as the temptress and the laws punishing her putative seducer as laws that are meant to "strengthen, by the very firm abutment of the breeches-pocket, both him and his good resolutions against the temptations and force of designing women."[18] The question of who seduced whom reflected the image of the female as sexual predator which permeated late nineteenth-century thought.[19] Argued to its final stage, it would provide the ultimate rationale for considering the prepubescent female as the cause of her own seduction. Her sexuality was seen as pathological and externally directed.

The ambiguous view of childhood sexual activity found in the public health literature of the nineteenth century has a remarkable parallel in late nineteenth-century Austrian law. Paragraph 127 of the *Austrian Criminal Code* makes it a crime to have sexual relations with any one under the age of 14 *(Nothzucht)*.[20] This seems clear and absolute, paralleling as it does the minimum age for the registration of prostitutes and the presumed age of menarche.[21] (Fourteen was also the age of consent in Austria and was the lowest on the continent in the nineteenth century. As puberty and the age of consent were held to be coterminus in both Roman and Canon Law, one can assume an implied legal equivalency in Austrian law.)

Paragraph 128 concerning cases of sexual abuse other than penetration *(Schändung)* with children under the age of 14 was the subject of a court decision which modified its interpretation, as well as that of the preceding paragraph. The Highest Court *(Oberster Gerichts- und Cassationshof)* held on February 3, 1858, that in order to prove a case of indecent assault it was necessary to prove that "the minor with whom the immoral act was performed, had been the passive participant." This ruling seems to recognize the potential of the minor as the seductress. The law reflected at least some of the stereotypical perceptions of the female child held by medicine during the fin-de-siècle. Both medicine and law assumed a potential sexual pathology in the female which could manifest itself even in the female child.

THE PORNOGRAPHIC VIEW

In 1906, shortly after Freud published his *Three Essays on Sexuality*, a work appeared in Vienna which has established itself as the classic work of pornography in German. *Josefine Mutzenbacher, or the History of a Viennese Whore As Told by Herself* reflects the mock autobiographic structure of the numerous fictional accounts of the lives of prostitutes beginning at least as early as *Moll Flanders* (or perhaps as far back as Rojas' *The Spanish Bawd*). In eighteenth-century Vienna, a series of pornographic novels had appeared written in the same autobiographic mode purporting to chronicle the lives of the lower-class serving girl in Vienna.[22] In these reverse *Pamelas* the seduction of the serving girl prepares her for a rich (and varied) life as a prostitute. However, all these works deal with female characters above the legal age of consent. Here *Josefine Mutzenbacher* is the exception. The novel presents the sexual history of a female child from the ages of five to 14. Indeed, the novel closes at the very age and the very moment when Josefine enters into the life of a registered prostitute in Vienna.

The uniqueness of the age and adventures of the most successful pornographic heroine in German letters can to no little extent be judged by the sequels to the novel. Published during the 1930s and evidently written by hands other than the author of the original, *My 365 Lovers* as well as *My Daughter Peperl* dealt with heroines who were at least at the age of consent.[23] The latter work, chronicling the pornographic adventures of Josefine's daughter, consciously rejects the pattern established by the earlier novel and begins with a pubescent protagonist. One further criterion for an evaluation of the uniqueness of *Josefine Mutzenbacher*'s stress on the youth of its protagonist is the demographic fact that the average age of first marriage for females in Austria during the fin-de-siècle was the mid-twenties (between 26.3 in 1871 to 25.3 in 1910).[24] Indeed, a contemporary writing on the question in 1904 sees the "natural" age for marriage for the female as 20.[25] The youth of the protagonist would have thus seemed an even greater factor distancing her from normal women.

Josefine Mutzenbacher is set in the world of the Viennese proletariat, a world that, according to a contemporary, supplies the majority of Vienna's criminals and prostitutes.[26] The tiny apartment of the Mutzenbachers is crowded with the five-member family (two brothers in addition to Josephine) and a boarder. The novel, as with all pornographic works, is a series of sexual scenes, beginning with Josephine's "seduction" by a boarder at the age of five. The seducer, part of the extended family, plays the role of a voyeur, observing but not touching the child. The five-year-old's reaction is mixed. She "wanted to scream but he said to her 'Be good. I won't do anything.' "[27] Her second reaction mirrors the insight attributed to the fictional character when she retrospectively observes that she "did not understand any of this and as is a child's want, I did not think about it. Today I know what it means, and I refer to the carpenter's apprentice as my first lover" (p. 10).

Fear of sexuality and its repression through feigned ignorance are implied by Josefine's sense of her own sexual curiosity, at least as perceived by the anonymous but certainly male author.[28] If the carpenter's seduction has nourished the psychological seed of polymorphous sexuality present in the child, the second episode of the work brings her sexuality to full flower. At the age of seven she is introduced into the world of heterosexuality by a brother and sister, 13 and nine years old respectively, who have been engaging in incestuous coupling. She observes the sexual acts of the two "with a feeling, composed of curiosity, amazement, horror, and yet an up-to-now strange excitement" (p. 12). The world of Josefine's playmates is that of poverty. Their home has been shattered by the death of their mother and the absence of the father. The nine-year-old girl seduces Josefine's brother, who is approximately the same age. Yet their sexuality is adult, concluding with mutual orgasm. The child has become the adult *in nuce*.

According to Josefine's account, at the age of seven, confronted with the sexuality of her peers, she became aware of her own sexuality:

> Since that day I see children and adults, men and women through other eyes. I was only seven years old, but my sexuality was fully present. It could be read in my eyes. My face, my mouth, my gait must have been a single invitation to grab me and lay me down. I can only explain the effect which emanated from me . . . which made strange and, it seemed to me, prudent men after meeting me, lose all sense of prudence and risk everything without a second thought (p. 17).

This is the voice of the woman as temptress at the age of seven. Within the opening pages of the novel, the newly discovered sexuality of the child seduces other members of her extended family, her brother and her cousins. But Josefine's physical immaturity, her inability to engage in genital sexual contact are stressed by the author and paralleled to her demand for sexual stimulation. The sexual acts in which Josefine engages with her brother and cousins run the gamut of nongenital sexual variations. The polymorphous quality of Josefine's sexual interest is evident when she attempts to blackmail Horak, the beer deliveryman, into having genital sex with her. When this proves to be impossible, her desire for the sexual act encourages the adult to introduce her into anal sexuality. Within the first 40 pages of the novel, Josefine has had various sexual misadventures with three adults, including an anonymous soldier, as well as two other children—Robert, who had been earlier seduced by his stepmother, and a nameless seven-year-old who pounces upon her in a field. Sexuality permeates Josefine's world. Her siblings, her neighbors, even the strangers on the street, see her as a sexual object. All of this precoital sexuality leads to Josefine's seduction by the new boarder, Herr Ekhard. The question arises as to who is seducing whom:

> When we were alone again, I became very excited, because it occurred to me that we could do everything without being disturbed. I went into the kitchen to Herr Ekhard—that was his name—let him stroke my hair again and I ran my hands through his beard, which excited me even more. And again it must have been something in my glance, something which robbed him of his rationality. He pressed his hand on my dress, at exactly the critical point. I stood in front of him, he sat on a chair, and he pressed his hand against me. If I did not know what was happening nothing would have occurred to me. But I smiled at him and my smile must have said everything (p. 37).

Josefine's seduction by the boarder is clearly not one of a passive, asexual being. By the end of the first half of the novel Josefine is completely sexual, although not yet ten. Her mother, having herself been seduced by Herr Ekhard, summarizes the author's view of the sexual potential of the child, when she states "Children are evil. . . . One cannot supervise them enough" (p. 104). The proletarian child, the potential lower-class prostitute, is congenitally predisposed to the perversities of adult sexuality.

The second half of the novel, beginning after the sudden death of Josefine's mother, moves outside the world of the family and the immediate neighborhood. Josefine is seduced by her priest and her catechist. The entire world seems to sense her sexual presence and be

attracted by it. Indeed, after her seduction by the catechist is revealed
through the report of a naive playmate, she is seduced by her own
widowed father. The introduction of a new boarder, Rudolf, moves the
incestuous relationship to a new plane, for Rudolf also has a liaison with
a young girl, Zensi, whom he had seduced at the age of eight. Rudolf
and Zensi, encouraged by her unemployed father, initiate Josefine into
the world of the Viennese demimonde.

It is only in the final third of the novel that the economic imperative
is presented. While all the social evils of poverty are reflected in the
earlier segments of the novel, from the abandonment of children by
working parents to the immorality of the boarders, it is the inherent
sexual nature of the child which is central to the novel. While Josefine's
polymorphous sexuality is triggered by her seduction at the age of five,
she indulges in sexual acts out of the pleasure which they bring her.
The financial aspect of carnality delights her, for she finds that she can
be paid for that which she enjoys. The beginnings of her life as a prostitute reflect the economic relationship between the upper-class males,
who pay her for her favors, and the poverty of her life at that time. Here
is the third level. Having moved from sexuality within the family to that
within the social structure associated with the child, she moves into the
demimonde.

Here the novel ends. Like other prostitutes in pseudo-autobiogra-
phies, Josefine has achieved the pinnacle of her desires. She is able to
live off of that aspect of her existence which gives her the most pleasure.
Here the male fantasy of the lower-class prostitute and her accessibility
on the fringes of the upper class is played out in Josefine's life. For her,
her childhood experiences were paramount in shaping her successful
life as a whore, at least seen in retrospect. She ends the novel with the
observation that "my childhood memories, as colorful and exciting as
they are, have remained in my memory and I have reported them. In
the final instance they are childhood memories, even if they are sexual
and not at all childlike. But they remain in all cases more deeply and
permanently engraved in our memory than everything that we later
experience" (p. 272).

The image of the sexual life of the child under the age of consent
present in *Josefine Mutzenbacher* reflects many of the sexual stereotypes
of the female present in fin-de-siècle Viennese thought. The sexuality
of the child, at least that of the proletarian child, is presupposed. The
tawdriness and horror associated with child prostitution are missing, as
is the sense of debauchery of the seducer present in earlier images of
the seduction of the innocent female.[29] For these female children are in

no way perceived as innocent. In *Josefine Mutzenbacher*, as well as in works of English Victorian child pornography, the child is the active participant if not the initiator of the sexual act.[30] The accessibility of the child as sexual object is emphasized. But it is not any child. It is specifically, at least in the world of Vienna, the female proletarian child. The sexuality attributed to the proletarian is the sexuality of the other. The distance between the perceived self and this other is equivalent to the distance perceived between the races. In Jefferson's Virginia it was the sexuality of the black as the other which made the black female the sexual object *par excellence*; in Freud's Vienna, it is the lower-class female, the proletariat, as the source of all debauchery.[31]

THE LITERARY VIEW

The image of the child as sexual object in the belles lettres of fin-de-siècle Vienna is somewhat more subtle and complex than that found in *Josefine Mutzenbacher*, but the similarity of the basic structure is unmistakable. An examination of the role of the female child in the creative writing of this period can contribute some greater subtlety to the use of this stereotype in the literature of the parlor rather than the smoking room. In the work of Peter Altenberg (1859-1919), the figure of the prepubescent female assumes a central role. Even a cursory glance at Altenberg's first volume of sketches, *As I See It* (1896), shows a preoccupation with the child. The first sketch, "Nine and Eleven," begins:

Margueritta stood close to him.
She leaned up against him.
She took his hand in her little hands and held it tightly.
Sometimes she pressed it softly against her breast.
And yet she was only eleven years old.[32]

The opening of this essay is consciously ambiguous. The child is revealed only in the fifth sentence to be a child. The opening lines refer to the physical attractiveness of the female, not the innocent woman but the seductress. Altenberg contrasts the two children in the essay, the older child, outgoing and responsive, and the younger, withdrawn and quiet. The narrator finds himself seated between the two, staring out to sea, and he reflects on the younger child Rositta "above whom fate was poised. . . . And yet she kissed him so softly and said: 'You, Herr Alberti . . . !'" (p. 5). For Altenberg the child contains the hidden woman, with all her seductive powers. In the child it is masked, but the female child acts in concert with these subliminal emotional patterns. In the sketch "Music" the male narrator ("he") listens to the completely unself-conscious piano playing of a 12-year-old, which brings forth a hidden level of meaning to the piece:

> "What are you playing? !" The man asked.
> "Why do you ask? ! That is my Albert-Étude, Bertini
> No. 18. When I play it I always think about you—"
> "Why? !"
> "I don't know; it is so pretty."
> As if a child had suddenly become a woman [ein Weib] (p. 57).

With that self-conscious declaration of her emotions, the child loses her innocence "and the soul was lost from the music." Here the innocence of the child, its spontaneity, is destroyed by that moment of conscious reflection lacking in the first sketch. There the nine- and eleven-year-old do not differentiate their flirtatiousness. They flaunt their unself-conscious coquetry before every male. In the sketch "Music," innocence is lost because of the specific interest of the child in "him," the narrator. But even here, as in all the essays set among the Viennese petite bourgeoisie the role of the child as sexual object is suppressed. While the child, either actively or passively, assumes the role of innocent seductress in relationship to the narrator, any blatant sexual moment is missing, at least until the author's imagination leaves the confines of the Ringstrasse. In the epiphany entitled "The Greek," Altenberg provides a new persona for the narrator. He is now the Greek. The sketch is set in Greece, in a park, and the narrator observes:

> A white batiste dress flying by. —Ash-blond, long, loose, silken hair. Slender delicate legs in black stockings. She is thirteen-years-old. One sees above the knee white underpants. She flies across the path with her hoop (p. 119).

The narrator's reaction to this child is sexual. He enters into an interior monologue triggered by the sight of the child pushing her hoop across the path, a child whose description is that of a Viennese schoolgirl. The narrator ruminates:

> Oh, you, nude, completely nude, on a perfumed, velvet field in the evening shadows, pushing your hoop and flying—flying! And then you stand there and throw in a rounded movement your blond hair backwards and we drink with our eyes, with the artist-

soul's organ of love [*Liebesorgan*], your slender white body—in the love of beauty! (p. 119)

The titillation registered by the sight of the child is recorded in the fantasy of the observer. Like Aschenbach's fantasy about the androgynous 14-year-old boy observed on the Lido in Thomas Mann's "Death in Venice" (1912), the child, by its very movement, is perceived as a sexual object.[33] The playful chasing after the hoop transforms this child into the mythological Diana of the hunt, with all the sexual implications of that equation, just as Tadzio is associated with Hyacinthus.

Altenberg, like Mann, must flee the confines of the stereotypical children of northern or central Europe to find his idealized child in the south. Mann's ironic use of the Polish child in a Venetian setting underlines his awareness of this fact. Altenberg simply transplants his fantasy from Vienna to Greece. His Greek narrator can in no way be differentiated from his other narrators and his child figure is identical to the other girl-children in appearance and intuitive ability to create beauty in art (here the dance with the hoop). But in Altenberg's Greece, as in Aschenbach's Venice, the exoticism of place, like the exoticism of class in *Josefine Mutzenbacher*, enables the character to articulate, in sexual metaphors, his vision of the child as sexual object.

Altenberg's stereotypical image of the child as inherently pure but with clearly sexual overtones was evident to his more radicalized contemporaries. Ria Claassen, in her pamphlet "The Female Phantom of the Male" (1898), condemns Altenberg, among others, for having created the "phantom of the woman as virgin-mother, as a saint, as the intercessor with a transcendental principle."[34] As is evident, this stereotype simply provided another distancing technique with which the male could rationalize his attraction to the seemingly unthreatening sexuality of the female child.

In a different genre, Felix Salten (1869-1947) saw many of the same characteristics in the prepubescent female.[35] In 1911 Salten published a commentary to a volume of photographs taken by Emil Mayer at the Prater, Vienna's public amusement park. These candid photographs included a series of four entitled "Young Love," in which Mayer captured two young girls flirting their way through the park. Salten's commentary is quite enlightening as how a contemporary saw these photographs: "Yes, this little group also belongs here. Children . . . but there will be strict individuals who will shake their heads at this scene and say 'There aren't any children any more! And yet they are children, evidently completely innocent children who do not know that this 'eye-play' [*Augenspiel*] is called coquetery, that their laughter, winking, gossiping, their little, graceful, as well as affected mode of presentation is the prelude to the comedy of love, toward which they are maturing."[36]

For Salten, as for the general Viennese public, the coquetry, the sexual playfulness of the female child, is the sign of her innate nature. Indeed, in an article some three decades earlier, an anonymous reporter in the Viennese *Illustrated Extra* condemned the casting of a 12-year-old as an adultress in a Prater penny theater. Even more appalling than the child actress mimicking adult immorality, was her audience—an audience of peers, children titillated by a child imitating adult sexual misdeeds.[37] By 1911, and for a more sophisticated audience, Salten's voice loses the condemnatory note found in the earlier newspaper article, but the sense of his message remains the same. Adult sexuality is omnipresent in unconscious form in children: "Here [in the Prater] young beauties celebrate their first successes. Developing coquettes experience their first triumphs. Future fickle hearts commit their first betrayals. . . . Here there is pain, disappointment and in all the childish lack of experience, bitter experiences. Twelve-year-old girls sigh 'I will never believe a man again.' Fourteen-year-old boys shout ironically: 'Stop already with women.' [*Weiber*] When they sit at home in the evening, childish sleepiness in their eyes, all is forgotten, And when their parents ask them: 'Where were you?' they answer innocently and simply: 'Out walking . . .' " (p. 115).

For Altenberg and Salten the mask of the naive child is precisely what fascinates and excites the adult. For Arthur Schnitzler (1862-1931), the image of the seductive child is embedded in a more highly colored context, revealing a subtle reworking of this theme.[38] Especially in his long novella "Casanova's Return Home" (1918), the seduction of the child plays an interesting, if marginal, role. Schnitzler uses the historical character of Casanova in a totally fictional re-creation of the aged roué's attempt to return to the city of his birth, Venice, from which he had been banned for his political associations. The 53-year-old and penniless Casanova arrives on the outskirts of Venice disguised as the noble Chevalier de Seingalt. He is recognized by Olivio, whose marriage to Amalia Casanova had been made possible on a whim some 16 years before by contributing a dowry to the couple. Amalia expressed her gratefulness to the young and handsome stranger by spending her wedding night with him. In the past 16 years Olivio had managed to raise himself up into the fringe of the bourgeoisie and his wife had borne him three daughters, the oldest of which, Teresina, is 13 at the time of Casanova's return to the scene. Olivio sees his daughters, "thirteen, ten, and eight . . . thus none of them old enough to have their heads—if I may be so bold—none of them old enough to have their heads turned by Casanova."[39]

Indeed, none of the daughters captures Casanova's fancy, but rather it is their cousin Marcolina, who appears to Casanova not much older than the oldest daughter. The story focuses on the fascination of the older man for this young girl. Olivio's wife Amalia can see in the aged and destitute Casanova only the young, rich, and noble individual with whom she had slept almost two decades earlier; Marcolina sees before her only a wreck of a man masquerading as a nobleman. When the aged Casanova is stymied in his attempt to seduce the child-woman Marcolina, he turns to the oldest child, the 13-year-old Teresina. This tangential episode is prefigured in the meeting of the children with Casanova in which "the oldest, Teresina, still appearing like a child, stared at the stranger with unconstrained, somewhat peasant-like curiosity" (p. 252). Rather than kissing the children's proffered hands, he takes "each of the children around their heads and kisses each on both cheeks." This seemingly paternal act, as seen from Casanova's viewpoint, has sexual overtones.

Toward the conclusion of the novella Teresina is sent to fetch Casanova for a dinner party of the local noteworthies. Her absence is noted by the assembled group, who begin to joke to her discomfitted father about her presence in Casanova's chambers. In the chambers a seduction occurs:

> Olivio's oldest little daughter [*Töchterlein*], the thirteen-year-old, entered [his chambers] and announced that the entire party was assembled and awaiting the Chevalier to begin their gambling. Her eyes glowed strangely, her cheeks blushed, her woman-like, thick tresses played blue-black about her temples, her childish mouth was agape. "Have you drunk some wine, Teresina?" Casanova asked and took a long step towards her. "Indeed—and the Chevalier saw that at once?" She grew even redder and as if in embarrassment she licked her lower lip with her tongue. Casanova grabbed her by the shoulders, breathed into her face, pulled her to him and threw her on the bed. She looked at him with large, helpless eyes, from which the glow had vanished. But when she opened her mouth as if to scream, Casanova threw her such a threatening glance that she almost froze and permitted him to do anything he pleased with her. He kissed her tenderly yet wildly and whispered: "You must not tell the priest, Teresina, not even in the confessional. When you have a lover or fiancé or even a husband, no one needs to know about this. You should always lie,

you should lie to your father and mother and sisters, so that you shall do well here on earth. Note this."—Thus he blasphemed and Teresina must have held this for a blessing which he spoke over her for she took his hand and piously kissed it like that of a priest. He laughed loudly. "Come," he said, "My little woman [*Frau*], we shall appear in the salon arm-in-arm." She became a bit affected, but smiled not at all unpleased (p. 323).

Perceived by the reader, Casanova's act is that of an aging roué committed at a moment of self-doubt about his attractiveness and one which violated his host's hospitality. It is a condemnation of Casanova. Yet the image of the child Teresina, as perceived by Casanova, alters the implications of this passage. She is a child-woman from a lower class (at least a class lower than that of the invented Chevalier de Seingalt), who is captivated by the myth of Casanova the lover without being completely prepared for the physical reality implied by that myth. In Casanova's eyes she initially appears the coquette, standing on the edge of maturity. She has womanlike [*frauenhaft*] hair but a childish [*kindlich*] mouth. Her physiognomy is that of the child-woman.

While Casanova's act must be condemned, for in Schnitzler's Vienna no sexual intercourse, even by mutual consent, was legally permitted under the age of 14, the implicit rationale for Casanova's act lies within the nature of the child seduced. Teresina is the seductive country girl, Schnitzler's sweet girl [*süsses Mädl*], his woman of the suburban Viennese demimonde, at the moment of defloration. Her sexual precociousness, at least as perceived by Casanova, is the mitigating factor in this seduction, and this precociousness is to no little degree the result of her belonging to another class. Here Schnitzler's irony can be felt, for of course the Chevalier de Seingalt does not exist. It is a title assumed by Casanova, as he states, to show his innate nobility. Indeed, it is the fecundity of the rising bourgeoisie, typified by Olivio and his family, against which the stagnant world of Venetian noble intrigue is contrasted. Teresina is perceived by Casanova to be below him in class.

Gordon Allport has noted that "liaisons with members of lower classes seem particularly attractive to people with higher status. The daughter of the patrician family who runs away with the coachman is almost as familiar a theme in literature as the prodigal son who wastes his substance in riotous living with lower-class women. Both reveal the same truth."[40] The truth is the implied sexual libertinage of the other. In "Casanova's Return Home," the other is both of a lower class and a child.

The writers of fin-de-siècle Vienna perceived the hidden woman within the child as her determining factor. The female child conceals within herself the seductress. The prepubescent figure of Lucile in the tale "Lucidor" (1910) by Hugo von Hofmannsthal (1847-1929), which served as the basis for Richard Strauss' opera *Arabella*, illustrates this even within the androgynous mask of the heroine, for Lucile's sexuality breaks through the barriers of both her youth and her disguise as a young boy to seduce her sister's lover.[41] Here Hofmannsthal has also labeled Lucile as the attractive exotic, the Polish (albeit noble) child in imperial Vienna. As in the earlier cases it is the seducer who is seduced, at least as perceived by the middle-class male authors and their characters.

FREUD AGAIN

Now that we have "framed the context" for Freud's statement concerning infantile polymorphous perversity in terms of the fin-de-siècle Viennese understanding of the female child, a recapitulation of Freud's argument may be helpful. The seduction of the child leads to polymorphous perverse activity in the form of "sexual irregularities" because an "aptitude for them is innately present in [the child's] disposition." Although the nature of the child is inherently sexual, in both the narrow as well as the broad use of the term, the very immaturity of this sexuality has not yet permitted the child to create those "mental dams" against "sexual excesses." These are the structures typified by the bourgeoise attitude toward sexuality. Freud labels them as "shame, disgust and morality." The antithesis of these qualities has been ascribed to the stereotype of the female child. She is unself-conscious, totally without a sense of the implications of her acts, and beyond proscriptive morality. Thus, the child is like the adult female, whom she has concealed within her. Here the analogy is exposed as faulty, for within all children the potential for polymorphous perversity is hidden.

Freud has simply extended the image of the female child to all children and is thus able to move from this implied equation to the adult female with ease. While in every female the act of seduction may bring forth the disguised tendency toward perversion, it is most evident in those females belonging to the proleteriat, "the average uncultivated female." She has not developed a strong identification with the moral system of the dominant economic and social class and can thus be seduced into a life of perversity. Her seduction releases her polymorphous nature and she becomes like the prostitute, for most women "have an aptitude for prostitution." The prostitute is therefore the natural extension of the female child.

Freud's view concerning the prostitute was not that of the dominant public opinion during the latter nineteenth century. The general consensus isolated the prostitute and placed her in the category of the congenital degenerate. As framed in the title of Cesare Lombroso's classic study *The Delinquent Female: The Prostitute and the Normal Woman* (1893), the prostitute was reduced to a degenerate form of female sexuality.[42] Christian Ströhmberg, Lombroso's most vociferous German supporter, stated it quite baldly: "[The prostitute] fills her ranks from the degenerate females [*Weiber*], who are clearly differentiated from the normal woman [*Frau*]. Their abnormal predisposition can be seen in the gradations from occasional prostitution to moral insanity."[43] The prostitute is both physically and psychologically predetermined to her future from the moment of conception. Freud intimates, however, that all women possess this tendency as part of their nature.

In a quintessentially Viennese work of the fin de siècle, the answer to Lombroso can be found. Otto Weininger's *Sex and Character* (1903), which appeared while Freud was formulating his views on female sexuality, abandoned the older Romantic antithesis between the "virgin" and the "whore" as found in Lombroso's theory.[44] Weininger's work is a mad diatribe against the spectres of the woman and the Jew which haunted his imagination. But this work of pseudoscience had an overwhelming influence on the shaping of the Viennese view of the biological nature of the woman. Weininger argued: "I have come to regard the prostitute element as a possibility in all women just as much as the merely animal capacity for motherhood."[45] "We do not have to face the general occurrence of women as one or the other of two distinct inborn types, the maternal and the prostitute. The reality is found between the two" (p. 217). Prostitution is not the result of seduction per se or of social conditions for "where there is no inclination for a certain course, the course will not be adopted" (p. 217). Weininger also answers the question as to the etiology of this inclination: "Schopenhauer said that a man's existence dates from the moment when his father and mother fell in love. That is not true. The birth of a human being, ideally considered, dates from the moment when the mother first saw or heard the voice of the father of the child" (p. 217). The female child has the potential for the degenerate life of the prostitute from before the moment of conception.

The enigma of Freud's statement falls within the general Viennese understanding of the sexuality ascribed to the stereotypes of the female child, the female proletarian, and the prostitute. It is also indebted to such other views as his own earlier understanding of the role of seduction in the etiology of hysteria and the general problem of the incestuous overtones present in hysterical patients. However, with his exposition of his views in the *Three Essays on the Theory of Sexuality*, residual elements of the Viennese stereotypes of the female remained trapped.

Thinking about Freud's assimilation of late nineteenth-century ideas of the woman into his theory of infantile sexuality (or at least into the language in which the theory is couched) creates yet another puzzle which is even more complex. The stereotype of the seductive child in turn-of-the-century Vienna was projected in exactly those years of sexual latency in which any overt sexuality is missing. The need for the most neutral mirror possible for the projections of the male authors is evident. In latency neither the uninhibited sexuality of the infant nor the emerging sexuality of puberty conflicts with the projected sexual interests of the adult male.

Freud's own concerns of the late 1890s, during his formulation of the idea of infantile sexuality, are reflected in an understanding of this same mirroring effect. In a letter to Wilhelm Fliess of May 31, 1897, Freud recounted a dream concerning his ten-year-old daughter Mathilde:

> Not long ago I dreamt that I was feeling over-affectionately towards Mathilde, but her name was "Hella," and then I saw the word "Hella" in heavy type before me. The solution is that Hella is the name of an American niece whose photograph we have been sent. Mathilde may have been called Hella because she has been weeping so bitterly recently over the Greek defeats. She has a passion for mythology of ancient Hellas and naturally regards all Hellenes as heroes. The dream of course fulfils my wish to pin down a father as the originator of neurosis and put an end to my persistent doubts.[46]

These "over-affectionate feelings" [*"über-zärtliche Gefühle"*] which Freud attributes to his desire to make the father the seducer in his theory of neurosis are clearly sexual in nature. He conflates his daughter with his teenage niece, relating the asexual to the sexual, and rationalizing this relationship in the intensity of Mathilde's asexual feelings. Does the intense desire to see the seductiveness of the child reflect a wish on Freud's part to resolve his own sexual projection concerning himself as the seducer? Indeed, the reality of the sexual interest of the adult male in the prepubescent female posits an antithetical structure to the Oedipal triangle, the trauma theory which Freud initially acknowledged but then replaced with the theory of the fantasy connected with infantile sexuality. Both exist simultaneously but as reflections of the male perception of female sexuality. Freud's rejection of the symmetry between male and female sexuality has its evident locus in the sexual projections of the adult male. This in no way vitiates the validity of Freud's formulation of infantile sexuality but it does alter the rationale for its "discovery." This lies in the dual needs of the adult male fantasy for the projections of female child and the innocent male seducer. Freud's assimilation of the stereotypes of female sexuality of fin-de-siècle Vienna provided both images.

The other aspect of the sexual attractiveness of the projection of the other, her exoticism and concomitant availability, is also amalgamated by Freud into his understanding of the Viennese middle-class female's self-image. He commented in a note to Fliess that much of the problem of female sexual neurosis lies in the presence of the serving girl in the middle-class family:

> An immense load of self-reproaches (e.g., for theft, abortion, etc.) is made possible for a woman by identification with these people of low morals, who are so often remembered by her as worthless women connected sexually with her father or brother. And, as a result of the sublimation of these girls in phantasies, highly improbable charges are made in these same phantasies against other people. Fears of prostitution (fears of walking in the street alone), fears of a man being hidden under the bed, and so on, also point in the direction of servant-girls. There is tragic justice in the fact that the action of the head of the family in stooping to relations with a servant-girl is atoned for by his daughter's self-abasement.[48]

The identification of the problem of female hysteria lies in the seduction by the adult male of the serving girl [*Dienstmädchen*]. The image of unacceptable sexual contact is seen existing across class lines. The middle-class female is perceived as having accepted this sexual structure, which provides for a seductress as her source of self-castigation. The source of this image lies in the adult male's projection of his own potential guilt in the seduction of those within his extended family (here the stress on the serving *girl*). This is parallel to his sense of anxiety in his seductive desire for his daughter. Class and family interconnect to provide the model for the male's projection.

The relationship between male projections of female sexuality and realities of female sexuality is, at best, tenuous. It is, however, of importance in understanding the dominant fantasies concerning the female. The seductive child and the lower-class female are figments of the masculine imagination in turn-of-the-century Vienna, yet because they were articulated through works of art they became central metaphors for sexuality in Viennese society. They thus became the sexual fantasies, or nightmares, of an entire society.

NOTES

[1] Steven Marcus, "Introduction," to Sigmund Freud, *Three Essays on the Theory of Sexuality*, trans. James Strachey (New York: Basic Books, 1962), p. xxxix. Unless otherwise noted all translations cited in this essay are mine.

[2] Two points of view which provide some general psychological background to the problems of stereotyping are Renato Tagiuri and Luigi Petrullo, eds., *Person Perception and Interpersonal Behavior* (Stanford: Stanford University Press, 1958) and Peter W. Sheehan, ed., *The Function and Nature of Imagery* (New York: Academic Press, 1972).

[3] The relationship between Freud's idea of infantile sexuality and earlier medical and theological views of masturbation has been well documented in Henri F. Ellenberger, *The Discovery of the Unconscious: The History and Evolution of Dynamic Psychiatry* (New York: Basic Books, 1970), pp. 295-303. The general background is outlined in E. H. Hare, "Masturbatory Insanity: The History of an Idea," *The Journal of Mental Science*, 108 (1962), 1-25. For the more general background see Jos van Ussel, *Sexualunterdrückung: Geschichte der Sexualfeindschaft* (Reinbek: Rowohlt, 1970) and Michel Foucault, *Histoire de la sexualité* (Paris: Gallimard, 1976).

[4] Voltaire, "Onan, Onanisme," *Oeuvres complètes, Dictionnaire philosophique*, IV (Paris: Garnier, 1879), 133-135.

[5] D. M. Rozier, *Lettres médicales et morales* (Paris: Bechet, 1822).

[6] Richard Krafft-Ebing, *Psychopathia Sexualis with a special reference to antipathic sexual instinct*, trans. C. G. Chaddock (London: Rebman, 1899), pp. 48-49. For the general background to this question see Annemarie Wettley, *Von der "Psychopathia sexualis" zur Sexualwissenschaft*. Beiträge zur Sexualforschung 17 (Stuttgart: Enke, 1959).

[7] Hermann Rohleder, *Vorlesungen über Sexualtrieb und Sexualleben des Menschen* (Berlin: Fischer, 1901), pp. 15-16.

[8] Albert Fuchs, "Zwei Fälle von sexueller Paradoxie", *Jahrbuch für Psychiatrie und Neurologie*, 23 (1903), 207-213.

[9] The Romantic image of childhood in German letters is best summarized in Rainer Stöcklie, *Die Rückkehr des romantischen Romanhelden in seine Kindheit* (Diss., Fribourg, 1970). More specific but skeletal is the chapter "Jugend in Wien", in Hermann Glaser, *Literatur des 20. Jahrhunderts in Motiven* (München: Beck, 1978), pp. 21-25 and his chapter on sex and culture in his book *Sigmund Freud's zwanzigstes Jahrhundert* (München: Hanser, 1976), pp. 51-168. The general literature on this topic is collected in Manuel Lopez, "A Guide to the Interdisciplinary Literature of the History of Childhood," *History of the Child Quarterly*, 1 (1974), 463-494.

[10] Jakob Christoph Santlus, *Zur Psychologie der menschlichen Triebe* (Neuwied: Heuser, 1864), pp. 87ff. The idea that female sexuality begins at the moment of menarche continues throughout the nineteenth century. In one of the standard textbooks of German clinical psychiatry during the 1890s, Theodor Kirchhof observed the close relationship between "faulty education" and insanity in "very young girls" as the etiology of insanity could not be caused by "unsatisfied sexual desire, in as much as so many of the patients have hardly entered upon the period of puberty." This is contrasted with domination of sexuality even in the equivalently young male. Theodore (sic) Kirchhof, *Handbook of Insanity for Practitioners and Students* (New York: William Word, 1893), p. 24.

[11]Frances Finnegan, *Poverty and Prostitution: A Study of Victorian Prostitutes in York* (Cambridge: University Press, 1979), p. 81n.

[12]Josef Schrank, *Die Prostitution in Wien in historischer, administrativer und hygienischer Beziehung* (Wien: Selbstverlag, 1886), II, 202-207.

[13]William Tait, *Magdalenism, An Inquiry into the Extent, Causes, and Consequences of Prostitution in Edinburgh* (Edinburgh: Rickard, 1852), p. 32.

[14]Abraham Flexner, *Prostitution in Europe* (New York: Century, 1914), p. 430.

[15]Friedrich Hügel, *Zur Geschichte, Statistik und Regelung der Prostitution. Social-medicinische Studien in ihrer praktischen Behandlung und Anwendung auf Wien und andere Großstädte* (Wien: Zamarski und Dittmarsch, 1865), pp. 155-156.

[16]Hügel, pp. 205-217.

[17]William Acton, *Prostitution, considered in its moral, social, and sanitary aspects* (London: Churchill, 1857), pp. 165-166. Acton's comments on the immorality on Vienna are indicative of that city's reputation in the 1850s (pp. 147-148). The majority of useful studies on late nineteenth-century cultural attitudes towards sexuality have dealt with British views, but the British experience is not unique. The major studies and rebuttals in this area which have been of use are: Steven Marcus, *The Other Victorians: A Study of Sexuality and Pornography in Mid-Nineteenth Century England* (New York: Meridian, 1974); Morse Peckham, "Victorian Counterculture," *Victorian Studies*, 18 (1975), 257-276; Flavia Alaya, "Victorian Science and the 'Genius' of Woman," *Journal of the History of Ideas*, 38 (1977), 261-280; Peter Gay, "Victorian Sexuality: Old Texts and New Insights," *American Scholar*, 49 (1980), 372-378. The major study of fin-de-siècle Austrian thought which deals with parallel issues is Carl Schorske, *Fin de Siècle Vienna: Politics and Culture* (New York: Knopf, 1980).

[18]Acton, p. 73.

[19]The roots of this concept are exposed by Ursula Friess, *Buhlerin und Zauberin: Eine Untersuchung zur deutschen Literatur des 18. Jahrhunderts* (München: Fink, 1970). The problem in the late nineteenth century is sketched in the structure of one literary type by Ariane Thomalla, *Die 'femme fragile': Ein literarischer Frauentypus um die Jahrhundertwende*. Literatur in der Gesellschaft 15. (Düsseldorf: Bertelsmann, 1972). More recently, the polemical implications of this problem have been stressed by Silvia Bovenschen, *Imaginierte Weiblichkeit und weibliche Imagination: Die Frau in literarischer Diskurs* (Frankfurt: Suhrkamp, 1978)

[20]Schrank, II, 324-325.

[21]The question of the relationship between the real age of menarche in the late nineteenth century to the legal fiction of the age of consent has never been properly discussed. While the age of menarche dropped, the general fertility rates in the large cities, especially among the lower classes also dropped. See John E. Knodel, *The Decline of Fertility in Germany, 1871-1939* (Princeton: Princeton University Press, 1974), pp. 88-90. See also J. Richard Udry, "Age at menarche, at first intercourse, and at first pregnancy," *Journal of Biosocial Science*, 11 (1979), 433-442. For the cultural background of this question see Janice Delaney et al., *The Curse: A Cultural History of Menstruation* (New York: Dutton, 1976), and Penelope Shuttle and Peter Redgrove, *The Wise Wound: Eve's Curse and Everywoman* (New York: Marek, 1978). See also V. Bullough and M. Voght, "Women, Menstruation and Nineteenth-Century Medicine," *Bulletin of the History of Medicine*, 47, (1973), 66-82.

[22]The standard history remains Paul Englisch, *Geschichte der erotischen Literatur* (1927; reprint Magstadt: Verlag für Kultur und Wissenschaft, 1963), pp. 290-293. See also Gustav Gugitz, "Die Wiener Stubenmädchenliteratur von 1784," *Zeitschrift für Bücherfreunde*, 6 (1902), 137-150.

[23]See Oswald Wiener's introduction to the reprint of *Meine 365 Liebhaber* (Reinbek: Rowohlt, 1979), pp. 5-7.

[24]Knodel, p. 70.

[25]Gottlieb Schnapper-Arndt, *Sozialstatistik* (Leipzig: Werner Klinkhardt, 1908), p. 235.

[26]"Aus dem Proletariate recrutiren sich die Verbrecher und die Prostituirten" (Schrank, I, 308).

[27]All references are to the reprint *Josefine Mutzenbacher: Geschichte einer wienerischen Dirne* (München: Non-Stop, 1971) here, p. 10. This has been compared with the first edition (1906) and with other reprints.

[28]The author of *Josefine Mutzenbacher* is unknown. While Felix Salten is mentioned by many reference books—as well as by the editor of the reprint cited above—as the reputed author, he clearly denied this to a contemporary, see Englisch, p. 291.

[29]Some sense of the social reality can be seen in Ronald Pearsall, *The Worm in the Bud: The World of Victorian Sexuality* (New York: Macmillan, 1969), as well as in Hans Ostwald's turn-of-the-century series *Großstadt-Dokumente*: Alfred Deutsch-German, *Wiener Mädel*, Großstadt-Dokumente 17 (Berlin: Hermann Seemann, n.d.); Alfred Lasson, *Gefährdete und verwahrloste Jugend*, Großstadt-Dokumente 49 (Berlin: Hermann Seemann, n.d.); Wilhelm Hammer, *Zehn Lebensläufe Berliner Kontrollmädchen*, Großstadt-Dokumente 23 (Berlin: Hermann Seemann, n.d.) Compare Theodor Herzl's fascination with the Other as the blond, blue-eyed child-woman as presented in Amos Elon's discussion of the 1880s (Amos Elon, *Herzl* [New York: Holt, Rinehart and Winston, 1975], pp. 44-48, 81).

[30]See the various tales which appeared in the pornographic journal *The Pearl* during 1879-1880. The modern reprint (New York: Grove, 1968) does not reprint the "Christmas number" for 1879 which has an extensive fantasy concerning the sexual nature of children. Here and in other pornographic sources the sexual fantasies of adults concerning children obviously revolve around the incest taboo. The literature on this question, both the historical perception of incest and the statistical occurrence, has been summarized by Herbert Maisch, *Inzest* (Reinbek: Rowohlt, 1968).

[31]See Alexander Thomas and Samuel Sillen, *Racism and Psychiatry* (New York: Brunner/Mazel, 1972), pp. 101-102.

[32]All references are to the first edition, Peter Altenberg, *Wie ich es sehe* (Berlin: S. Fischer, 1896), here p. 3.

[33]See Inta Miske Ezergailis, *Male and Female: An Approach to Thomas Mann's Dialectic* (The Hague: Martinus Nijhoff, 1975), esp. pp. 47-71.

[34]Ria Claassen, *Das Frauenphantom des Mannes*, Züricher Diskussionen, 4 (Zürich: n.p., 1898), p. 4.

[35]See K. Riedmüller, "Felix Salten als Mensch, Dichter und Kritiker" (Diss., Wien, 1950).

[36]Felix Salten, *Wurstelprater* (Wien: Rosenbaum, 1911), pp. 111-115.

[37]*Illustrirtes Extrablatt*, June 23, 1880, cited by Schrank, I, 308.

[38]A first-rate study of Schnitzler's stereotypical perception of the female is available in Barbara Gutt, *Emanzipation bei Arthur Schnitzler* (Berlin: Volker Spiess, 1978).

[39]All references are to Arthur Schnitzler, *Gesammelte Werke: Erzählende Schriften, Ergänzungsband IV* (Berlin: S. Fischer, 1922), here p. 246.

[40]Gordon Allport, *The Nature of Prejudice* (Garden City, N.Y.: Doubleday, 1958), p. 351.

[41]Hugo von Hofmannsthal, *Gesammelte Werke: Die Erzählungen* (Stockholm: Bermann-Fischer, 1946), pp. 117 ff.

[42]Cesare Lombroso and Guglielmo Ferrero, *La donna deliquente: La prostituta e la donna normale* (Torino: Roux, 1893). In this context see Annemarie Wettley, "Bemerkungen zum Entartungs-begriff im Hinblick auf den Alkoholismus und die sexuellen Perversionen," *Archivo ibero-americano de historia de la medicina*, 9 (1957), 539-542.

[43]Christian Ströhmberg, *Die Prostitution . . . Eine social-medicinische Studie* (Stuttgart: Enke, 1899), p. 65.

[44]See Gisela Brude-Firnau, "Wissenschaft von der Frau? Zum Einfluß von Otto Weiningers 'Geschlecht und Charakter' auf den deutschen Roman," in Wolfgang Paulsen, ed., *Die Frau als Heldin und Autorin* (Bern: Francke, 1979), pp. 136-149.

[45]All references are to Otto Weininger, *Sex and Character* (London: William Heinemann, 1906), here p. 235.

[46]*The Origins of Psycho-analysis: Letters to Wilhelm Fliess, Drafts and Notes 1887-1902*, ed.
Maria Bonaparte, Anna Freud, Ernst Kris, trans. Eric Mosbacher and James Strachey
(New York, Basic Books, 1954), p. 206.

[47]I am here drawing from the more detailed discussion of this question in Juliet Mitchell's
Psychoanalysis and Feminism: Freud, Reich, Laing and Women (New York: Vintage,
1975), esp. pp. 5-16, 401-435. For a more comprehensive study of one specific aspect
of Freud's views discussed by Mitchell, see also Stephen Kern, "The Discovery of
Child Sexuality: Freud and the Emergence of Child Psychology," Diss., Columbia,
1972.

[48]The Origins of Psycho-analysis, p. 198.

Chapter 11

Freud and Hoffmann:
"The Sandman"

Bernard Rubin

Freud's paper "The Uncanny,"[1] published in 1919, appeared just prior to the important theoretical landmarks of his structural theory, characterized by the tripartite model of id, ego, and superego, and the concept of signal anxiety. These monographs, "The Ego and the Id," published in 1923, and "Inhibition, Symptom and Anxiety," published in 1926, summarized his thinking and arguments in favor of a model of the mind with its central causality of Oedipal conflict, castration anxiety, and resultant organization into a three-part psyche. It was the elaboration of a theory that was central to Freud's thinking and to psychoanalysis since its theoretical beginnings.

On first reading, Freud's essay "The Uncanny" seems to be a curiously elliptical way of explaining the uncanny effect in literature, for the essay combines an analysis of an E.T.A. Hoffmann story, "The Sandman,"[2] and the lexical and etymological use of the word *unheimlich*. Freud concludes that the uncanny effect is due to "something which is secretly familiar, which has undergone repression and then returns from it," that is, the castration complex. In particular, Freud takes the many and peculiar literary use of eyes, both real and mechanical, in the Hoffmann story as substitutes for the penis, and, therefore, of ocular anxiety as a substitute for castration anxiety. He states:

> We may try to reject the derivation of fears about the eye from the fear of castration on rationalistic grounds . . . but this view does not account adequately for the substitutive relation between the eye and male member which is seen to exist in dreams and myths and fantasies (*SE* vol. 17, 231).

Freud posits a substitutive relationship, eye = penis, and then proceeds as if it has been proven. In fact, Freud's essay has itself qualities of the uncanny in that the Oedipus theme is presented as known and familiar while another idea, somewhat unfamiliar and strange, but known to us (and Freud), keeps intruding in a series of footnotes: Freud's theory of narcissism.[3] The first footnote (*SE* vol. 17, 232-234) describes Olympia, the mechanical doll of the Sandman story with whom Nathanael has fallen in love, as a narcissistic love object. The second footnote (pp. 235-236) is the rudimentary notion of a vertical ego split, and its relationship to the double, which anticipates the ego (= self) as central in personality development. The third footnote (p. 248) is the description of Freud's experience of seeing himself as his own double in a mirror. That uncanny moment seemed to demonstrate the awareness of a split-off part of his self. For Freud this other self was at first a disagreeable intruder who needed to be hurried out, but it was also a part of himself, an aspect of his creative self, from which he turned away.[4]

What appears at first to be a short excursion by Freud into the literary world to further bolster his theory of a universal castration complex now appears to represent a shift between familiar and unfamiliar, ordinary and novel, central and peripheral, animate and inanimate, object-centered and self-centered. Although Freud quickly and certainly indicates his preference for the return of the repressed—particularly the Oedipal conflict—as productive of uncanny feelings, his recurrent shifting of positions produces an effect of uncertainty. This uncertainty is apparent from the first lines of the essay. Freud begins with an apology for investigating aesthetics—but he notes that the uncanny is one area where psychoanalysis has some claim, particularly because it is so remote, that is, *abseits*[5] (not central). Freud continues to apologize: "It is long since he [Freud] had experienced or heard anything which has given him an uncanny impression." Nevertheless, what is uncanny, his peripheral theorizing on narcissism, continues to come to light and to be set aside by Freud.

In Part I of "The Uncanny," Freud laboriously examines the lexicography and etymology of the word uncanny *(unheimlich)*. From a number of possible definitions, Freud prefers the one by Schelling: "Unheimlich is the name for everything that ought to have remained hidden and secret and has become visible." Freud concludes that the meaning of *unheimlich* is contained within its apparent opposite—*heimlich*. (The difficulty with the English "uncanny" is that its opposite—"canny"—has no such equivalent possibilities.) Freud's use of etymology, though intriguing, is not entirely convincing because it seems to work only for the German. He ends this part of the essay with the idea that the uncanny response in the reader is a recognition of the return of the repressed. "Un" is the token of repression added to "heimlich," which, when removed, results in the (re)cognition of Oedipus.

Part II consists of a summary of the Hoffmann story, the use of which is stimulated in part by a 1906 paper on the uncanny by the psychologist Jentsch. He wrote that the uncanny might be caused by doubts about whether an apparently animate being is really alive, or, conversely, whether a lifeless object is in fact really inanimate. The Hoffmann story deals with just this question—Nathanael, the hero, falls in love with a mechanical doll, Olympia. Yet Freud dismisses Jentsch's point connecting the uncanny with uncertainty, with the following remark: "Uncertainty whether an object is living or inanimate, which admittedly applies to the doll Olympia, is quite irrelevant in connection with this other, more striking instance of uncanniness" (*SE* vol. 17, 230). For Freud the uncanny is directly attached to the figure of the Sandman and to being robbed of one's eyes by him—that is, to being castrated by him. But just as there are two separate theses of the uncanny in the paper, one central, the other *abseits,* so too there are two stories of the Sandman, one Freud's, the other Hoffmann's.

In Freud's summary the story begins with the student Nathanael's recollections of his father's mysterious death. It continues: On certain evenings his mother would send him to bed early because the Sandman was coming. The Sandman was a wicked person who, when children refused to go to bed, threw sand in their eyes which then caused them "to jump out of their heads." Nathanael, determined to find out more, hides in his father's study one night, and sees that the Sandman is in fact the lawyer Coppelius, a man who occasionally came to their home for dinner. Nathanael has been repelled by him, as well as frightened of him. He is discovered, and his eyes threatened with hot coals by Coppelius. His father intervenes, the boy swoons and falls into a long illness. A year later, after Nathanael has recovered, the Sandman reappears, his father dies in an explosion, and Coppelius disappears.

Nathanael, now at the university, is afraid that an itinerant spyglass salesman, Coppola, is in reality Coppelius. However, his fears are allayed, and he finally buys a glass for himself. With it he can see into the home of one of his professors, Spalanzani, who lives across the way. There Nathanael spies the professor's daughter, Olympia, with whom he falls in love. One day he surprises Spalanzani and Coppola fighting over Olympia, who is their handiwork, an automaton. Coppola runs off with the eyeless doll, and Spalanzani throws the doll's eyes at Nathanael. Again Nathanael becomes ill, recovers with Klara at his side, whom he now plans to marry. One day, while walking in the marketplace, Nathanael goes with Klara to the top of the clock tower. He looks through his spyglass at a curious object, which he sees to be Coppelius. He goes mad, tries to throw Klara from the tower, but she is rescued by her brother. Nathanael, looking at Coppelius, throws himself from the parapet screaming of eyes. This is what Freud retains from the story.

But here is the "real" story. Hoffmann begins with three letters: one from Nathanael to his friend Lothar, misdirected to Klara, his fiancée; another, her response to Nathanael; and a third from Nathanael to Lothar. In these letters Nathanael tells the story of his father's mysterious death, and of the return of this memory with the appearance at his school of Coppola, an itinerant seller of lenses and glasses, and who Nathanael is afraid might be Coppelius. Klara, in her letter, insists that his fears are not outside of, but within, himself. The narrator then speaks to us, the readers, of his wish to tell the story of Nathanael in as compelling and creative a manner as possible. He says:

> If, like an audacious painter, you had initially sketched the outline of the picture within you in a few bold strokes, you would have easily been able to make the colors deeper and more intense until the multifarious crowd of living shapes swept your friends away and they saw themselves, as you see yourself, in the midst of the scene that had issued from your soul. . . . I tormented myself to devise a way to begin Nathanael's story in a manner at once creative and stirring (*The Sandman*, pp. 104-105)

The letters are his means to that end. He says:

> I was most strongly compelled to tell you about Nathanael's disastrous life . . . there were no words I could find which were appropriate to describe, even in the most feeble way, the brilliant colors of my inner vision . . . so, . . .do accept the three letters . . . (*The Sandman*, p. 105).

The story continues with Nathanael's return to his home and Klara. He complains to her of Coppelius as an evil principle, and she again insists that it exists only in his mind. Nathanael then attempts to write a perfect poem that will transport Klara in her feelings for, and understanding of, him. In that poem, however, he sees only death in her eyes, and accuses her of being an automaton. After a near duel with her brother, his friend Lothar, he is reconciled to all, and returns to school. There he buys the spyglass from Coppola, spies Olympia, who is perfect, he thinks, and falls in love. Nathanael discovers that she is an automaton, the handiwork of Professor Spalanzani and Coppola, who are fighting over her parts. Nathanael again falls ill, and is recovering with Klara by his side. They go for a walk and climb to the top of the clocktower. From there Klara sees a "strange little grey bush." Nathanael, looking through his glass, instead sees Klara, and crying out "Whirl, wooden doll," tries to kill her. After she is saved by her brother, Nathanael hurls himself from the tower, crushing his skull, while Coppelius looks on.

Freud's summary is as interesting for its omissions as for its inclusions. He has left out the three letters, the narrator, Klara as double of Olympia, Klara's regulating function with Nathanael, Coppelius' "unscrewing Nathanael's hands and feet, and putting them together one way and then another," the little grey bush, and Klara's role in Nathanael's last madness and death. He has emphasized Coppelius as castrator, rather than as mechanician. Whatever Coppelius does or threatens to do to Nathanael is interpreted by Freud as destructive of some part of Nathanael. However, the story itself emphasizes that Coppelius (and Coppola) want to know, or have secrets about, how parts go together, that is, the mysteries of creation.[6]

Freud then continues to examine a number of other factors that he connects to the uncanny: first, the double [Doppelgänger]. He speaks of its relation to the ego (= self) and narcissism. Here he comes closest to the possibility of expanding his earlier ideas on narcissism by stating:

> . . . theme of the double. . . . They are a harking-back to particular phases in the evolution of the self-regarding feeling, a regression to the time when the ego was not yet sharply differentiated from the external world and from other people. I believe that these factors are partly responsible for the impression of uncanniness, although it is not easy to isolate and determine exactly their share in it (SE vol. 17, 236).

So Freud emphasizes that self-regard develops prior to the system ego, and also connects it in some way to the uncanny. Freud leaves that theme and goes on to examine feelings of helplessness, the compulsion to repeat, and the omnipotence of thoughts. He then completes his thesis by stating that every emotional affect is transformed by repression into morbid anxiety, and that it reoccurs.

> At this point I will put forward two considerations which, I think, contain the gist of this short study. In the first place—every affect belonging to an emotional impulse, whatever its kind, is transformed, if it is repressed, into anxiety, then among instances of frightening things there must be one class in which the frightening element can be shown to be something repressed which recurs. This class of frightening things would then constitute the uncanny—In the second place, if this is indeed the secret nature of the uncanny, we can understand why linguistic usage has extended Das Heimliche (homely) into its opposite Das Unheimliche . . . (SE vol. 17, 241).

In Part III, Freud, as if dissatisfied with his own arguments supporting castration anxiety as central to the uncanny, continues to examine others. In so doing, he adds more and more uncertainty, and the sense that the uncanny (re)enters his essay, for, while he seems to believe that he has demonstrated that repressed desires and archaic forms of thought may lead to uncanny feelings, he has not always done so in the essay. Freud says: "Nor shall we conceal the fact that for almost every example adduced in support of our hypothesis one may be found which rebuts it" (SE vol. 17, 245-246).

He notes that fiction is a particularly fertile source of the uncanny, and that the fictional context is especially determinative of uncanny feelings. He says further on: "It is evident therefore, that we must be prepared to admit that there are other elements besides those which we have so far laid down as determining the production of uncanny feelings . . . what remains probably calls for an *aesthetic* enquiry. But that would open the door to doubts . . ." (SE vol. 17, 247). Eschewing his doubts, Freud returns to, and opts for, repressed complexes as being the most significant in creating the uncanny feeling in the reader. And so the essay ends.

Although much has been said to try to explain creativity, most psychoanalytic writing has tended to narrow the approach to describing the creative work as symptomatic of the writer's psychological problems, or to analyze the characters of his work as parental imagos, or to see them as representations of psychic structures in conflict. Another direction has come from Freud's earlier paper "On Narcissism—An Introduction," published in 1914.[7] From that time to the present the view of narcissism[8] has enlarged to that of a system, with its own line of development in which there are hypothesized operations including drive regulation, self-nonself distinctions, the repository of self-esteem, and creativity. While much of this theorizing has been directed to the understanding of narcissistic disorders and their treatment, I wish to explore that aspect of the self-system which is useful in understanding the functioning of the mind as it thinks, creates, and observes itself creating. The evidence for that particular observation is to be found in the text of the creative product itself, that is, the story, essay, etc. The text reveals the story of its creation.

One further aside before returning to those texts of Freud and Hoffmann. The concept of the representational world as developed by Sandler and Rosenblatt is particularly helpful in this study.[9] For Sandler and Rosenblatt the representational world of the child is a gradually differentiated psychic world, for the most part unconscious. The child creates within an organized whole of its internal "I" and external "not-I," each of which consists of a range of images, the relationship and vicissitudes of which make up the self. A specialized part of the representational world consists of symbols which are used in the ego function of thinking. A more specialized part of the representational world is the ideal shape of self-images, the assumption of which, in fantasy or creativity, gives the greatest degree of narcissistic gratification. Thus, in the text, the story of its creation will be directed toward the achievement of an ideal shape. That is, the authors, Freud and Hoffmann, will demonstrate in their respective texts the problem of creation, and how successfully they approximate an ideal shape.

Now, I shall return to "The Uncanny" of Freud and to "The Sandman" of Hoffmann. Freud's concept of narcissism first appeared in 1910 as a footnote to the second edition of his "Three Essays on the Theory of Sexuality," and in his text on Leonardo. In 1912 it was footnoted in "Totem and Taboo." "The Uncanny" was begun in 1913. Although narcissism appeared as a major organized thesis in 1914, in "The Uncanny" it remains *abseits*. Freud once said that the essay showed evidence of a difficult birth, perhaps because of his age at the time the essay appeared. He was 63, and he had spent most of his creative life developing a literature for psychoanalysis.[10] It may have been his concern with originality as the creator of psychoanalysis, that is, with literary priority—was he first?—and with immortality—would his theories live on after him? All these questions seem to have been of some concern to him, and I think appear as three issues in the creative writing of "The Uncanny." These issues, then, are primacy, centrality, and continuity.

The first is . . . what was first, or who was first? Neil Hertz, in his essay on "The Uncanny," emphasizes particular aspects of Freud's interpersonal relationships just before and during the period of his publication of "The Uncanny."[11] In particular, he singles out the triangle of Freud, Helene Deutsch, and Victor Tausk (who killed himself just prior to the completion of "The Uncanny") as determinative of Freud's concern about his originality. Plagiarism is the theme, with Freud being reported as fearful that Tausk wanted to steal his ideas. Undoubtedly, Hertz has demonstrated some interpersonal forces that may have played a part in Freud's completion of "The Uncanny." Yet, the ideas in the paper were begun before World War I. It would be an error to consider the problem exclusively an interpersonal one, in which Freud was concerned about being recognized as the originator of psychoanalysis. The problem was also intrapsychic. There were split-off aspects of the self which reappear uncannily in his theorizing in this essay. Those split-off aspects are in the three footnotes, already described, in which he speaks of a theory, narcissism, which conflicts with the main textual thesis of Oedipus and castration anxiety. Split-off aspects also occur in Part III of "The Uncanny," which deals with doubt. All doubts concerning the main thesis are recounted and dismissed. The essay ends on a curious note, however, with Freud's admission that he went where he had not planned nor wished to go: "We have drifted into this field of research half-involuntarily, through the temptation to explain certain instances which contradicted our theory of the causes of the uncanny" (*SE* vol. 17, 251-252). The central question that appears in the text, it seems to me, is what theory has primacy—Oedipus or Narcissus? At the conclusion of the essay the answer still remains in doubt.

The second issue of creativity is one of distinguishing what is central, and important, from what is peripheral, and therefore less cogent. In his article, "The Sideshow, or Remarks on a Canny Moment," Samuel Weber takes Freud's opening wording about the psychoanalytic reason for examining the uncanny—it is *remote* from aesthetics (*SE*, p. 219). This remoteness—*abseits* (what is aside) is developed into a Lacanian thesis by Weber, who sees Freud as *repeatedly* trying to prove that what is uncanny is caused by a return of the repressed castration anxiety, and that it is repeatedly set aside. What is central is the maternal phallus. It cannot be *looked at straight on*, as Nathanael could not look at the "strange little grey bush," so Weber's Freud is repeatedly compelled to look away in a chain of signifiers, which are both indicative of the fear of castration and the attempts to re-repress it.

What is *abseits*, it seems to me, is rather the theory of narcissism, set off into the three footnotes as a separate and not-successfully-resolved peripheral series of ideas. Uncannily, these three footnoted digressions on narcissism explain that theory more succinctly and successfully than the essentially earlier article by Freud devoted to that subject. By elaborating the concept of Nathanael as self, with parts provided by his father, and Olympia as self-object, mirroring Nathanael's defective creative self, and by indicating that the ego has various states, particularly those in which the self is experienced as other, the double, Freud has freed his theory of narcissism from its nineteenth-century, mechanistic, hydraulic principles.

Third, there is the issue of continuity or its lack. Sheldon Bach,[12] in a recent article on the absence of a sense of continuity in the thinking of persons with narcissistic character problems, emphasizes uncanny feelings as the hallmark of such persons. They feel a lack of continuity between their internalized self and others, and a concomitant loss of distinction between imagination and reality. Bach feels that this can also arise in creative states which involve a "regression to narcissistic modes." For the creative person such as regression can result in these discontinuities. Sometimes the creative act can be experienced as an other, and, if successful, the continuity is reexperienced. However, with such regression there is always the threat of discontinuity—and uncertainty.

These three issues of primacy, centrality, and (dis)continuity result in intellectual uncertainty. In spite of Freud's dismissal of Jentsch's thesis, the result in "The Uncanny" is intellectual uncertainty. It is my belief that the uncanny is the affective experience of the reader engaged through the text in the narcissistic aspects of the author's creative uncertainties.

"The Sandman" too can be considered a story of the self—and of the creative self failing in an attempt to organize some of its disparate elements. In "The Sandman" Hoffmann quickly states in the first few pages the problem to be solved. The central character, Nathanael, writes:

> I have only to tell you now about the most terrible moment in all the years of my youth; then you will be convinced that it *is not because of faulty vision that everything seems devoid of color to me*, but that a somber destiny has really hung a murky veil over my life, which I will perhaps tear through only when I die ("The Sandman," pp. 98-99, emphasis mine).

Thus something is seen (experienced), but Nathanael despairs of being able to organize it within his self.

In a second letter, this time from Klara to Nathanael, a solution is prescribed:

> I will frankly confess that in my opinion all the fears and terrors of which you speak took place only in your mind and had very little to do with the true, external world.
>
> If there is a dark power . . . it must form inside us, from part of us, must be identical with ourselves; only in this way can we believe in it. . . . If our mind is firm enough and adequately fortified by the joys of life to be able to recognize alien and hostile influences as such, and to proceed tranquilly along the path of our own choosing and propensities, then this mysterious power will perish in its futile attempt to assume a shape that is supposed to be a reflection of ourselves ("The Sandman," p. 102).

And so the self is exquisitely described as doubled in relation to a loss, which might be thought of as innocence, immortality, or primary narcissism.

After this exchange of letters by the characters in the story, the narrator interjects himself, discussing with the reader the difficulty of putting into words what the writer perceives (sees) as an inner experience:

> Have you, gentle reader, ever experienced anything that totally possessed your heart, your thoughts and your senses to the exclusion of all else? . . . Your gaze was peculiar, as if seeking forms in empty space invisible to other eyes . . .
>
> Then your friends asked you . . . what is it . . . what is the matter? And, wishing to describe the picture in your mind with all its vivid colors, the light and the shade, you struggled vainly to find words ("The Sandman," p. 104).

This emphasis on the inner self in the Hoffmann story is not idiosyncratic, but rather emphasizes what is explicit for the author. It is the problem of artistic reation, the problem of seeing what is inside and putting together words that can capture and communicate that spark to the reader. For this reason the story hovers between dream and reality, between the supernatural and natural, between inside and outside; for this is the nature of the struggle of the creative self, and how it is viewed by the self. Also for this reason the characters are at the same time the characters of the story, the actors in a dream, and self- and object-representations. Then one can say that *the experience of the mind looking at itself creating is the story of the story.* Hoffmann's text, as Freud's text, can be read so as to visualize the self in its creative and disrupted aspects. For Nathanael it is difficult to create because in the process of trying to *see* what is inside he experiences an alienation from reality. With this alienation there is a threat of insanity or death. Nathanael becomes a self-representation, and Klara an object-representation. Their coalescence has a soothing effect on Nathanael, but also causes the loss of his creativity. But Klara as narcissistic object, as also Olympia, only temporarily helps with the basic instability of the self, perhaps because it lacked an ideal shape. Instead there is an oscillation between the soothed, childlike Nathanael, and the passionate, creative, but distracted Nathanael, with attempts by Nathanael's (or the narrator's) mind to handle the discontinuity. Both Olympia and Klara are self-objects in that sense. They serve as unremitting admirers of his artistic self. Hoffmann describes the most perfect of narcissistic reflections in Nathanael's description of Olympia, as follows:

> Nathanael had dug up everything he had ever written—poems, fantasies, visions, romances, tales—. . . . Never before had he such a splendid listener. She neither embroidered nor knitted; she did not look out of the window nor feed a bird nor play with a lapdog or kitten; she did not twist slips of paper or anything else around her fingers; she had no need to disguise a yawn by forcing a cough. In brief, she sat for hours on end without moving, staring directly into his eyes, and her gaze grew ever more ardent and animated. . . .
>
> When Nathanael returned to his own room, he cried, "How beautiful, how profound is her mind! Only you, only you truly understand me" ("The Sandman," p. 118).

When this use of Olympia—and Klara—fails, as it does on three occasions—first when Nathanael spies on Coppelius, second when he falls in love with Olympia, and third when he returns to Klara to convalesce—it leads to narcissistic rage, fragmentation, and finally death. The self-object cannot fill the gap of that which seems to be missing: the ideal self as artist. And so, too, in Freud's "The Uncanny." He cannot resolve its thesis of narcissism, and so the thesis is split off, only to reappear uncannily and repetitively. What is uncanny for the reader is a resonance with what has been split off and then reappears in the text. Hoffmann, in "The Sandman," describes the process more directly: "As a good portrait painter, I may possibly succeed in making Nathanael recognizable even if the original is unknown to you" ("The Sandman," p. 105).

The portraits do appear in their various aspects in both authors' works. The self in its narcissistic peregrinations is painted with different degrees of clarity, and in various states of order and disorganization. It is my contention that Freud, in struggling with an inability to resolve the intrusion of a new and theoretical concept with an older and more cherished one, chose a Hoffmann story that illustrated the title of his monograph by example, and that he also demonstrated, repeatedly within his own text of that story, the uncertain struggle of the self to create. The texts then repeat each other.

NOTES

[1]*SE* vol. 17, 217-256.

[2]All references to "The Sandman" are from *The Tales of E.T.A. Hoffmann*, ed. and trans. Leonard J. Kent and Elizabeth C. Knight (Chicago: University of Chicago Press, 1969), pp. 93-125.

[3]Freud used the term for years to describe a developmental stage intermediate between autoerotism and object-love in the organization of the ego (= self = person). The first printed notation was a footnote in the second edition (1910) of his "Three Essays on the Theory of Sexuality."

[4]Freud's concern with the uncanny effect of a "double" increased as he grew older and took the form of a fear of meeting those he felt were his doubles: Arthur Schnitzler and Josef Popper, both of whom lived in Vienna (see Ernest S. Wolf and Harry Trosman, "Freud and Popper-Lynkeus," *Journal Amer. Psychoanal. Assn.*, 22 [1974], 123-141). Freud wrote to Schnitzler (May 14, 1922) that he was motivated in avoiding a meeting "by shyness at the thought of seeing my double"—the poet—"who found by intuition what I uncovered by hard labor" (Sigmund Freud, *Letters, 1873-1939* [ed. E. L. Freud], New York: Basic Books, 1960.)

Josef Popper published "Phantasien eines Realisten" in 1899 a short time before Freud's "Interpretation of Dreams" appeared in 1900. Freud credited him with insights about dream psychology, yet seemed concerned about scientific priority. He distinguished between two separate paths to the discovery of a common truth in relation to Popper's and his insights regarding dreaming (see Josef Popper-Lynkeus and the Theory of Dreams, *SE* vol. 19, 259-263). Freud returned to this concern in a 1932 paper ("My Contact with Josef Popper-Lynkeus," *SE* vol. 22, 217-224) in which a particularly revealing statement closes that short essay:

> But I never sought him [Popper] out. My innovations in psychology had estranged me from my contemporaries, and especially from the older among them: often enough when I approached some man whom I had honored from a distance, I found myself repelled, as it were, by his lack of understanding for what had become my whole life to me. . . . I was anxious that the happy impression of our agreement upon the problem of dream-distortion should not be spoilt (*SE* vol. 22, 224).

Wolf and Trosman add that Popper's works gave Freud a feeling of uncanny familiarity. I think that Freud's avoidance of what he thought was his double was to avoid questioning his creativity. (Also see Ralph Tymms, *Doubles in Literary Psychology*, Cambridge: Bowes & Bowes, 1949, in which the double in literature is characterized as the unconscious self.)

[5]*Abseits* becomes the word around which Samuel Weber develops a thesis elaborating a Lacanian view of "The Uncanny" essay. See "The Sideshow, or: Remarks on a Canny Moment," *MLN*, 88 (1973), 1102-1133.

[6]The problem of the mysteries of life—how things go together, how they work, and how machines approximate living organisms, that is, essentially, to know the unknowable—is found in all of Hoffmann's tales. Implied is the question of how can one make knowable and mechanical the inner self. This is ignored by Freud in the main text of his uncanny essay.

[7]In 1914 Freud summarized his thinking on the concept of narcissism in "On Narcissism: An Introduction," *SE* vol. 14, 73-102. He never returned to it as the formal subject of any later paper.

[8]The concept of narcissism was elaborated by a number of theorists in terms of the self, which was variously placed within the system ego or described as requiring consideration as a system in its own right. See Heinz Hartmann, "Comments on the Psychoanalytic Theory of the Ego" (1950), in *Essays on Ego Psychology* (New York: International Universities Press, 1964), pp. 113-141; Edith Jacobson, "The Self and the Object World," *Psychoanalytic Study of the Child*, 9 (1954), 75-127; Joseph Sandler and Bernard Rosenblatt, "The Concept of the Representational World," *Psychoanalytic Study of the Child*, 17 (1962), 128-148; and Heinz Kohut, "Forms and Transformation of Narcissism," *Journal Amer. Psychoanal. Assn.*, 14 (1966) 243-272. These views of the self indicate an organization of the earliest somatic and psychical experiences of the child, which are later related to self-integrity, self-esteem, and ideals. Hartmann, Jacobson, and Kohut each attempt to integrate Freud's libido theory into their theses, a circumstance which tends to obscure some of their concepts of the self.

[9]In the representational world of Sandler and Rosenblatt (see note 8), the model is spatial. Taking care that it is considered only as a model, one can postulate that the more pleasing the shape, the more successful is the creative effort. This does not help to understand uncanny effects, yet one can theorize that discontinuities may be part of the cause of the uncanny, whether the creative effort is successful or not. See the text in reference to Bach (n. 12).

[10]In a letter to Helene Deutsch Freud wrote: "I invented psychoanalysis because it had no literature."

[11]"Freud and the Sandman," in *Textual Strategies*, ed. J. V. Harari (Ithaca: Cornell University Press, 1979), pp. 296-321.

[12]"Narcissism, Continuity and The Uncanny," *Int. Journal Psychoanal.*, 56 (1975), 77-86.

Chapter 12

The Uncanny Rendered Canny: Freud's Blind Spot in Reading Hoffmann's "Sandman"

Françoise Meltzer

I

> He who does not expect the unexpected will not find it out,
> for it is trackless and unexplored.
>
> —Heraclitus, *Fragments*

Freud's essay "The Uncanny" has recently elicited much critical attention.[1] The essay certainly is sufficiently compelling and confusing to warrant the attention it has received. Not only does Freud repeat himself in a surprising display of stylistic fallacy (the *Wiederholungszwang* of which he speaks in this work thus manifesting itself even at the level of his prose), but he further makes a blatant use of *recusatio*, insisting that he is guilty of a "special obtuseness in the matter," that it has been long since he himself has experienced an uncanny moment, and then proceeding vividly to tell of several incidents in which he had.[2] Given that one concern of the essay is repression, such protestations take on an intriguing light.

The definition of the uncanny begins with a discussion of the etymology of the word *unheimlich*. Using the same points as in "The Antithetical Sense of Primal Words," Freud demonstrates how the word *unheimlich* in German also can mean its opposite—"canny" can also mean "uncanny" in certain parts of Germany. But it is upon Schelling's definition of the uncanny that Freud's most frequent usage of the word will rest. For Schelling, the uncanny "is the name for everything that ought to have remained secret and hidden and has come to light."[3] The *recusatio* which informs the text would seem, then, to make Schelling's point.

Two further definitions are added to the term uncanny: the first is a refutation of Jentsch's concept that the uncanny is grounded in intellectual uncertainty. Jentsch had used the writings of E.T.A. Hoffmann to prove his point. Freud therefore takes as his central concern Hoffmann's short story "The Sandman," and goes about showing that we know the true identity of the mysterious Sandman in the tale: "For the conclusion of the story makes it quite clear that Coppola the optician really *is* the lawyer Coppelius and also, therefore, the Sandman" (*SE* vol. 17, 230). Freud's conclusion is a rejection of Jentsch:

> There is no question, therefore, of any intellectual uncertainty here. We know now that we are not supposed to be looking on at the products of a madman's imagination . . . and yet this knowledge does not lessen the impression of uncanniness in the least degree. The theory of intellectual uncertainty is thus incapable of explaining that impression (*SE* vol. 17, 230-231).

Nevertheless, as Freud's essay begins to unravel the complex knot which forms the uncanny, as he begins to explore such aspects as the double, the automaton, and death, he is led to a different possibility: "And are we after all justified in entirely ignoring the intellectual uncertainty as a factor, seeing that we have admitted its importance in relation to death?" Freud's conclusion is acknowledged repression:

> It is evident therefore, that we must be prepared to admit that there are other elements besides those which we have so far laid down as determining the production of uncanny feelings. We might say that these preliminary results have satisfied *psycho-analytic* interest in the problem of the uncanny, and that what remains

probably calls for an *aesthetic* enquiry. But that would be to open the door to doubts about what exactly is the value of our general contention that the uncanny proceeds from something familiar which has been repressed (*SE*, p. 247).

Freud keeps the door on his doubts firmly closed, so that the intellectual certainty which he professes is here admitted to be founded upon the repression of uncertainty. Freud's view on the "aesthetic," moreover, is quite low on his list of priorities, lest one take the preceding remarks as overly weighty in their admission of the limitations of psychoanalysis in the face of aesthetic considerations. Elsewhere, Freud notes:

> The science of aesthetics investigates the conditions under which things are felt as beautiful, but it has been unable to give any explanation of the nature and origin of beauty and, as usually happens, lack of success is concealed beneath a flood of resounding and empty words. Psychoanalysis, unfortunately, has scarcely anything to say about beauty either (*SE* vol. 21, 82-83).

The "unfortunately" connected with psychoanalysis should not be taken too seriously, since Freud sees in his science silence which differentiates it from the "lack of success" which aesthetics conceals beneath its empty words. And yet the "remainder" to which Freud admits in the Hoffmann story is much more than "an aesthetic valuation"—it is a reminder of that aspect of the uncanny with which Freud refuses to deal: the insistence upon intellectual certainty, even if its attainment results in horror, or in death. This is not to say with Freud that the uncanny does not include intellectual uncertainty—quite the contrary. It is rather to say that such uncertainty in uncanny moments is tolerated because of the subject's secret motivation: the desire to know.

It is uncanny indeed that while Freud repressed such curiosity in himself, he deals with a tale which is grounded in curiosity, and yet he never addresses that drive. For Freud the uncanny occurs when something which *ought* to have remained "secret and hidden" manages to surmount the repression barrier, which brings us to the third definition which Freud accepts for the term: "An uncanny experience occurs either when infantile complexes which have been repressed are once more revived by some impression, or when primitive beliefs which have been surmounted seem once more to be confirmed" (*SE* vol. 17, 249). In both cases, what is "discovered" has been long familiar, though repressed.

And in both cases, Freud assumes that the discovery occurs in spite of the subject, that is to say, against his will. The insistence upon curiosity, despite knowledge of its possible consequences, is the part of the uncanny which Freud chooses to ignore, and is precisely the area which this essay will examine.

It is curiosity that sets into action the Hoffmann story which Freud considers. The protagonist, Nathanael, remembers that as boy a mysterious person would come to the house. His mother called this individual "The Sandman," and put the children to bed early when he came to see Nathanael's father. In his summary of the tale, Freud says, "When questioned about the Sandman, his mother, it is true, denied that such a person existed except as a figure of speech." Nathanael's nurse, however, tells him that the Sandman is terrible, that he gathers children's bleeding eyes in a sack and carries the eyes "off to the half-moon to feed his children" (*SE* vol. 17, 227-228). Dread of the Sandman becomes fixed in Nathanael's breast, says Freud, adding: "he determined to find out what the Sandman looked like." It is clear that the boy's curiosity is more compelling than his fear; it is equally clear that Freud overlooks this fact. Nathanael says of his boyhood: "but if only I—if only I could solve the mystery and get to see this fantastic Sandman with my own eyes—that was the desire which increased in me year by year."[4] To solve the mystery and to see with one's own eyes—these are Nathanael's obsessions. In his own words, "As my curiosity to know the Sandman grew, so did my courage" (pp. 95-96). The boy hides in a dark closet and satisfies his curiosity with two discoveries: first, that the Sandman is the old lawyer Coppelius "who frequently had dinner with us!" and second, that his father bears a striking resemblance to this terrible friend: "As my old father now bent over the fire, he looked completely different. His mild and honest features seemed to have been distorted into a repulsive and diabolical mask by some horrible convulsive pain. He looked like Coppelius . . ." (pp. 97-98). The boy screams and is discovered in his hiding place. Coppelius wants to take out his eyes with hot coals from the fire, but the father saves his son with his entreaties, "Master! Master!. . . leave my Nathanael his eyes!" The boy is saved, and spends the rest of his life obsessed with the fear that the Sandman (whether it be in the form of the lawyer Coppelius, or of his double, the spyglass salesman Coppola) will appear to rob him of his eyes.

Freud's interpretation is straightforward: the fear of losing one's eyes is a displacement for the fear of castration: "A study of dreams, phantasies and myths has taught us that anxiety about one's eyes, the fear

of going blind, is often enough a substitute for the dread of being castrated." Nathanael is simply repeating the gesture of Oedipus "the
mythical criminal" who, in blinding himself was merely carrying out
"a mitigated form of the punishment of castration—the only punishment
that was adequate for him by the *lex talionis*" (*SE* vol. 17, 231).

But Freud's interpretation imposes upon the Hoffmann tale an axiom
which is drawn from another—that of Oedipus. For Freud, the eye is
a substitute for the male member in both cases, and in both cases the-
knowing-too-much having seen-too-much must result in self-inflicted
punishment by the Law of Retaliation. As with the "easy" dismissal of
Jentsch, however, Freud seems a bit uncomfortable, with the eyes = penis
equation. The eyes are precious organs, he admits, and it is natural that
they be guarded "by a proportionate dread." Fear of castration itself
may contain "no other significance and no deeper secret than a justifiable
dread of this kind." And yet Freud is adamant:

> But this view does not account adequately for the substitutive re-
> lation between the eye and the male member which is seen to exist
> in dreams and myths and phantasies; nor can it dispel the impres-
> sion that the threat of being castrated in especial excites a peculiarly
> violent and obscure emotion, and that this emotion is what first
> gives the ideas of losing other organs its intense colouring. *All
> further doubts are removed* when we learn the details of their "cas-
> tration-complex" from the analysis of neurotic patients, and realize
> its immense importance in their mental life (*SE* vol. 17, 231).

So it is clinical evidence which finally functions to "remove all doubts."
What remains unconvincing, however, is that the specifically optical
quality which the satisfaction of curiosity entails (in both Nathanael and
Oedipus)—the desire to *see* in order to know—can be arguably viewed
as transgression in retrospect by the subject—a transgression of the law
for the sake of curiosity and an act therefore to be punished by the
expulsion of the guilty organs. That in the case of Oedipus both the eyes
and the male member may be called "guilty" does not obviate the equally
weighty fact that for Oedipus the gouging of the eyes may have been
punishment for the primary sin—that of seeing too much—and not
substitution of the "real" organ to be singled out. Indeed, when Oedipus
finally realizes what his insistence for knowledge, his obsessive curiosity,
has made him "see" and know, his apostrophe to his eyes is as logically
acceptable in the realm of transgression by vision as that of incest:

No more shall you
Behold the evils I have suffered and done.
Be dark from now on, since you saw before
What you should not, and knew not what you should.[5]

The refusal to repress curiosity results in the cases of both Nathanael and Oedipus in crimes against nature. The crime of Oedipus is evident; that of Nathanael is less so and we will return to it below. The natural desire to know is in direct contradiction with the natural law, and the transgressor must take his punishment with the wisdom his curiosity imparts to him. This is how Nietzsche reads the Oedipus story as well:

> . . . for how should man force nature to yield up her secrets but by successfully resisting her, that is to say, by unnatural acts? This is the recognition I find expressed in the terrible triad of Oedipean fates; the same man who solved the riddle of nature (the ambiguous Sphinx) must also, as murderer of his father and husband of his mother, break the consecrated tables of the natural order. It is as though the myth whispered to us that wisdom, and especially Dionysiac *wisdom, is an unnatural crime*, and that whoever, in pride of knowledge, hurls nature into the abyss of destruction, must himself experience nature's disintegration.[6]

We may further say of Nathanael what Nietzsche adds of Oedipus: "he presents us in the beginning with a complicated legal knot, in the slow unravelling of which the *judge brings about his own destruction*."[7] This is the double movement of the uncanny; that on the one hand, curiosity insists upon itself, the Aristotelian notion that man's natural desire is to know; and that on the other hand, the Symbolic Order (in Lacan's sense) is ruptured by the penetrating gaze, so that the *lex talionis* inexorably imposes itself upon the subject who has seen what ought to have remained hidden and secret and has become visible.[8] The uncanny then is at once a moment of discovery and one of recognition—it is this paradox which creates an *unheimlich* episode in the history of the subject. This doubling imposes itself on the subject as well, in whom the doubling is interiorized such that he becomes at one and the same time the judge and the accused. With Oedipus, the judgment is exile and the gouging of the eyes; with Nathanael, the judgment takes the form of a lifelong obsessive fear of losing his eyes, a fear which culminates in suicide.

The compulsion of curiosity—of the *intellectus cupidus*—is, as we have noted, repressed in Freud on several levels: the refusal to "open the door" to Jentsch's definition of the uncanny as grounded in the question of intellectual uncertainty; the refusal to question the eyes = male member equation; the initial refusal to admit to any memorable uncanny experiences of his own; and the refusal to acknowledge the curiosity which can motivate the uncanny experience. The role of the eyes is thus solely substitutive for castration anxiety in the Freud text. We are arguing here that the doubling movement of the uncanny is rather born of the clash of two drives: the will to know and the taboos of the Symbolic Order. An Athenian in Plato's *Laws* speaks of the law of incest with the notion of the natural order which remains unquestioned in Freud and which is problematized by Nietzsche:

> Once suppose this law perpetual and effective—let it be, as it ought to be, no less effective in the remaining cases than it actually is against incest with parents—and the result will be untold good. It is dictated, to begin with, by *nature's own voice*, leads to the suppression of the mad frenzy of sex, as well as marriage breach of all kinds, and *all manner of excess* in meats and drinks, and wins men to affection of their wedded wives.[9]

All excess is to be suppressed for the sake of the race. The excess of knowledge, compelling though it is, is to be punished by the Law of the Race, the preordained order into which the subject is situated *before* he acquires knowledge of his relation to "others" in his drama. The knowledge of both Oedipus and Nathanael that they have transgressed that law ruptures the veil of repression. It is this same rupturing which Freud refuses to consider in his own uncovering of the uncanny essay, even though he states that repression produces the uncanny: "repression . . . the necessary condition of a primitive feeling recurring in the shape of something uncanny" (*SE* vol. 17, 242).

Thus Freud's essay is uncanny by his own definition, except that it *does not emerge* from the uncanny moment, unlike the tales of Oedipus and Nathanael: "It may be true that the uncanny is something which is secretly familiar, which has undergone repression and then returned [emerged] from it" (*SE* vol. 17, 245). But Freud continues to "overlook," among other things, the primal significance of the eyes. It is not by accident that Nietzsche, for example, describes Oedipus' drama in ocular imagery: "And now we see that the poet's (Sophocles) entire conception was nothing more nor less than the *luminous afterimage* which *kind nature provides our eyes after a look into the abyss.*"[10] Freud turns away from the abyss; but the protagonists of the texts he examines do not. The insistence upon witnessing the primal scene in both texts entails, as we have said, a doubling. Such a doubling is necessary in the contemplation of origin. Jacques Derrida says of creative imagination the same thing: "One must be separate from oneself in order to be reunited with the blind origin of the work in its darkness."[11] The French term for the primal scene links the concept of origin and "doubling" overtly: *la scène originaire*. And origins are at the heart of Freud's definition of the uncanny, it will be remembered: "An uncanny experience occurs either when repressed infantile complexes have been revived by some impressed, or when primitive beliefs we have surmounted seem once more to be confirmed."

What Freud "leaves out" of his examination of the uncanny is the will to know. The uncanny moment in the Hoffmann text, that moment which will inscribe Nathanael's fate upon him for the rest of his life, does not occur by chance: He chooses it, and the disintegration of his self which follows is the other side of the knowledge/Law, seeing/rupturing dialectic. To return to Nietzsche: "whoever, *in pride of knowledge*, hurls nature into the abyss of destruction, must himself experience nature's disintegration." The doubles which permeate the Hoffmann text now take on another meaning: They are not only fragmentations of Nathanael's self; with their gazes and fixed stares, they are also various forms of scopic knowledge with which he is struggling. Seeing has become for him deautomatized, and the *Verfremdungseffekt* which follows the night of discovery is the double movement of the uncanny.

Lacan, while he accepts Freud's equation of eyes = male member, himself traces this moment of the estranged gaze: "The world is all-seeing, but it is not exhibitionistic—it does not provoke our gaze. When it begins to provoke it, the *feeling of strangeness* begins too."[12] Why does Nathanael, in the story, fear the automaton Olympia? Because, it will be shown, he fears that he himself is an automaton. And in a sense, he is, for his flight from the glazed eyes of both Klara and Olympia (significantly, both names meaning "light"—*nomen est omen*) is the denial of the judge within himself before whom only he knows he stands accused. The sentence is irrevocable—it needs only to be set into motion—and it is thus no wonder that Nathanael stands terrified before machinery, and before instruments of vision—telescopes, eyes, spyglasses, eyeglasses. His prolonged denial of the judge is the movement of the story; but his doubles and the various instruments of vision accumulate into *anamorphosis*—a distorted vision which looks normal when viewed with a special device.

The story is not one of growing distortion, but of seeing increasingly clearly.

II

> They do not comprehend how a thing agrees at variance with itself; it is an attunement turning back on itself, like that of the bow and the lyre.
>
> —Heraclitus, *Fragment #51*

For Freud, anxiety about the loss of the eyes is in "intimate connection" with Nathanael's father's death, and the Sandman appears, not only as the manifestation of this anxiety, but apparently to keep Nathanael from love—first with Klara, then with the doll Olympia. The events of the story, says Freud, "become intelligible as soon as we replace the Sandman by the dreaded father at whose hands castration is expected" (*SE* vol. 17, 232).

Of significance here is the need to render something "intelligible"—a need which manifests itself in Freud, as we have seen, by the insistence upon control and certainty, at the expense of further exploration, which might "open the door to doubts about the exact value of our general contention. . . ." The psychoanalytic mode, then, serves to control not only uncertainty, but any arbitrariness as well. Indeed, Freud's view of the arbitrary, as delimited in the *"Gradiva,"* is resoundingly explicit: "There is far less freedom and arbitrariness in mental life, however, than we are inclined to assume—There may be none at all. What we call chance in the world outside can, as is well known, be resolved into laws, which we are now beginning only dimly to suspect" (*SE* vol. 9, 9). Freud's "desire to know the truth," his own curiosity, is grounded in the need for control, the need to establish empirical laws which will force out the random, the arbitrary, even freedom. Psychoanalysis, says Freud in "The Uncanny," "is concerned with laying bare these hidden forces" (*SE* vol. 17, 243). And yet the uncanny is a moment which cannot, at least initially, be explained, for it presents a scopic knowledge which is at odds with one's cognition of the present. But Freud must impose destiny here too: The uncanny, he says, is an involuntary repetition. Where otherwise we would have spoken of chance, we now have a sense "of something fateful and inescapable." In other words, the immediate experience of the uncanny, the moment of horror and incomprehensibility, is "sublated" by Freud by a mechanistic axiom: The moment is not "chosen" or random; it is rather "returned to," a "fateful and inescapable" destiny.

Thus Freud insists upon sacrificing freedom on the altar of intellectual certainty. Curiosity becomes, not the subject's willingness to face uncertainty, but the inexorable hand of an *a priori* law. Order, says Freud in "Civilization and Its Discontents," is the compulsion to repeat. Thus Nathanael's moment of triumph, his courage to uncover the identity of the Sandman—"Summoning up every drop of my courage, I cautiously peeped out" —is effectively annihilated, translated instead into an automistic compulsion to repeat, *precisely like an automaton.* To Oedipus' question, "Why would I renounce knowing by whom I am born?" Freud answers that "fate" is the compulsion to repeat, a desire for origin in which memory is rooted.

In "Beyond the Pleasure Principle," Freud declares, and in italics, *"It seems, then, that an instinct is an urge inherent in organic life to restore an earlier stage of things . . ." (SE* vol. 18, 36). In the same paper, written in the same month during which the paper on "The Uncanny" was completed (1919), Freud discusses "fate":

> What psycho-analysis reveals in the transference phenomena of neurotics can also be observed in the lives of some normal people. The impression they give is of being pursued by a malignant fate or possessed by some "daemonic power"; but psycho-analysis has always taken the view that their fate is for the most part arranged by themselves and determined by early infantile influences. The compulsion which is here in evidence differs in no way from the compulsion to repeat which we have found in neurotics . . . (*SE* vol. 18, 21-22).

Thus the Freudian reading of Hoffmann's tale would hold that Nathanael, pursued by the fate of having his eyes popped out, is in fact only repeating the trauma of the conceptual primal scene which he witnessed from the closet (his father and the Sandman). Moreover, he himself has arranged this fate for himself, determined as he was by early infantile influences. Even the highly uncanny quality of Olympia, whom both Nathanael and the reader gradually come to realize is an automaton, is rejected by Freud as the heart of the uncanny experience. Far "uncannier" for him is the connection between the Sandman and the robbing of eyes—an uncanniness which he will dispel with the explanation of castration anxiety:

> This short summary [of Hoffmann's tale] leaves, I think, *no doubt* that the feeling of something uncanny is directly attached to the figure of the Sand-Man, that is, to the idea of being robbed of one's

eyes; and that Jentsch's point of an intellectual uncertainty has nothing to do with this effect. Uncertainty whether an object is living or inanimate, which *we must admit* in regard to the doll Olympia, is quite irrelevant in connection with this other, *more striking* instance of uncanniness (*SE* vol. 17, 230, emphases mine).

Freud situates the uncanny, then, only in the overtly bizarre connection between the Sandman and the eyes he seems to want to rob. This moment, moreover, is for him the convergence of the return of the repressed and the recognition of the "once familiar" it entails. The irony is that psychoanalytic destiny becomes an inexorable machine of predictably moving parts, precluding all randomness—a machine of which the doll Olympia becomes the "living" metaphor, though Freud of course never says or admits this. But one is rather tempted to see in the uncanny precisely the *deautomatization* of sight: In the fleeting moment between discovery (from curiosity) and recognition (from memory), there occurs the collision of two aspects of the self; past/present, judge/accused. And this is so, I would argue, even if we accept the Freudian reading. When the world begins to provoke our gaze, said Lacan, "a feeling of strangeness begins too." If the judge needs only time to set his machinery into motion, to make, as we have said, of Nathanael an automaton, the Freudian notion of controlling the uncanny moment is still a turning away from the risk the experience of the uncanny entails, and from the insistence upon exploring the uncertainty the uncanny embodies. The horror of incomprehensible cognitive experience can be neatly explained for Freud by drives and infantile influences.

And yet there is something which Freud admits is universally and eternally ungraspable: the concept of death. On this subject, Freud writes in "The Uncanny": "There is scarcely any other matter, however, upon which our thoughts and feelings have changed so little since the very earliest times, and in which discarded forms have been so completely preserved under thin disguise." Here Freud is quick to say that language and laws are of no use to help us understand: "It is true that the statement 'All men are mortal' is paraded in text-books of logic as an example of a general proposition, but no human being really grasps it, and our unconscious has as little use now as it ever had for the idea of its own mortality" (*SE* vol. 17, 241-242). And it is in connection with death that Freud introduces the role of the double. In the mind of a child, he says, as in that of primitive man, the double stems from primary narcissism: Unable to distinguish self from other, primary narcissism makes everything an extension of self, and so the double becomes, in Freud's words (which are actually taken from Rank), "an energetic denial of the power of death." Once this stage has been left behind, however, the double becomes terrifying. Freud is explicit: "From having been an assurance of immortality, he becomes the uncanny harbinger of death" (*SE* vol. 17, 235). It should be clear why this is the case: The necessary repression of mortality creates the state, more or less exaggerated in everyone, of vestigial narcissism. The self is seen as the single "real" subject; only the "other" is mortal, and must therefore not be acknowledged as being on equal footing. But the double entails the seeing of self as other, and thus forces the admission of mortality.

Doubling and multiplying take place for Nathanael immediately after he sees the Sandman. But there is also the problem of doubling in Klara and Olympia, the two women who are at various times the objects of Nathanael's love. Klara, despite the fact that she is overtly "real" and not a doll, like Olympia, is very much described as a robot herself. She is not beautiful, but "architects praised the perfect proportions of her figure, and painters considered her neck, shoulders, breasts almost too chastely formed" (p. 106). Form is Olympia's major attribute, but the words describing Klara have a vaguely engineering sound about them. Klara, like Olympia, is famous for not saying much (though she does say more than the latter's mechanical "ah, ah, ah!") and her gaze, like Olympia's, is "calm and steady." For this reason, the narrator goes on to say, "many chided Klara for being cold, without feeling, and unimaginative." This can be no coincidence: The reader begins to see the doubling of Klara and Olympia; Nathanael does not.

In the scene with his father and the Sandman, Nathanael becomes uncertain of his origins. To begin with, he sees a father whom he does not recognize—one who looks like Coppelius, the Sandman. To underscore Coppelius' sudden possibility as a father-double, the old lawyer does a very curious thing indeed. After agreeing, at the father's entreaties, to spare the boy's eyes, Coppelius proceeds to *screw off* his arms and legs as an "experiment." Freud says: "That is, he had worked on him as a mechanician would on a doll" (*SE* vol. 17, 232, n. 1). Coppelius wants in any case for the boy to believe that he is a doll—an automaton. The lawyer begins this hideous undertaking by saying, "we will at any rate examine the *mechanism* of the hand and the foot." Here is not Freud's conditional "as a mechanician would on a doll"—the text is rather declarative: Coppelius treats Nathanael precisely like an automaton. Even some sort of primal mechanician creator is alluded to by the lawyer. In examining the boy, Coppelius marvels at the former's build and says, finding that he has screwed the limbs back on poorly, "There's something wrong here! It's better the way they were! The Old Man knew his business!" (p. 98). A *scène originaire* is thus witnessed by the child—but the violence of the "father" is performed upon the boy, not the mother (indeed it is her warm breath which awakens him from "the sleep of death"). It is Nathanael's entrails which are violated; and it is he who is from that moment both literally and figuratively (the doubles) fragmented.

Nathanael now fears his origins, and fears that he is the other incarnate: the automaton. Punctually every evening at nine o'clock, he has to go to bed—he is unconscious in sleep, as if unwound. The original myth of the Sandman is, it will be remembered, the sleep bringer. He is the man who carries a bag of sand, throwing the sand into children's eyes to make them sleep—unconscious. The fear of unconsciousness not only is associated with death, but also with not knowing, uncertainty. It is while Nathanael sleeps that the Sandman Coppelius always comes.

Klara and Olympia, themselves doubles, are now feared by Nathanael to be his own doubles as well. Not insignificantly, in Nathanael's strange, "prophetic" poem, Klara's eyes leap into his own bosom. When in the last lines of the poem he looks into her eyes, the poem reads, "it was death that, with Klara's eyes, looked upon him kindly" (p. 109). Klara the familiar, the known, the fiancée, is the distant relation whose real origins are, significantly, not entirely clear. And the estrangement is doubled inside Nathanael after he reads his own poem aloud: "Whose horrible voice is that?" Klara and her brother, moreover, appear in Nathanael's life immediately after the death of his father—that is, shortly after the Sandman scene. That scene in itself is a prefiguration of a later episode in the story, in which Spalanzani (the clockworks maker, "father" of Olympia) and Coppola (the spyglass salesman) fight over the doll Olympia. "I made the eyes," says Coppola, "I the clockwork," shouts Spalanzani. In this type of automatized judgment of Solomon, Olympia is carted out a lifeless (even more so than usual) figure. Nathanael witnesses the Sandman *scène originaire* all over again—but he now is the spectator. Olympia is substituted for him, with her two "fathers" (and perhaps his) fighting over her parts. In horror, Nathanael is stupefied. The narrator says, "He had *only too clearly seen* that in the deathly pale waxen face of Olympia there were no eyes, but *merely black holes*. She was a lifeless doll" (p. 119, emphasis mine).

Freud claims, as we have noted, that the resolution of the intellectual uncertainty concerning Olympia's animate or inanimate nature "is quite irrelevant." But does not this scene precisely trace for us the movements of the uncanny; that is, is not the uncanny moment created when Nathanael becomes certain that Olympia is a doll, and when he simultaneously still sees her as the girl he loves? It is this moment of suspension, the collision of past and present; of two forms of cognition, the "long familiar" and the "forgotten"; of curiosity and the Symbolic Order; of the self and mortality; of the self and the double—it is this instant which informs the uncanny, for in that instant one is precisely "not at home" *(unheimlich)* in one's recognized world. In that instant, one sees only too clearly (or, significantly, too well): The empty sockets which once contained the eyes of the doll Olympia now show with all its horror the ripping of the veil, and the Nietzschean abyss, "whoever, in pride of knowledge, hurls nature into the abyss of destruction, must himself experience nature's disintegration." Disintegration occurs everywhere in the text. Olympia's eyes, now not only lifeless but also wrenched from their sockets, look up at Nathanael. "And now Nathanael saw something like a pair of bloody eyes staring up at him from the floor. Spalanzani seized them with his uninjured hand and flung them at Nathanael so that they hit his breast. Then madness racked Nathanael with scorching claws, *ripping to shreds* his mind and senses" (p. 120). The poem, of course, is repeated, as is the earlier Sandman scene. Shortly thereafter, Nathanael hurls himself from a tower and *shatters* his skull.

It would be tempting, of course, to see in this scene with Olympia only a reification (indeed, rectification) of the *scène originaire* with the Sandman. After all, Nathanael witnesses a violation of the entrails by the father, a clear basis for castration anxiety according to the psychoanalytic precept. But such a conclusion would, with its emphasis on psychoanalytic views of destiny and the dubious existence of random chance, add to the mechanistic aspects of the text—precisely those aspects which the Hoffmann tale, by showing them triumphant, ironizes. Throughout the story, after all, Nathanael is haunted by doubles, automata, clockmakers, eyemakers, various optical instruments, prophetic poems, duplicated scenes, and repeated gestures ("ah! ah! ah!"). The very society is satirized, with its tea parties and dances, and shown to us as comprised of a series of social models no less automatized than the unfortunate Olympia. In the midst of all of this duplication and cloning, the only character who fears this lifeless world of cuckoo clocks is Nathanael who, with his "lacerated soul," is in direct conflict with this apparently smoothly running machinery. All of the gazes around him are lifeless, glazed—only his gaze seems to penetrate behind the Potempkin Village which surrounds him. Are we then to apply to this world of absurd and orderly moving parts the deterministic architecture

of the psychoanalytic principles—castration anxiety and repetition compulsion—to explain away the uncanny? Freud would seem to have it
so:

> *How exactly we can trace back* to infantile psychology the uncanny
> effect of such similar recurrences. . . . For it is possible to recognize
> the dominance in the unconscious mind of a compulsion to repeat
> proceeding from the instinctual impulses and probably inherent
> in the very nature of the instincts—a compulsion powerful enough
> to overrule the pleasure-principle, lending to certain aspects of the
> mind their daemonic character, and still very clearly expressed in
> the impulses of small children. . . . All these considerations pre-
> pare us for the discovery that whatever reminds us of this inner
> "compulsion to repeat" is perceived as uncanny (*SE* vol. 17, p.
> 238).

Freud here refers his reader to "Beyond the Pleasure Principle," "now
ready for publication," that essay which deals directly with the compulsion to repeat, and with instinct as the restoration of an earlier state
(origin). But that Freud himself sees in Nathanael's story a repetition of
the Oedipal drama is in itself an interesting determination to return to
the origins of the psychoanalytic structure. Such a repetition, I have
been arguing, attempts to reautomatize the uncanny in the very opposite
manner in which the Hoffmann story seeks to deautomatize the same
moment. It is Freud, then, who is the real Sandman of the Hoffmann
story, for he "robs" it of the cognitive value of its eyes.

III

> The lord whose oracle is in Delphi neither declares nor con-
> ceals, but gives a sign.
>
> —Heraclitus, Fragment #93

> Self-consciousness is, to begin with, simple being-for-self, self-
> equal through the exclusion from itself of everything else. For
> it, its essence and absolute object is "I"; and in this immediacy,
> or in this (mere) being, of its being-for-self, it is an individual.
> What is "other" for it is an unessential, negatively, character-
> ized object. But the "other" is also a self-consciousness; one
> individual is confronted by another individual. . . . In so far
> as it is the action of the other, each seeks the death of the
> other.
>
> —Hegel, Phenomenology of Spirit

> The professor of poetry and rhetoric took a pinch of snuff,
> snapped the lid shut, cleared his throat, and solemnly de-
> clared: "Most honorable ladies and gentlemen, do you not see
> the point of it all? It is all an allegory, an extended metaphor.
> Do you understand? *Sapienti sat.*"
> —E.T.A. Hoffmann, "The Sandman"

If Freud is the "real" Sandman of the Hoffmann tale, we may also term the automaton Olympia the machinery of psychoanalysis—for at the basis of Freud's science is repetition compulsion [*Wiederholungszwang*]of which the automaton is "an allegory, an extended metaphor." Indeed, Olympia repeats not only her gestures (which are strangely mechanical, as even her admirers remark), but her speech as well ("ah, ah, ah!" she repeats upon "hearing" all of Nathanael's poetry). She is also the metaphor of the psychoanalytic machinery of destiny. For there can be no arbitrariness in an automaton, its "chance" behavior "resolved into laws," precisely as Freud notes about "freedom and arbitrariness" in the *Gradiva*.

Thus, Freud's essay unconsciously puts in the foreground the very figure, Olympia, who helps create the uncanny moments in "The Sandman," not only by resolving into psychoanalytic laws the apparently chance occurrences in the tale, but by controlling through the enunciation of those laws—repetition compulsion, self-imposed destiny, the return to infantile complexes and primitive beliefs, castration anxiety—that very experience which is by definition (before Freud gets hold of it) inexplicable. What emerge triumphant are the inexorable laws of psychoanalysis and control; what are "overlooked" in order to substantiate those laws are incomprehensibility and curiosity and, therefore, the eyes too are seen only as figures of speech—metaphors (substitutions, carrybacks) to the male member. The Delphic oracle for Freud, unlike as Heraclitus would have it, declares or conceals, according to what the subject wishes unconsciously. Mystery of all forms is "empiricized" into the science of psychoanalysis, into the superimposition of laws upon cognition. *Sapienti sat.*

We have said that because of the insistence upon control, Freud overlooks curiosity and represses uncertainty. One of the most striking examples of such repression occurs in the way in which Freud misreads the end of the Hoffmann tale. When Nathanael and Klara are atop the town hall tower Klara looks down and cries to Nathanael, "Just look at that strange little grey bush." Nathanael *automatically* (a significant adverb) feels his side pocket, gets out Coppola's spyglass and looks through it to one side. He goes mad and tries to throw Klara over the railing. The lawyer Coppelius suddenly approaches the tower, and Freud reads as follows: "We may suppose that it was his approach, seen through the spy-glass, which threw Nathanael into his fit of madness" (*SE* vol. 17, p. 229). In fact, however, it is Klara who is "standing in front of the glass." The text is clear: Nathanael's pulse begins to throb and, deathly pale, "he stared at Klara." It is upon seeing *her* through the glass, then, that he goes mad and tries to kill her. It is only when he later sees Coppelius (after Klara's brother has saved her from the mad Nathanael) that Nathanael freezes, screams "Ah, nice-a eyes, nice-a eyes" (Coppola's phrase), and jumps to his death over the railing. These two moments, forced, telescoped into one by Freud, must be separated: Nathanael's view of Klara through the telescope, inducing him to attempt killing her, and Nathanael's view of Coppelius below, inducing the former to kill himself. Again, it should be fairly evident why Freud sees only the second moment, since it concerns the "father figure" Coppelius, and the connection with self-imposed destiny based on castration anxiety. But the moment of seeing Klara through the telescope does not fit Freud's system, and is consequently ignored. It is this moment which we shall examine first.

Why does Nathanael, recovered from the previous fit of madness which resulted from the destruction of the doll Olympia, and once again betrothed to the lovely Klara—why does Nathanael go mad once again upon staring at Klara's eyes through the telescope? Upon viewing her thus, he screams at her, "Whirl wooden doll!" twice, a comment which should lead us to answer the question. The wooden doll, after all, was the automaton Olympia, and not Klara at all. But Klara and Olympia, we have noted, are in fact doubles of each other and, in many ways, of Nathanael himself. Through the telescope, Nathanael is suddenly able to see in Klara's fixed stare the eyes he had thought destroyed with the demise of Olympia.

In other words, it is through the telescope that Nathanael finally comes to see Klara as the automaton's double, something which he saw in Olympia only once it was too late. The *anamorphosis*, then, is completed: the distorted vision which Nathanael had had of Klara is seen for what it is through the device of the telescope. It is as though he had awakened himself from an *automatisme ambulatoire*.[13] But the doubling, as we know, does not end there. We have noted Nathanael's own possible automatistic origins: the screwing and unscrewing of his limbs in the scene with the Sandman, the allusion by Coppelius to a master creator ("The Old Man knew his business"), the repeated *scène originaire* which Nathanael shares with Olympia. Klara's too perfect form, her lack of imagination and feeling, and her "calm and steady" gaze suddenly come into focus through the telescope. She is for Nathanael the doll Olympia whom he thought destroyed. But the multiplication does not end there: He fears as well that she is *his* double. Freud says, it will be remembered, that once the subject has emerged from primary narcissism, the double becomes horrible: "From having been an assurance of immortality, he becomes the uncanny harbinger of death." Nathanael's poem, describing in its last lines the gaze of Klara, now becomes prophetic: "It was death that, with Klara's eyes, looked upon him kindly."

Klara, because he sees her as his double, now becomes a threat to the integrity of Nathanael's consciousness. It is the moment described by Hegel: "But the 'other' is also a self-consciousness; one individual is confronted by another individual. . . . In so far as it is the action of the other, each seeks the death of the other." However, the movement in the Hoffmann tale is not reciprocal, since Klara, with her dead gaze, sees and seeks presumably nothing. Moreover, Nathanael, in seeing in her glazed eyes his own, is fighting precisely to prove that he *is* self-consciousness, and not a wooden doll. Klara is the "uncanny harbinger of death," and the uncanniness of that moment, linked as it is to death, cannot be "reautomatized" by psychoanalytic control. Death, says Freud himself, cannot be understood. Of the proposition "All men are mortal," he had written ". . . no human being really grasps it, and our unconscious has as little use now as it ever had for the idea of its own mortality." The moment of the self confronting death, seeing itself as other, is the moment of the uncanny at its most powerful, and is precisely the moment from which Freud, in his reading of the tale, turns away.

Nathanael, in trying to kill Klara, is trying to preserve his own consciousness. Freud, in turning away from this moment, is preserving the laws of his science and insisting upon intellectual certainty even if it entails repression: "But that would be to open the door to doubts about what exactly is the value of our general contention that the uncanny proceeds from something familiar which has been repressed." There is nothing familiar about death.

The second moment on the tower now bears scrutiny. Nathanael sees Coppelius and throws himself over the railing. Here the uncanny fits neatly into Freud's definition: Coppelius, the familiar, the repressed figure of the Sandman, suddenly *returns*. Again on the subject of death Freud writes, "Most likely our fear still implies the old belief that the dead man becomes the enemy of his survivor and seeks to carry him off to share his new life with him" (*SE* vol. 17, 242). Who is deceased in this story whom Nathanael might fear would wish to carry him away with him? The father, of course; the Coppelius/Coppola/Spalanzani triad of "substitute fathers" merge into the figure of Coppelius, the *revenant*.[14] Here is not the ghastly double, but rather the return of the repressed. Why does Coppelius know that his presence will cause Nathanael to jump from the tower ("Ha, ha! Just wait," he says to the crowd, "he'll come down on his own.")? Because Coppelius witnessed Nathanael's "crime" of seeing too much in the Sandman scene—and thus *set into motion* the sentence for the crime. Is this for Nathanael his self-imposed destiny, as Freud would have it? Perhaps. But it is also the impossibility of continuing the denial of the judge on the part of the accused, of denying the past by "seeing" only the present. If Nathanael behaves like an automaton here, as if Coppelius were pulling his puppet strings from below, he is nevertheless standing accused before himself first and foremost. It is only that his witness makes him incapable of further repressing his crime, and "the judge brings about his own destruction."

Nathanael's fate—that is, the events which unravel themselves in the tale—are as inexorably imposed upon him as the signs uttered by the Delphic oracle. But his judgment is his own. Oedipus traces the same distinction, and insists that his punishment was of his own doing alone, even if the god Apollo decided his fate:

> Apollo it was, Apollo, friends
> Who brought to pass these evil, evil woes of mine.
> The hand of no one struck my eyes but wretched me.

We cannot be so clear, in the case of Nathanael, on the manifestation of an external or divine hand deciding his fate. Indeed, his may be viewed precisely as the self-imposed destiny for which Freud argues. But the judgment is Nathanael's alone, and it is this element of individualized choice which Freud's automatistic model of destiny denies.

In his discussion in the uncanny essay of "a special agency" (later to become the superego)—that internal *double* within the subject which "is able to treat the rest of the ego like an object," Freud adds: "There are also all the unfulfilled but possible futures to which we still cling in phantasy, all the strivings of the ego which adverse external circumstances have crushed, and all our suppressed acts of volition which nourish in us the illusion of Free Will" (*SE* vol. 17, 236). Free will must for Freud always be seen as illusion, and external fate, self-imposed destiny. Only death seems to escape the psychoanalytic dissection of the strange. "Considering our unchanged attitude towards death," writes Freud in "The Uncanny," "we might rather enquire what has become of the repression, which is the necessary condition of a primitive feeling to recurring in the shape of something uncanny. But repression is there, too" (*SE* vol. 17, 242). The statement is more than proven in Freud's own treatment of Nathanael's end, in his refusal to "see" two cognitive moments on the tower as separate, and as necessarily grounded in scopic knowledge, not metaphorical displacements of punishment.

Significantly, Freud uses a visual apparatus as a metaphor for psychical locality. In the "Interpretation of Dreams," he writes:

> I shall remain upon psychological ground and I propose simply to follow the suggestion that we should picture the instrument which carries out our mental functions as resembling a compound microscope or a photographic apparatus, or something of the kind. On that basis, psychical locality will correspond to a point inside the apparatus at which one of the preliminary stages of an image comes into being. In the microscope and telescope, as we know, these occur in part at ideal points, regions in which no tangible component of the apparatus is situated   (*SE* vol. 5, 536).

Psychical locality, then, exists somewhere *between* the lenses, as a convergence between two ideal points in an intangible realm. (Klara's gaze on the tower is *between* Nathanael's view through the telescope and Coppelius who waits behind and beneath her.) This quotation from Freud would serve as perhaps more palatable a definition of the uncanny, for is not the uncanny the convergence between two "lenses" (two visions, or self-aspects), a "region" in which there is no tangible or explicative component of the usual cognitive apparatus? It is the deautomatization of the gaze, of instruments, of repeated action which the Hoffmann story calls for. It is the reautomatization of all of these which Freud would seem to call for. Freud relies upon a metaphor to describe an abstraction—the psychical locality—but he cannot get even as close as such a usage of a figure of speech when he is considering an experience which is all too real: the (un)canny. Indeed, he rather uses metaphor in this case (eyes = male member; fear of the Sandman = castration anxiety) to distance himself from the phenomenon which the empiricism of psychoanalytic principles ("I shall *remain* upon psychological *ground* and I *propose simply* . . .") can accept in fiction, dreams, or a given psyche under scrutiny, but cannot admit within itself: intellectual uncertainty.

NOTES

[1]See, for example, Jacques Derrida's discussion of the "uncanny" in the chapter "La double séance" from *La Dissémination* (Paris, 1972), p. 300, n. 56. Other recent examples include: Friedrich A. Kittler's " 'Das Phantom unseres Ichs' und die Literaturpsychologie: E.T.A. Hoffmann-Freud-Lacan," *Urszenen: Literaturwissenschaft als Diskursanalyse und Diskurskritik*, ed. Kittler and Turk (Frankfurt, 1977); Samuel Weber's "The Sideshow, or: Remarks on a Canny Moment," *MLN*, 88 (1973), 1102-1133; Neil Hertz's "Freud and the Sandman," in *Textual Strategies*, J. V. Harari, ed. (Ithaca, 1979), pp. 296-321, which includes a superb analysis of Freud's insistence upon repetition compulsion; Hélène Cixous' "La fiction et ses fantômes: Une lecture de l'*Unheimliche* de Freud," *Poétique III*, (1972), 199-216; Sheldon Bach's "Narcissism, Continuity and the Uncanny," *International Journal of Psychoanalysis*, 56 (1975), 77-86.

[2]There is, for example, Freud's personal anecdote (significantly placed in a footnote) of sitting alone in a *wagon-lit* compartment and seeing his "double," which was in fact his reflection in the mirror. He claims to have thoroughly disliked this unrecognized stranger, rather than having been terrified of him. He adds: "Is it not possible, though, that our [his and E. Mach's similar response to a parallel situation] dislike of them was a vestigial trace of the archaic reaction which feels the double to be something uncanny?" (*SE* vol. 17, 248, n. 1). Freud also tells of another personal experience in which, lost in a town in Italy, he happened into the red light district. Each time that he tried to take a street leading out of this area, he found himself somehow back in it. The third time this occurred, he admits: "Now, however, a feeling overcame me which I can only describe as uncanny . . ." (*SE* vol. 17, 237).

[3]*SE* vol. 17, 224.

[4]*The Tales of E.T.A. Hoffmann*, ed. and trans. by Leonard J. Kent and Elizabeth C. Knight (Chicago, 1969), p. 95. All quotations of Hoffmann are taken from this edition and will henceforth be situated by page number only.

[5]*Oedipus Rex*, trans. Albert Cook, ed. L.R. Lind (Boston, 1957), p. 147

[6]Friedrich Nietzsche, *The Birth of Tragedy* and *The Geneology of Morals*, trans. Francis Golffing (New York, 1956), p. 61.

[7]Nietzsche, p. 60.

[8]For Lacan, the Subject is inserted into a preestablished order, which is the Symbolic. It is the relation of the Subject to signifiers, language, and speech (and therefore, of laws). This is to be contrasted with the Imaginary (prespeech), the realm of images. The Oedipal stage for Lacan is one of moving from the Imaginary into the linguistic and social registers of the Symbolic. See "The Function and Field of Speech and Language in Psychoanalysis," known as the "Discours de Rome," published first in *La psychanalyse*, P.U.F., vol. I (1956), pp. 81-166, and then in the *Ecrits* (Paris, 1966). The most thoroughly annotated English translation is Anthony Wilden's *The Language of the Self* (New York, 1968).

[9]*Plato, the Collected Dialogues*, ed. Edith Hamilton and Huntington Cairns (Princeton, 1961), p. 1404. My emphases.

[10]Nietzsche, p. 61.

[11]Jacques Derrida, *Writing and Difference*, trans. Alan Bass (Chicago, 1978), p. 8. A similar view of doubling with respect to artistic creation occurs in Proust's tea and madeleine episode as well, where the mind is described as being both the seeker and the obscure country to be explored: "What an abyss of uncertainty whenever the mind feels that some part of it has strayed beyond its own borders; when it, the seeker, is at once the dark region through which it must go seeking, where all its equipment will avail it nothing. Seek? More than that: create" (*Swann's Way*, trans. C. K. Scott Moncrieff [New York, 1970], p. 35). And Freud's own essay on the uncanny discusses such internal doubling, in a note to the introduction of the "special agency"

(later to be called the superego): "I believe that when poets complain that two souls dwell in the human breast, and when popular psychologists talk of the splitting of people's egos, what they are thinking of is this division (in the sphere of ego-psychology) between the critical agency and the rest of the ego" (*SE* vol. 17, 235, n. 2).

[12]Jacques Lacan, "The Eye and the Gaze," *The Four Fundamental Concepts of Psychoanalysis*, trans. Alan Sheridan (New York, 1978), p. 75.

[13]In *The Interpretation of Dreams*, Freud tells of his own dream within a dream in which he can only explain finding himself in a different train compartment by having walked in his sleep (during the dream in the dream): "We know of people who have gone upon railway journeys in a twilight state, without betraying their abnormal condition by any signs, till at some point in the journey they have suddenly *come to themselves completely* and been amazed at the gap in their memory. In the dream itself, accordingly, I was declaring myself to be one of these cases of '*automatisme ambulatoire*' " (*SE* vol. 5, 457).

[14]Hélène Cixous' article ("La fiction et ses fantômes") deals with the *revenant* at some length—as double, as E.T.A. Hoffmann himself. She also insists upon uncertainty as the basis of the uncanny, as the untraceable boundary (as Jentsch had said) between the animate and the inanimate: "le Revenant . . . efface la limite entre deux états: ni vivant ni mort." So the automaton becomes a double for the ghost, the *returned* from the dead (p. 213).

Chapter 13

Lacan and America:
The Problem of Discourse

Sherry Turkle

Jacques Lacan began writing in the early 1950s. Americans have never taken very warmly to his work. They have felt that his theory, elaborated through references to Hegel and Heidegger, not to mention through complex puns in another language, was not written for them. And more than that, they have felt (with good reason) that a lot of what Lacan had to say was written against them, against them as the country where ego psychology had its most dramatic successes.

In recent years, American interest in Lacan has grown. But discussion about him in the United States is already following the polemical tradition of a quarter century of French intellectual pyrotechnics. Is Lacan an irresponsible charlatan or Freud's most important heir? Is his exceedingly obscure style a Gallic vice or a potent method that incites self-analysis? Should transatlantic rumors about his five-minute analytic sessions be the occasion for mirth, theoretical reconsiderations, or indignant outrage? After a quarter of a century of ignoring Lacan, Americans have ended up fighting about him, and there ensues sharp polarization of opinion (for or against) and discussion that tends to alternate between lofty philosophical issues and quarreling over the details of his unorthodox practice. With some exceptions, there has been little room for understanding Lacan in terms of his intentions as psychoanalytic theorist at a particular historical moment.

Orienting oneself in otherwise hard-to-navigate seas is made easier by beginning with issues on which there is a square confrontation between Lacan's ideas and positions that are well-known in this country: Lacan's attack on the traditional forms of the psychoanalytic institution and his attack on ego psychology. Lacan believes that everything about how the "profession" of psychoanalysis has been organized (from the hierarchy within training institutes to the existence of an International Psychoanalytic Association) subverts the Freudian enterprise. Further, he believes that the idea of an autonomous ego, an idea that has held a central position in the development of American psychoanalytic thought, undermines Freud's most essential contribution: that people are "inhabited," constructed by language and society. The spirit of his arguments, both in the attack on the ego and on the psychoanalytic institution, evokes the metaphor of a "Psychoanalytic Protestantism" which asserts the purity and power of a return—in the one case to an early Freud, in the other to a personal, immediate relationship with the psychoanalytic calling.

For Lacanians, Freud's work is the psychoanalytic Bible and derivative commentaries must be cast aside, abandoned, as are institutional forms that support the established psychoanalytic "church" rather than psychoanalytic theory. Lacan's sessions of variable length and his belief that only an analyst can authorize his or her practice exemplify his iconoclasm in relation to the doctrine of the psychoanalytic establishment.

THE ATTACK ON THE PSYCHOANALYTIC ESTABLISHMENT

Somewhat paradoxically, this theorist of ecclesiastical tone framed one of his most powerful attacks on the psychoanalytic institution by accusing it of being a church. *The Four Fundamental Concepts of Psychoanalysis* brings together a series of seminars that Lacan gave in Paris in 1964. The setting for the first seminar on January 15 is dramatic. The psychoanalytic society to which Lacan belongs has just been told that in order to become affiliated with the International Association it must bar Lacan from its analytic training program. He must have no psychoanalytic "children." The ban is to be final, irrevocable. Lacan experiences it as an "excommunication" and uses the event to discuss what there is within the psychoanalytic community "that is so reminiscent of religious practice."[1]

As soon as there is a psychoanalytic institution, it, like a church, has to be able to define its doctrine in terms of visible acts. For the Catholic Church it is acts of worship. For the analytic church it is standard techniques of practice that can be transmitted and monitored by a bureaucracy. But Lacan believes that if there is to be a psychoanalytic science, it, like other sciences, requires criticism, experimentation, iconoclasm. There is no room for a notion of "heresy." There is no room for excommunication. There is no room for ritual observance. "One remains loyal to tradition because one has nothing to say about the doctrine itself."[2]

For Lacan the psychoanalytic church stands between psychoanalysis and its growth as a science and it stands between each analyst and his or her calling. Lacan began his 1964 seminar with the question, "Am I qualified?", a question provoked by the censure of the International Association. And he answered that he was qualified, but that the grounds for his and anyone else's qualification to speak as an analyst were personal. Validation by an official institution was irrelevant. Feeling oneself a psychoanalyst is an act of personal faith, or as Lacan put it, in a phrase that became a focus of controversy even as it passed into the French psychoanalytic world as cliché: "L'analyste ne s'autorise que de lui-même." Only the analyst can authorize him- or herself as an analyst.

When it came time for Lacan to set up some kind of psychoanalytic institution of his own, he tried to make it a psychoanalytic anti-institution. To say the least, Lacan's Freudian School, founded in 1964, was a psychoanalytic society unlike any other. In a traditional psychoanalytic society there are a special class of analysts, at the top of a hierarchy of clinicians, who are known as "training analysts." They alone are considered qualified to analyze "candidates" in "training analyses," analyses in which it is decided in advance that the product will be new analysts. At Lacan's Freudian School there was no such thing as a "training analysis." If an analysis led to the analysand's experiencing an analytic calling and feeling authorized to begin practice, this analysis had been a training analysis. Like Martin Luther, who cried out for personal faith against the dogmas of the Church, Lacan asserts a Psychoanalytic Protestant Reformation. Psychoanalysis is a calling. The authorization to practice as an analyst is placed squarely on the individual.

In the 1964 seminar Lacan spoke of the essential paradox of the psychoanalytic society, of how it can fundamentally undermine the Freudian message. In order to assume a true analytic stance, an analyst must refuse all certitudes, must absolutely refuse to be in the position of a "a subject who is presumed to know." But the existence of an analytic society undermines this radically agnostic position: "What does an organization of psychoanalysts mean when it confers certificates of ability, if not that it indicates to whom one may apply to represent this subject who is supposed to know?"[3] In the Freudian School there were no "certificates," but the lack of formal authorizations was not enough to break out of the vicious circle. Within his own Freudian School Lacan became enmeshed in the contradictions that he had been most brilliant at pointing out to others. The environment became rigid, authoritarian, intolerant.[4] There were "ins" and there were "outs" and the "outs" were excluded. In 1969 some of Lacan's closest disciples resigned in protest and formed another group, and by the mid-1970s the School was again badly divided. On January 5, 1980, faced with growing challenges to his authority, Lacan dissolved the School, demanding that each member make a new choice for or against him. Those who declared themselves faithful could join a new group, "La Cause Freudienne."

Why did all this happen? Some think that the problem was simply Lacan. At every point in the history of the French psychoanalytic movement, at each of the four schisms (each precipitated by Lacan), at each use of a quasi religious language with which Lacan demanded not so much a choice as a profession of faith, one can interpret what went on as an expression of Lacan's personality, his style, his taste for crisis and attention, his flair for the dramatic. But the history of psychoanalysis has always been marked by cycles of iconoclasm, church building, destruction of the temple, and call for its rebirth. These express something beyond the character of any one individual. If psychoanalysis is a subversive science, designed to undermine all truths, to question the meaning of all bonds, then the problem of how to organize psychoanalysts is akin to the problem of how to organize anarchists: Perhaps only permanent organizational revolution can break the contradiction. In the dissolution of the Freudian School and the ensuing scramble of its members to reconstitute themselves in a new relationship to Lacan's work, to the legitimacy of his disciples, and to the problem of a succession of power, and now with Lacan's death, the Lacanian enterprise is continuing to struggle with contradictions that seem inevitably to turn the psychoanalytic institution into a trap and the presence of a *Maître*, be it Freud or be it Lacan, into the center of a church. The problem lies deep within the paradoxes of the psychoanalytic institution; Lacan more than anyone else has provided the basis for its theorization.

THE CRITIQUE OF EGO PSYCHOLOGY

Lacan made his first attack on ego psychology in an essay that is the theoretical centerpiece of the *Ecrits*. This is "The Function and Field of Speech and Language in Psychoanalysis," usually referred to as the "Discourse of Rome." The "Discourse of Rome" put Lacan on a collision course with the international psychoanalytic community. Lacan wrote and revised the essay from 1949 to 1953. While most American analysts, influenced by Anna Freud, Heinz Hartmann, and Rudolf Loewenstein, were working toward a new ego psychology, Lacan was characterizing "the theory of the ego and the analysis of defenses" as "everything most contrary to the Freudian experience."[5] For Lacan, the Freudian vision destroys the "Cartesian subject," the "cogito." In its place, and like other writers in the French structuralist tradition, Lacan developed a notion of a constructed subject. For Lacan, people are constituted by language, by what he calls the "symbolic order." In "The Discourse of Rome" he states the case without equivocation: "Man speaks then, but it is because the symbol has made him man."[6]

The heart of Lacan's attack on ego psychology is philosophical. He traces most of ego psychology's problems to the idea that there is an "objective," "knowable" reality. Ego psychology is an unfortunate artifact. Lacan has written eloquently about how ego psychology has to follow, once you accept this philosophical fallacy: "I can well understand that to prop up so obviously precarious a conception, certain individuals on the other side of the Atlantic should have felt the need to introduce into it some stable value, some standard of the measure of the real: this turns out to be the autonomous ego . . . a down at the heels mirage. . . ."[7] In his essay on "The Mirror Stage," Lacan gives his own description of the ego, built out of the misidentifications, confusions, and alienations of a presymbolic stage of development.[8] This image of the ego has nothing in common with the sturdy, helpful being described by the ego psychologists. While the American school of ego psychology was calling for "therapeutic alliances" with the ego, Lacan insisted that the ego, trapped in the presymbolic mode of alienating identifications, is the carrier of neurosis. For an analyst, allying with the ego is consorting with the enemy.

In the attack on the "acting" ego, Lacan is attacking the idea that each of us has a "center." But most people want to believe in that "center." They want to believe that there is a reality that they can capture through language and which will remain unchanged by language. To sum up these "wants": They want to believe in a conscious, unified subject, with confident unquestioning access to the world of objects, and with access to language as a transparent means of reference to this world. In an only half joking way we could call these "wants" the "three reassuring rules of realism."

Philosophers from many different perspectives have long ago called each of these "rules" into question, but psychoanalysis is more than a philosophy. It is a philosophy-in-practice, a philosophy that struggles with the philosophy that is implicit in how people handle everyday life, a philosophy that pits itself against the "three rules" as they reassure each of us. In the course of my research on the sociology of psychoanalysis, I have interviewed many hundreds of analysts. In these interviews it is clear that they too want to believe in the "three rules," even as they struggle to hear another level of reality in the words of their patients. They want (often despite themselves) to believe that there is an "actor" that they can speak to on that couch. They want to and Lacan says "no." In his spoken and his written texts, Lacan tries to evoke in his readers and listeners an experience of what he feels was most subversive in the Freudian vision. To put it too simply—this is the destruction of the "three rules." People are "decentered" subjects. Nothing is as it seems. Our language reveals a reality where we lack control or autonomy. And, perhaps "worst" of all, we can never fully know this reality. Psychoanalysis is a knowledge about the impossibility of knowing. It not only is an "impossible profession," but also transmits an "impossible" message.

In a recent paper on Lacan, Stanley Leavy captures the essence of this "unacceptable" message, when he says that Lacan "demotes" language "to a source of systematic misrepresentation . . . the misrepresentation of objectifying, seeing oneself for example from some position prior to all one's defenses, hence being a reasonable person after all, a *belle âme*, in Hegel's phrase."[9] And then, Leavy states the core of why it is so difficult to accept Lacan, the heart of most resistance to Lacan. If you take Lacan's argument to its absolute limit, "the establishment of any kind of rational discourse in the analysis runs counter to the exposure of unconscious truth, and if there is no rational discourse, what then. . . ."[10]

The phrase "what then" brings us to the central problem raised by Lacan's challenge to psychoanalytic theory and clinical practice. It is a problem of discourse. What kind of discourse is appropriate to psychoanalysis? How does Lacan deal with the "what then"?

THE DISCOURSE OF PSYCHOANALYSIS

For Lacan the words of the analyst in the analytic session are not assertions requiring assent or disagreement. They are provocations to speech, to personal exploration. Further, Lacan believes that the writing of the psychoanalytic theorist must also be of this nature. The point of the psychoanalytic text is not to convey information, but to do something to the reader.

Lacan's critics have objected that his work lacks the rich texture of Freud's where examples from case histories and daily life abound. Freud's kind of "texturing" by examples (like somebody leaving an umbrella behind) have a reassuring earthiness. If you read Lacan looking for such, you will indeed be disappointed. Lacan has an altogether different idea of the kind of examples needed by his reader. It is the text itself—the plays on words, the play with words—which is the example of how language works in the shifting, slipping, associative chains of the unconscious. The reader gets a feeling for the workings of the unconscious by having a window onto Lacan's unconscious.

If Lacan's texts seem uncomfortable and disjointed, if they provoke the reader to considerable annoyance with Lacan for not "making up his mind," Lacan would say that in a psychoanalytic discourse this is as it should be and that, particularly in the United States where a "watered down" version of psychoanalysis has become established university truth and standard medical practice, a problematic discourse may be a good thing. Indeed, the question of the discourse appropriate to psychoanalysis (the discourse of poetry, of science, or of delirium) dominated most discussion during Lacan's 1975 visit to the United States. I illustrate with a vignette from that trip.

Lacan stood in front of an expanse of green chalkboard in a conference room at the Massachusetts Institute of Technology School of Engineering. Behind him, painstakingly sketched in colored chalk, was a series of knots.

These, he explained, were Borromean knots made of interlocking circles. When one of the circles is cut, the whole chain of circles becomes undone. Wherever Lacan had been in America, he had spoken of these knots. Before each talk, in New Haven, New York, and Cambridge, he had spent hours drawing the knots in four colors, designating the Imaginary, the Real, the Symbolic, and a fourth circle which he called the "symptom" (symptôme). When Lacan was speaking to audiences of psychoanalysts, the drawings of complex knots and the language of topology were themselves a barrier to communication. But now, at MIT, formal representation and mathematical rigor presented no problem. The problem was in what Lacan was saying. After carefully describing manipulations to prove that a series of representations on the board were all the same knot, Lacan went on to give the knot a name:

> I call the knot with three circles the figure of psychic reality, and epsilon is the symptom. The symptom is the special mark of the human dimension. Perhaps God has symptoms, but his understanding is most probably paranoid . . . We encounter the Trinity all the time. Notably in the sexual domain. There it is not held fixed by an individual alone but also by an other . . . The pretended mystery of the divine Trinity reflects what is in each of us; what it illustrates best is paranoid knowledge . . .[11]

For most of the mathematicians, linguists, and philosophers in the audience, the question of whether this man was doing poetry or science did not even present itself. He simply seemed incomprehensible. But Lacan was trying to say something very important through his attempt to pull together topology, trinities, and symptoms.

There are several ways in which mathematics might enter a theoretical discussion about human nature. Mathematics can be used metaphorically or it can be used very literally in the construction of precise mathematical models. Lacan's use of topology fits neither of these familiar categories. It is too sustained on a technical level to be dismissed as "pure metaphor." It is not delimited enough to be a model. What is it? Understanding some ways in which it is different from more typical mathematical models in psychology provides a start towards an answer and towards an appreciation of what Lacan is trying to say about the discourse appropriate to psychoanalysis.

Often the purpose of a mathematical model in psychology is to calculate the consequences of a given manipulation on a given situation. The formula is the instrument that lets you "crank the handle." There is nothing of this predictive intent in what Lacan is doing with the knots. Sometimes the psychologist's use of a mathematical model is more conceptual than predictive: Certain problems are elucidated by being presented entirely within the framework of a mathematizable "microworld." The mathematizable phenomena are factored out of the rest of reality, which is left for another time and another theory. They have deliberately been made functionally invisible to the scientist. Lacan wants to capture some aspect of the mind through mathematization, what he calls a "mathematizable minimum," but he is not willing to filter out the rest even temporarily. Thus, he might begin a paragraph with a description of how to manipulate knots and end it with a question about God. For the mathematical psychologist, the justification for his theory is its product, that is, the true statements it will generate. For Lacan, the process of theorizing itself takes on a privileged role. He speaks of how manipulating and perforating spheres in the "praxis of knots" is "the thing to which the spirit is most rebel." The circles that make up the knots are sections of spheres, "man's first representations of his own body and his first conceptions of science." The knots "so contradict our global sense of our bodies as enveloped and enveloping that to try onself in the praxis of knots is to shatter inhibition," perhaps because it threatens our images of our bodies and our images of our science by reminding us of a connection between them.

It is clear that for Lacan, doing mathematical theory—working on the knots, practicing the manipulations—enters as an integral element —indeed, as the critical element—in the emergence of insight about the self, in the same sense that psychoanalytic insight grows out of the lived relationship with an analyst.

The mathematical modeler often sees his enterprise as scientific and precise, as opposed to literary or poetic. Lacan refuses this dichotomy. He cuts across a line between poetry and science that has become axiomatic in the philosophy if not in the practice of Western science.

Occasionally, a physicist or mathematician describes what he or she does in poetic terms. This discourse may be seen as interesting, but it is judged peripheral to the fundamentals of his or her "science." Even if its relation to philosophical issues is granted, it is considered to be irrelevant to scientific practice For the physicist, the question of the line between poetry and science can be a matter for Sunday morning rumination because on Monday morning it can be relegated to the philosophers of science and the physicist can get back to the "real business" of science. Poetry can be factored out from scientific function because the physicist experiences a clear distinction between his or her creative, partly intuitive mental processes which lead to the discovery of fundamental particles and the fundamental particles themselves. For the psychoanalyst, the division is less clear: Process and product may be one.

Lacan's MIT audience, primed for the arrival of a visiting intellectual "dignitary" and expecting a polished "university talk," found Lacan's presentation confusing. Many even interpreted it as the result of an insulting lack of preparation. The discussion period made matters worse. Lacan answered a question about the relationship between "interior and exterior" by stating that, as an analyst, he was not at all certain that man even had an interior:

> The only thing that seems to me to testify to it is that which we produce as excrement. The characteristic of a human is that—and this is very much in contrast with other animals—he doesn't know what to do with his shit. He is encumbered by his shit. Why is he so encumbered while these things are so discreet in nature? Of course it is true that we are always coming across cat shit, but a cat counts as a civilized animal. But if you take elephants, it is striking how little space their leavings take up in nature, whereas when you think of it, elephant turds could be enormous. The discretion of the elephant is a curious thing. Civilization means shit. Cloaca maxima.

The seminar came to an end soon after this digression on the excrement of elephants and others. By the time his audience shuffled out of the seminar and on to dinner at the Ritz, grumblings about Lacanian incomprehensibility had given way to protests about his deliriousness or senility. A rational discourse, the kind of discourse that would be accepted in the university, can be about topology, or it can be about elephant shit as an example of Dadaist poetry. But Lacan was not speaking about mathematics or poetry or psychoanalysis. He was trying to do them.

POETRY, SCIENCE, AND PLAY

When Americans heard Lacan speak of Borromean knots, Greek science, paranoia, the concept of number, symptoms, phonemes, spheres, and elephant shit, they were baffled. They tried to find a code to decipher the communication. In the main, they had missed Lacan's point. Lacan wanted his audence to enter into the circle of his language without trying to understand it from the "outside." Lacan wanted them to take his structuralism seriously—not just as a theory (it is relatively easy to say that you like Claude Lévi-Strauss who only asks you to theorize about myth and kinship), but as a practice. If you assume that people are inhabited by language, constituted by language, then the suggestion that you relate to a psychoanalytic discourse by letting it inhabit you makes sense. And as in any psychoanalytic experience, there should be no expectation that things will happen quickly. Lacan has always made it clear that understanding him requires time and a process of "working through": "It is empirical fact . . . that after ten years' time, what I have written becomes clear to everyone."

Americans think of themselves as a pragmatic people. They also like to think of themselves as responsive to intellectual humility. They found little comfort in Lacan's assurance that with ten years' work they could be sure to understand him. The American audience was expecting an expert who would spell out his new theory of the mind; instead they got a man who simply spoke and who made it clear that, despite their expectations, "I don't have a conception of the world; I have a style." This, too, was little comfort.

Americans fear that when style is stressed it is at the expense of substance. Lacan the stylist was mistrusted, seen as frivolous and un-interested in "getting a message across." Lacan was trying to get a message across, but he was trying to do it across an ocean of differences in cultural and intellectual traditions.

Americans are quick to equate the gestural with the superficial; but in France, a nation of stylists, style and substance are not so sharply dichotomized. Style of dress, speech, and physical bearing are seen as expressions of the inner man; gesture is studied and significant. Even small differences in the formulas for closing a letter carry subtle nuances. In France, stylized gesture becomes art: mime. Charlie Chaplin and Buster Keaton are beloved.

French structuralism has legitimated the French national preoccupation with style by erasing the line between what is said and how it is said and by arguing that style is the key to substance. While American behavioral scientists are encouraged to "get their results out" in easily abstractable articles, the model that is set by the dean of French structuralism, Claude Lévi-Strauss, is to write one's books in elaborate homologies with their subject matters. So, for example, Lévi-Strauss structured *The Raw and the Cooked* in the form of a musical concerto. Scholars justified his extrapolation from music to myth on intellectual grounds, but it can also be seen as consonant with a long French tradition of intellectual play, even intellectual teasing.

In the early years of the twentieth century, a group of young French mathematicians invented Nicholas Bourbaki, and by signing their collaborative articles in his name, they made "him" the founder of one of the most important movements in twentieth-century mathematical thought. Lévi-Strauss put the picture of a wild pansy on the cover of his masterwork on primitive thought, *La pensée sauvage*, punning "wild pansy" *(pensée)* with "wild thought" *(pensée)*. When Americans are faced with Lévi-Strauss' "overtures" and pansies, with the Bourbaki School, or with the infinite regress of Lacanian literary conceits, they want to know if this is "play" or if this is "serious." They usually express the idea that if it is not the one it must be the other. But for Lacan himself, wit, word games, jokes, myth-making, the materials of the poet, are all part of a kind of play that is inseparable from the psychoanalytic enterprise. If analysts do not subvert the line between work and play, they are doing neither science nor poetry, and if analysts do not subvert the line between science and poetry, they are not psychoanalysts at all.

Anglo-American critics of Lacan find all of this very hard to take. For example, the English philosopher Richard Wollheim, writing in *The New York Review of Books,* dismissed Lacan as a philosopher for his lack of originality (to oversimplify his argument, he claimed that Hegel had said it all before and better) and added that Lacan's mode of discourse distorted the essential clarity of Freud's contribution.[11] When challenged on the grounds that Lacan is trying to use language to capture the quality of the object he is describing (which by its very nature eludes both clarity and "capture"), Wollheim presented a widely shared objection. He claimed that defending Lacan's discourse by alluding to its irrational object was like saying that "a thin man cannot drive fat oxen." In other words, you don't have to be confused to describe confusion. This argument is persuasive, but reveals a commitment to the premise that the world is such that clear language can picture it, if only approximately. Lacan is not committed to this premise. In the clinical situation and in the psychoanalytic text, the kind of statement that you make suggests something about the world. Language does something. Discourse acts. Clear language, irrespective of its content, carries a message in its clarity. And for Lacan, it is precisely the message about the subject that you do not want to convey. To return to Wollheim's oxen, it is as if being thin or fat were contagious. If being thin or fat were contagious, you would need to have a whole different way of talking about who would or could or should drive a fat ox.

The Lacanian thesis is precisely a thesis of contagion by discourse, that the unconscious and the language used to talk about it, in the clinical situation and in psychoanalytic theory, are not independent.

Lacan's writing and seminars are in no way "irrational." They are not free associations. They are painstakingly prepared texts. But the text is designed not to transmit "clear" content but to evoke a process within the reader or listener—most centrally, to help him or her reject standard notions about the nature of knowing. Wittgenstein takes up a related idea in the *Tractatus,* where he compares his work to a ladder that is to be discarded after the reader has used it to reach a new level of understanding.[12] The *Ecrits* are not meant to be read; they are meant to be lived with.

LACAN AND CONTEMPORARY CULTURE

Lacan's ideas on the discourse appropriate to psychoanalysis are one with his critique of the sturdy and "knowing" ego. And Lacan's message about the ego has particular contemporary relevance. Many people feel that a critique of ego psychology is not relevant to current concerns. They feel that what Lacan had to say was all well and good in the context of the 1950s, but that shrill denunciations of the "first wave" ego theorists are no longer to the point. I think they are wrong. I see several forces at work that make Lacan's critique of ego psychology more relevant than ever before. All of them have led to a resurgence of the notion of "free will."

First, even if "ego psychology" per se seems out of mode, there is the continued growth and popular presence of all its descendents: the plethora of theories and therapies which assume the presence of an active, autonomous "self." These run the gamut from what has come to be called American "humanistic" psychology to the flowering of such optimistic offshoots as bioenergetics, biorhythms, and "being your own best friend." They all talk a somewhat different language, but their messages have something fundamental in common. They promise self-improvement without calling society into question. They stress the reassuring and the individualistic. And they can do so because they share a model of the "self" not dissimilar to that of the autonomous ego that Lacan took to task over a quarter of a century ago.

Added to the noise of the "psychobabble" is the way in which sociobiology has captured the popular imagination. It has happened in the United States, and even more remarkably in France, where it is hard to imagine a sharper shift than this biologization of the land of the structuralists. On a first level of analysis, the message of sociobiology is like that of the structuralists: the individual "is not his or her own center." The individual is simply inhabited by instinct rather than by language. But as it has passed into the popular culture, sociobiology has taken on a very different cast. For example, the French director Alain Resnais recently made a film, *My American Uncle,* in which the central metaphor for the psychology of his characters is the behavior of a laboratory rat. Resnais' *Last Year at Marienbad* was the "psychoanalytic" film of the sixties, and *My American Uncle* is the "sociobiological" film for the eighties. The "voice of authority" in the film is that of French biologist

Henri Laborit. His version of sociobiology rejects the symbolic in favor of a biological causality and it goes far towards a view similar to ego psychology: with conscious effort we can use knowledge of instinctual processes to dominate them. The rat's behavior is programmed, conditioned, but it is also conditionable. We have come full circle back to voluntarism.

Third, the growing presence of increasingly "intelligent" computers in everyday life has given the whole question of free will a new salience. Our culture is just now starting to meet the idea of "artificial intelligences" in the plans of industrialists, educators and toymakers, that is, meeting them outside the realm of science fiction. Computer metaphors for thinking about people, long present in the jargon of engineers and in the technical writings of cognitive psychologists, are just now starting to make their way into the popular culture. A lot of people are reacting to intelligent machines and to machine images for thinking about people by asserting the opposite: that people can never be captured in code, in program. In the face of and before the threat of intelligent machines they insist that people, unlike the machines, are not deterministic systems. They insist that there is free will, an acting ego that slips through the net of science.

Lacan and his French followers have looked at ego psychology as the "Americanization" of psychoanalysis, as the "bastardization" of psychoanalysis, as the "watering down" of psychoanalysis. But here I have suggested that you can look at ego psychology in another way: as the psychological model that is closest to "common sense," as the psychological model that it closest to the way that most people like to think about themselves. It is the version of the unconscious most acceptable to the conscious.

Seen from this perspective, controversy about ego psychology relates directly to a struggle that touches each individual. Lacan's critique of ego psychology raises the question of the extent to which each of us is willing to accept the presence within of another, an alien, whether that other be psychoanalytic, linguistic, or historical. It raises the question of the extent to which each of us is willing to accept a subversion of our everyday sense of ourselves as actors, the makers of our own lives.

For generations, people have argued about whether or not Freud's theory was "revolutionary," and the debate has usually centered on Freud's ideas about sexuality. These days, the idea that our sexual selves are present in everything we do, say, and think has passed into the world of things that most people take for granted. But Lacan's work underscores that part of the psychoanalytic message that is revolutionary for our time. The individual is "decentered." There is no autonomous ego. What sex was to the Victorians, the question of free will is to our new "fin-de-siècle."

NOTES

[1] Jacques Lacan, *The Four Fundamental Concepts of Psychoanalysis*, translated from the French by Alan Sheridan (New York: W. W. Norton and Company, 1978), p. 4.

[2] Jacques Lacan, "The Function and Field of Speech and Language in Psychoanalysis," in *Ecrits: A Selection*, translated from the French by Alan Sheridan (New York: W. W. Norton and Company, 1977), p. 64.

[3] Jacques Lacan, "Of the Subject Who is Supposed to Know," in *The Four Fundamental Concepts of Psychoanalysis*, p. 232.

[4] For an analysis of the history of the Freudian School in relation to the paradoxes of the psychoanalytic institution, see Sherry Turkle, *Psychoanalytic Politics: Freud's French Revolution* (New York: Basic Books, 1978; MIT paperback, 1981).

[5] Jacques Lacan, "The Function and Field of Speech and Language in Psychoanalysis," in *Ecrits: A Selection*, p. 64.

[6] Ibid., p. 65.

[7] Jacques Lacan, "The Direction of the Treatment and the Principles of Its Power," in *Ecrits: A Selection*, pp. 230-231.

[8] Jacques Lacan, "The Mirror Stage as Formative of the Function of the I," in *Ecrits: A Selection*, pp. 230-231.

[9] Stanley Leavy, "The Theme and the Word: Further Reflections on Jacques Lacan," paper delivered to the New York Freudian Society, November 13, 1981, p. 11.

[10] Ibid., p. 12.

[11] *The New York Review of Books*, January 1979.

[12] See the discussion in the *Tractatus Logico-Philosophicus* (London: Routledge & Kegan Paul, 1933).

Index

255